TRUNDLEBERRY MANOR

MR. BOUNCER'S HOUSE

FIRE STATION

BLODGER'S GATEHOUSE

SIGMUND SWAMP'S HOUSE & BOATHOUSE

FERNYBANK FERRY

BROCK GRUFFY'S SHOP

BRAMBLE'S FARM

CHURCH

VICARAGE

RAILWAY STATION

P.C. HOPPIT'S HOUSE

POLICE STATION

DR. BUSHY'S HOUSE

N
W   E
S

This book belongs to :

.... Jonathan ....

SIGMUND'S BIRTHDAY SURPRISE

Written & Illustrated by John Patience

DERRYDALE BOOKS
New York
Copyright © 1984 by Fern Hollow Productions Ltd.
This 1984 edition is published by Derrydale Books,
distributed by Crown Publishers, Inc.
Printed in Italy
ISBN 0-517-445719

The birds were singing and the early morning sunshine was glinting through the trees, as Mr. Periwinkle, the postman, came driving along the lane in his mail truck. Normally Mr. Periwinkle did his rounds on his bicycle, but this morning he had an especially large birthday present to deliver to Sigmund Swamp. It was a long wooden crate, and rather strange snorting noises were coming out of it! The crate was very heavy and Sigmund had to help Mr. Periwinkle to carry it into the house.

"It says, 'From Uncle Oscar to Sigmund on his birthday'," said Sigmund, reading the label. "I wonder what it can be."

Carefully, Sigmund began to pry the lid off the crate. As he did this, the snorting noises from inside grew louder and louder, until at last the lid popped open and out crawled an enormous crocodile! In the twinkling of an eye, Mr. Periwinkle rushed out to his van and drove away, and Sigmund scrambled up on top of a cupboard. Meanwhile, the crocodile began to gobble up the poor toad's breakfast. He was very hungry. In fact, he hadn't had a bite to eat since he left the Amazon jungle, where Uncle Oscar had caught him!

Having polished off Sigmund's breakfast, the crocodile still felt hungry and went off looking for more. He made his way through the garden and slid into the Ferny River. As he swam past the school, the children were playing football. Spike Willowbank gave the ball an extra hard kick, which sent it flying over the playground wall. It would have landed in the river, but the crocodile caught it in his mouth and made a nice little snack of it.

When the crocodile reached the dam at Mr. Croaker's watermill, he climbed out of the river and wandered around until he came upon Mrs. Prickles, who was hanging out her wash.

"Good gracious," cried Mrs.
Prickles, almost jumping out of
her shoes. "It's a crocodile!"
And she scurried into her house
and bolted the door behind her.

As for the crocodile, he took
a fancy to the wash and ate the
lot, sheets, pillowcases and all.

Mrs. Prickles's wash had been very tasty, but now the crocodile sniffed the air and caught a scent that was absolutely delicious. It was coming from the bakery where Mr. Acorn had just finished baking a batch of cream buns and jam tarts. What a feast they made! The crocodile ate every last one of them, smacked his lips, and then devoured a shelf of crusty loaves.

"Go away at once," shouted Mr. Acorn, waving his rolling pin angrily. But the greedy animal didn't leave until he had eaten everything in sight.

By this time, Sigmund had informed P.C. Hoppit about the escaped crocodile, and together they set out to track him down. They hadn't been searching long when Sigmund heard an odd little sound coming from behind a tree.

"Boo-hoo. Boo-hoo-oo." It was the crocodile and he was crying.

"Dear me," whispered P.C. Hoppit. "What can be the matter with him?"

"I expect he's feeling lonely," replied Sigmund. "After all, he is the only crocodile in Fern Hollow."

"Yes," agreed P.C. Hoppit. "I think I'd better telephone Poppletown Zoo to come and take him away. There are bound to be other crocodiles at the zoo to keep him company."

Before long, a zookeeper arrived in a large van with a
cage on the back. On the zookeeper's instructions the
cage was baited with a tray of hot Swiss rolls, supplied by
Mr. Acorn. Then everyone hid themselves and waited.
The crocodile was still crying behind his tree, but when

he caught the delicious smell of the Swiss rolls, he quickly perked up and crawled out to investigate. The moment he was in the cage the zookeeper leapt out from his hiding place and locked the door.

"Hooray!" cried everyone.

"Mmmm," said the crocodile, munching the Swiss rolls.

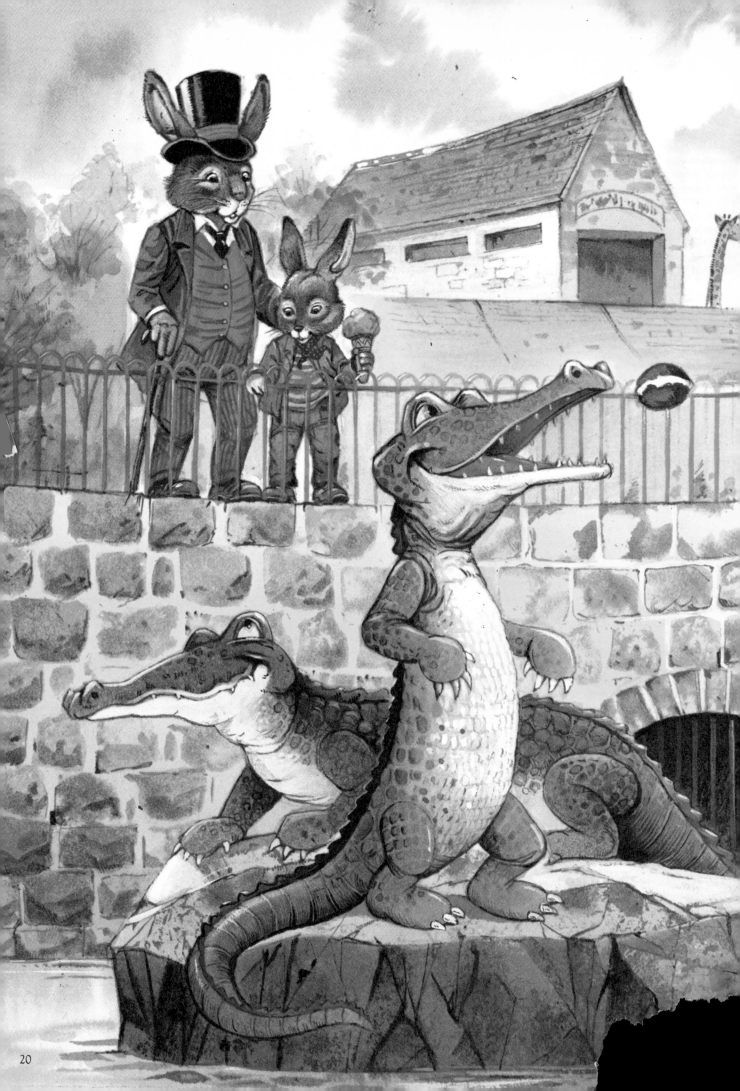

It turned out that Sigmund's Uncle Oscar had intended
to send the crocodile to the zoo in any case, instead of
which he had sent them a crate of Amazon honey, which
was really Sigmund's birthday present. He had simply
mixed up the labels. The crocodile settled in nicely at the
zoo, where Sigmund visited him from time to time and
fed him a few of Mr. Acorn's cream buns!

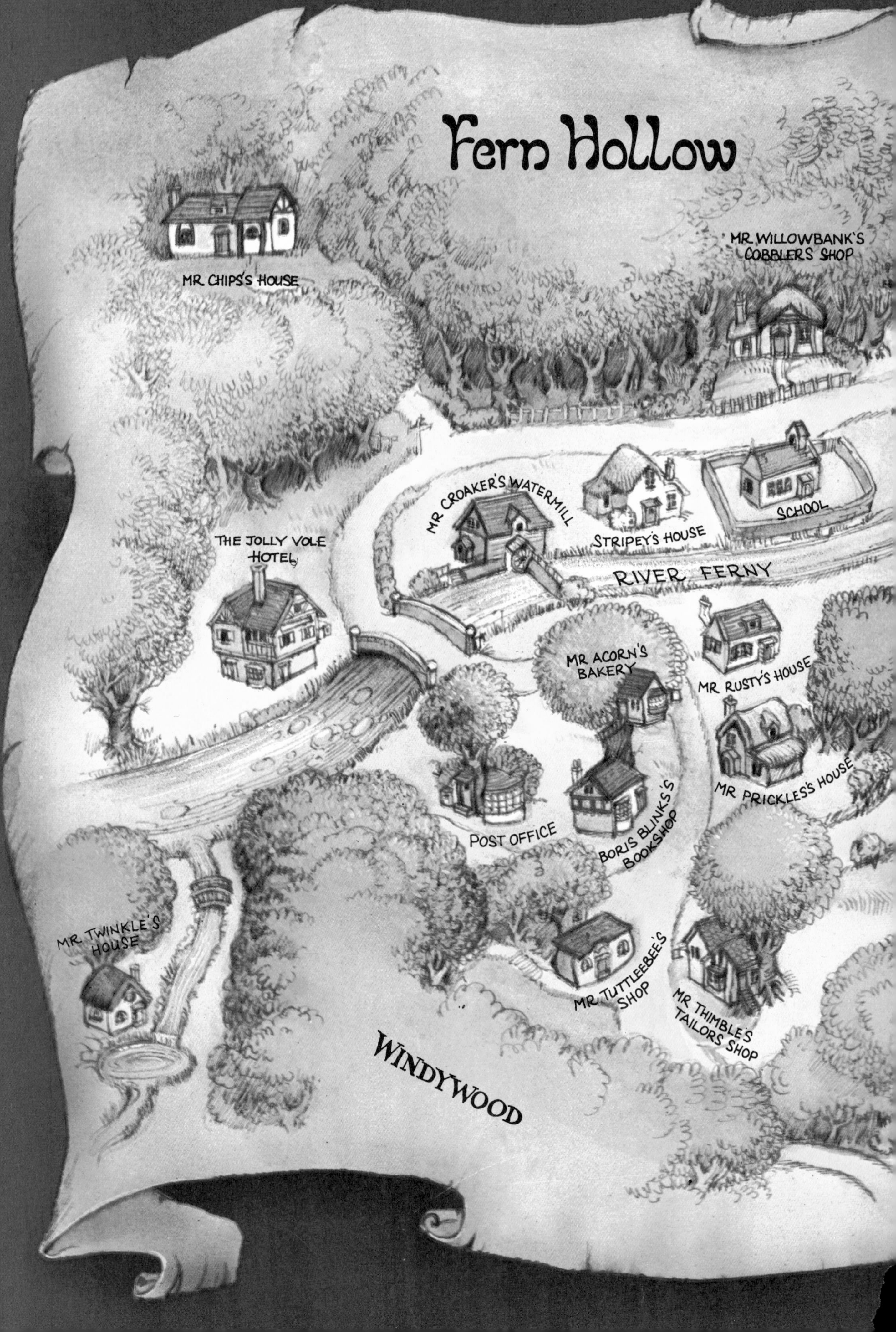

Fern Hollow

MR. CHIPS'S HOUSE

MR. WILLOWBANK'S COBBLER'S SHOP

MR. CROAKER'S WATERMILL

STRIPEY'S HOUSE

SCHOOL

THE JOLLY VOLE HOTEL

RIVER FERNY

MR. ACORN'S BAKERY

MR. RUSTY'S HOUSE

MR. PRICKLES'S HOUSE

POST OFFICE

BORIS BLINKS'S BOOKSHOP

MR. TWINKLE'S HOUSE

MR. TUTTLEBEE'S SHOP

MR. THIMBLE'S TAILORS SHOP

WINDYWOOD

everyday
VEGETARIAN

Oxmoor
House®

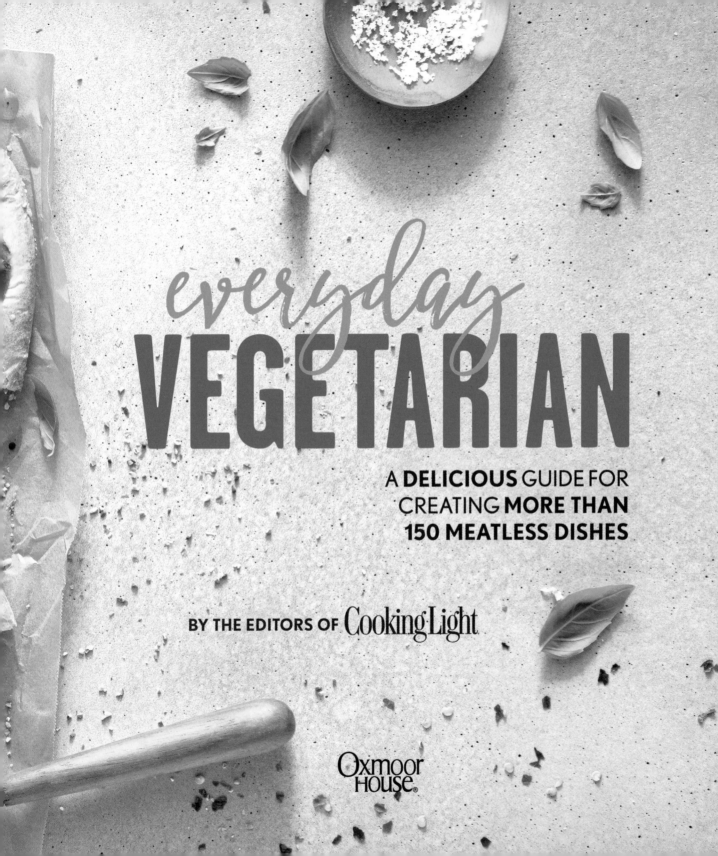

everyday VEGETARIAN

A **DELICIOUS** GUIDE FOR CREATING **MORE THAN** 150 MEATLESS DISHES

BY THE EDITORS OF CookingLight

Oxmoor House®

©2017 Time Inc. Books

Published by Oxmoor House, an imprint of Time Inc. Books
225 Liberty Street, New York, NY 10281

Senior Editor: Rachel Quinlivan West, R.D.
Assistant Editor: April Smitherman
Project Editor: Lacie Pinyan
Designers: Amy Bickell, Maribeth Jones
Junior Designer: AnnaMaria Jacob
Photographers: Daniel Agee, Iain Bagwell, Caitlin Bensel, Jen Causey, Greg Dupree, Alison Miksch, Victor Protasio, Mary Britton Senseney, Becky Stayner
Prop Stylists: Jessica Baude, Kay Clarke, Audrey Davis, Lindsey Lower
Food Stylists: Torie Cox, Margaret Dickey, Rishon Hanners, Kellie Kelley, Angie Mosier, Tori Prendergast, Catherine Steele, Chelsea Zimmer
Recipe Developers and Testers: Adam Hickman, Julia Levy, Karen Rankin, Deb Wise
Assistant Production Manager: Diane Rose Keener
Associate Manager for Project Management and Production: Anna Riego
Copy Editors: Jacqueline Giovanelli, Adrienne Davis
Indexer: Carol Roberts
Fellows: Helena Joseph, Kyle Grace Mills

ISBN-13: 978-0-8487-4951-4

Library of Congress Control Number: 2016955291

First Edition 2017

Printed in China

10 9 8 7 6 5 4 3 2 1

Time Inc. Books products may be purchased for business or promotional use. For information on bulk purchases, please contact Christi Crowley in the Special Sales Department at (845) 895-9858.

We welcome your comments and suggestions about Time Inc. Books.
Please write to us at:
Time Inc. Books
Attention: Book Editors
P.O. Box 62310
Tampa, Florida 33662-2310

contents

Sweet Potato and
Pesto Lasagna,
page 166

welcome

MEAT-FREE MEALS AREN'T JUST FOR VEGETARIANS ANYMORE.
In a time when Michael Pollan's now-famous advice—"Eat food. Not too much. Mostly plants."—is an increasingly common mantra, many people are opting to go meatless. If you're one of those who are incorporating more fruits, vegetables, and whole grains into your meals and omitting meat, even just occasionally, this book has you covered.

Beyond the wide-ranging health benefits, one of the many reasons to cook more plant-based meals is that it's simply an immensely satisfying way to eat. Limiting meat doesn't mean forgoing flavor. It means exploring new ingredients and ways of cooking that may not be in your current wheelhouse. And thanks to the ever-growing variety of products and produce available, vegetarian cuisine is more interesting now than ever.

Many restaurants have started moving meat from the center of the plate to the sidelines or omitting it altogether, giving home cooks new sources for meat-free inspiration to inform their at-home dinner plans. Farmers' markets make finding exceptional in-season (and often local) produce possible year-round, which always yields better-tasting food, and grocery stores are stocking an increasing variety of whole grains, which can make meals more hearty, satisfying, and healthful.

There's plenty of room at the meatless table for everyone, and we hope *Everyday Vegetarian* helps you find your place.

—the editors of *Cooking Light*

the everyday
vegetarian kitchen

the everyday vegetarian kitchen

The recipes in this book may be vegetarian but they're not just for vegetarians. They're for anyone who wants to eat more vegetables and less meat—or for those who just want to eat really good food that happens to be meat free. You'll find varied dishes bursting with wonderful colors, textures, and flavors.

Here are some tips for making amazing meatless meals:

1. MAKE MORE MEALS AT HOME

Vegetarian options at many fast-casual and fast-food restaurants are often limited and aren't always healthy. Instead, cook at home more often. It gives you the freedom to try new recipes while also controlling the ingredients that you consume. The result will be more nutritious, satisfying meals.

2. TRY NEW FOODS

One of the best parts about eating differently is trying foods that are new to you or that you may have overlooked previously. So, if you want to eat less meat or just explore vegetarianism a bit more, use it as an opportunity to taste new cuisines (Ethiopian, Thai, Indian, to name a few) or try that unfamiliar vegetable in the produce section. You'll bring new flavors and textures to mealtime, and that always keeps things interesting.

3. EAT SEASONALLY

The simple truth is that food tastes better when it's in season. Nothing compares to a perfectly ripe fruit or vegetable at the peak of its season—think of juicy peaches and bright tomatoes in summer, sweet peas in spring, crisp apples in the fall, and comforting root vegetables in winter. Another perk is that in-season fruits and vegetables don't require much work to make them taste amazing. There are times, however, when a dish doesn't hinge on using fresh produce; then you can visit the frozen-food aisle for many vegetables, such as peas and corn, which retain their nutrients and much of their sweet nature.

4. USE WHOLE GRAINS MORE OFTEN

Beyond the fact that whole grains offer a host of good-for-you nutrients, they're also a tasty way to expand your culinary horizons. Many whole grains are much more widely available than they used to be, making it easy to try something new. If your grocery store has bulk bins, purchase the exact amount of whole grains you need; that way you're not committing to a whole package that you may or may not use.

Why are whole grains so good for you? Here's the story: All grains start out as whole grains, which means that they still contain the germ, endosperm, and bran. The bran is full of fiber, which keeps you full, while the germ and endosperm contain beneficial antioxidants, vitamins, minerals, and other healthful compounds. Processing, however, can remove one or more of these components, making refined grains less healthful.

Super Crunchy
Tofu Tacos,
page 270

protein — Whether you've decided to go meatless on occasion or become a vegetarian full time, you need to keep nutrition on the front burner. Protein helps build and maintain your body, fight off disease, and keep energy levels high so you can stay alert all day. You can easily meet your daily protein needs (on average 46g for women, 56g for men) with a vegetarian diet, and you don't have to get it all from cheese. A variety of plant-based foods can get you there: beans, lentils, nuts, rice, and soy products like tofu and tempeh. On the following page are the numbers for a handful of these high-protein, meat-free foods.

EGGS | 6g per egg

Eggs are ideal for any meal, particularly those you need to get on the table quickly. You can start your day with them; they'll give you an a.m. boost and fuel you until lunch. If you need a meal that's portable, make hard-boiled eggs ahead and toss them into salads or enjoy alone. Omelets and quiche are also great for dinner, as are poached or sunny-side-up eggs served on top of a wide variety of dishes—you'll find a number of recipes in this book that do just that.

COTTAGE CHEESE | 12g per ½ cup

Cottage cheese is a versatile snack option. It's affordable, comes in reduced-fat versions, and also contains calcium. It often makes appearances in lasagna, but you can mix it into a variety of dishes to add creaminess, or use it as a substitute for ricotta cheese or sour cream, or eat it as you would yogurt topped with fruit and honey.

PUMPKIN SEEDS | 8g per 1 ounce

Also known as pepitas, roasted pumpkin seeds are a convenient grab-and-go snack or crunchy topping for salads and soups. While they're available year-round in stores, you can roast fresh seeds at home in the fall, when pumpkins are in season. Nuts and seeds can be high in calories so be mindful of your serving sizes.

BEANS | 6-10g per ½ cup, depending on the bean

Black beans, kidney beans, lentils, chickpeas, great Northern, and pinto beans are all delicious choices for low-fat, fiber-filled protein. You can use dried or canned beans. Dried beans allow you to control the sodium and additives that go into the dish, but take longer to prepare. If you use canned, you can choose an unsalted variety to keep sodium in check.

GREEK YOGURT | 14g per 6-ounce container

Greek yogurt packs as much as double the protein of regular yogurt. It's also thick, filling, tart, and less sweet than some regular varieties, all while staying in the low-calorie range. It's delicious on its own, with fruit or honey, or as a substitute for sour cream.

PEANUT BUTTER | 4g per tablespoon

No matter if you prefer crunchy or creamy, this childhood favorite is still a great way to add protein to your meals. Spread it on toast, stir it into oatmeal, add it to smoothies and baked goods, and use it in a classic PB&J. Or, keep some stashed with some whole-wheat crackers when you need a snack.

NUTS | 4-7g per 1 ounce, depending on the nut

Nuts offer a lot in their tiny package, including protein and healthy fats. They're calorically dense (about 160 to 190 calories per ounce depending on the type), so keeping an eye on the portion size is key. Have them for a snack by themselves or as a topping for salads, vegetables, or main dishes.

QUINOA | 8g per 1 cup cooked

This whole grain is not only high in protein, but also a good source of fiber and iron. Some varieties of quinoa take only 20 minutes or less to cook. You can use it as a base for salads or in place of rice, or stir it into soups and stews.

TOFU | 8g per 4 ounces

Neutral-tasting tofu is known for absorbing flavor from other ingredients, which makes it adaptable and versatile. Different varieties (silken to super firm) work best in different applications: Silken tofu works well in blended foods like smoothies and puddings while firmer varieties work better in stir-fries or when grilled or crumbled. It's important to note that the firmer the tofu, the more difficult it is to infuse with flavor.

TEMPEH | 16g per 3 ounces

Fermented soybeans packed into cakes, this tofu counterpart is not only an anti-inflammatory but also a great source of plant-based protein. The whole bean is used (making it less processed than tofu), and it has a nutty, slightly sour, savory flavor. Fermentation reduces the amount of phytic acid, a substance found in soy that prevents your body from absorbing good-for-you nutrients. Another reason we love tempeh: It packs 9g fiber (a third of your daily needs) into just 3 ounces.

vegetarian cheese — If you're a new vegetarian, take note: Not all cheeses are vegetarian. Traditional animal-based rennet is an enzyme derived from the stomach lining of calves, lambs, or goats. It's added to cheeses such as Parmesan, Gorgonzola, and Grana Padano to help the proteins in the milk separate into curds and the liquid to separate as whey. The curds are then processed and matured to make a variety of cheeses.

By law, some cheeses must be made with animal rennet in order to be called by that name. For example, "Parmigiano-Reggiano" has to be made using traditional methods, which includes using calf rennet. However, there is vegetable rennet that's made from either fungal or bacterial sources or from genetically modified microorganisms that's used in a number of cheeses. These include Parmesan-style cheeses and variations of others that are suitable for vegetarians; we use them often in this book.

HERE ARE SOME CHEESES THAT CONTAIN ANIMAL RENNET:

Parmigiano-Reggiano	Gorgonzola	Emmenthaler	Boucheron
Pecorino	Gruyère	Mimolette	Vacherin
Grana Padano	Manchego	Camembert	Asiago

vegans — In this book, we've used a broad interpretation of vegetarianism, which includes eggs and dairy products. For those who follow a vegan diet, which means no animal products of any kind including eggs, milk, cheese, yogurt, other dairy products, and honey, we've identified recipes that meet this criteria with this icon: **V**
They're also noted in the recipe index, which starts on page 347.

vegetarian pantry

To create delicious meals at home, the first step is having a solid pantry and fridge loaded with the staples that you use often. The following is our list. These kitchen staples are the basis of many recipes in this book. They're versatile ingredients that deliver big flavor in a healthy way. But, consider this a starting point and feel free to add and subtract from it based on your preferences and the dishes you like to prepare.

CITRUS: Lemons and limes (juice and rind) provide flavor and depth without added salt in sweet and savory dishes. Adding citrus to a dish has a similar effect to adding vinegar, but it's less tangy in flavor. Store whole citrus in the refrigerator for longer life.

GARLIC: Stirring in fresh garlic at the beginning of cooking transforms vegetables, pasta sauces, marinades, soups, and more with no added calories. Aromatic garlic adds complexity to ingredients and livens otherwise plain dishes. Store unused minced garlic in the refrigerator.

GREENS: Convenient, nutritious, and low-calorie, greens of all varieties are a must. Romaine or mesclun lettuces are good choices, but we love the versatility of leafy greens such as spinach, kale, Swiss chard, bok choy, and arugula. Keep one or two of your favorite types on hand each week to use for salads and sandwich toppings or to mix into stir fries, pastas, frittatas, or whole-grain based dishes.

NUTS AND NUT BUTTERS: Nuts and nut butters (such as peanut or almond butters) are great sources of protein (see page 13), but also provide a lot of flavor in an array of dishes. Nuts can be toasted and used as a topping or stirred into any number of dishes for added crunch, while nut butters can be the basis of a host of sauces that are flavorful and satiating.

CANNED BASICS: Although canned vegetables are higher in sodium than fresh, having a few on hand can significantly speed up meal prep when needed. Canned black beans, chickpeas, kidney beans, and cannellini beans are high-quality, inexpensive sources of fiber and protein that can be tossed in salads and soups, made into dips, and more. You can drain and rinse beans to cut the sodium by 40 percent or purchase unsalted varieties which have significantly less sodium than salted versions. Canned tomatoes can form the base of many recipes and there are lots of options to choose from—diced, crushed, whole. Look for unsalted varieties and use them in soups, sauces, egg dishes, pastas, and more.

HEART-HEALTHY OILS: Olive oil and canola oil are essentials for sautéing and roasting, using in salad dressings, and more. Both are high in heart-healthy unsaturated fats and low in artery-clogging saturated fats. Canola oil is a more neutral-flavored oil, while olive oil will lend a more assertive flavor.

VINEGARS: Use vinegar to add tanginess or to brighten the flavor of salad dressings, marinades, sauces, pastas, and even soups. Vinegars are strong, so add them to dishes in small amounts and taste to decide if you need more. Many of the recipes in this book use red wine vinegar, balsamic vinegar, rice vinegar, or cider vinegar.

GREEK YOGURT: In addition to the protein boost, Greek yogurt's creamy, rich texture makes it the perfect healthy replacement for sour cream or mayo in recipes. Stir in honey, nuts, or dried fruit for a quick snack, spoon over baked potatoes, or use as a dip or spread. Choose plain, fat-free or 2% Greek yogurt to save fat and calories.

FROZEN FRUITS AND VEGETABLES: When fresh fruits and vegetables aren't in season or convenient, opt for frozen. Not only does freezing retain most of the nutrients, but frozen produce can be an easy way to reduce food waste since you can use only what you need in recipes. Choose packages that don't have added sauces or seasonings to keep sodium, fat, and calories in check—you can season them as they cook to suit the dish you are making. Use frozen berries, mango, or pineapple in smoothies; add frozen edamame, broccoli, peppers, and a wide range of other vegetables to stir-fries and sautés for an instant boost of color, flavor, and nutrients.

QUICK-COOKING WHOLE GRAINS: Ready in as little as 10 minutes, quinoa, old-fashioned oats, instant brown rice, and whole-grain pastas can quickly become the center or side dish to any meal. Filled with essential vitamins, minerals, and antioxidants, the fiber in whole grains can also help you stay full longer after meals. Serve alone or toss with veggies, beans, toasted nuts, fresh herbs, or dried fruit.

salads

SPRING SALAD WITH GRAPES
AND PISTACHIO-CRUSTED GOAT CHEESE

HANDS-ON: **15 MINUTES**   TOTAL: **15 MINUTES**   SERVES **4**

¼ cup shelled dry-roasted pistachios, finely chopped

4 ounces goat cheese (about 1 cup)

¼ cup Easy Herb Vinaigrette

1 (5-ounce) package gourmet salad greens or spring lettuce mix

1 cup seedless red grapes, halved

¼ teaspoon freshly ground black pepper

Sure, you could simplify this by just topping the salad with crumbled goat cheese and chopped pistachios. But this method ensures that each grassy, creamy bite of cheese contrasts with the salty, crunchy nuts.

1. Place the pistachios in a shallow dish. Divide the cheese into 12 equal portions, rolling to form 12 balls. Roll each ball in the pistachios until well coated. Set the pistachio-crusted cheese balls aside.

2. Combine the Easy Herb Vinaigrette and greens in a large mixing bowl, and toss gently to coat evenly. Place the greens mixture on each of 4 salad plates. Top each serving with the grapes and cheese balls. Sprinkle the salads evenly with pepper, and serve immediately.

(serving size: 1¼ ounces greens, ¼ cup grapes, and 3 cheese balls): **CALORIES** 235; **FAT** 18.4g (sat 5.2g, mono 8.4g, poly 3.9g); **PROTEIN** 8g; **CARB** 12g; **FIBER** 2g; **SUGARS** 8g (est. added sugars 1g); **CHOL** 13mg; **IRON** 1mg; **SODIUM** 192mg; **CALCIUM** 67mg

EASY HERB VINAIGRETTE

HANDS-ON: **5 MINUTES**   TOTAL: **5 MINUTES**
MAKES **ABOUT 1⅔ CUPS VINAIGRETTE, ENOUGH FOR 13 SALADS**

9 tablespoons white wine vinegar

1½ tablespoons honey

½ teaspoon fine sea salt

1 cup canola oil

3 tablespoons chopped fresh basil

3 tablespoons minced fresh chives

This recipe makes plenty of dressing to keep on hand, so having a salad with dinner is effortless any night of the week.

Combine the first 3 ingredients in a medium bowl; slowly whisk in the oil until combined. Stir in the basil and chives. Store, covered, in a refrigerator for up to 5 days.

(serving size: 2 tablespoons): **CALORIES** 160; **FAT** 17.2g (sat 1.2g, mono 10.2g, poly 5.1g); **PROTEIN** 0g; **CARB** 2g; **FIBER** 0g; **SUGARS** 1g (est. added sugars 1g); **CHOL** 0mg; **IRON** 0mg; **SODIUM** 89mg; **CALCIUM** 2mg

INDIAN CHOPPED SALAD ♥

HANDS-ON: **25 MINUTES**   TOTAL: **25 MINUTES**   SERVES **6**

1 cup quartered radishes

1 cup finely chopped red onion

½ cup chopped fresh cilantro

4 to 5 tablespoons fresh lime juice

¼ cup chopped fresh mint

1 teaspoon roasted ground cumin

½ teaspoon kosher salt

¼ teaspoon ground red pepper

¼ teaspoon cracked black peppercorns

2 large ripe tomatoes, chopped

3 Persian cucumbers, halved lengthwise and cut crosswise into ¼-inch-thick slices

1 Honeycrisp apple, cored and finely chopped (about 1½ cups)

1 serrano chile, finely diced (about 1 tablespoon)

Indian salads don't use oil. They're meant to be fresh, clean, and a little astringent to balance the richer cooked dishes that they're paired with.

Combine all the ingredients in a large bowl; toss well. Taste for seasoning, adding more lime juice if needed.

(serving size: 1⅓ cups): **CALORIES** 40; **FAT** 0.3g (sat 0g, mono 0.2g, poly 0.1g); **PROTEIN** 1g; **CARB** 9g; **FIBER** 2g; **SUGARS** 5g (est. added sugars 0g); **CHOL** 0mg; **IRON** 1mg; **SODIUM** 172mg; **CALCIUM** 32mg

radishes are at their peak in spring and fall, offering a flavor that's quite mild. Those harvested in the summer heat have a much sharper, almost biting taste.

RADICCHIO, FRISÉE, APPLE, AND MANCHEGO SALAD

HANDS-ON: **10 MINUTES**   TOTAL: **10 MINUTES**   SERVES **4**

2 tablespoons fresh lemon juice

2 tablespoons extra-virgin olive oil

1 teaspoon honey

¼ teaspoon salt

¼ teaspoon freshly ground black pepper

2 cups thinly sliced radicchio

2 cups frisée

1 cup thinly sliced Fuji apple

1 ounce vegetarian Manchego cheese, shaved (about ¼ cup)

Radicchio has a pleasantly bitter flavor that is a nice contrast to the sweetness of the honey and fresh apple. Manchego adds a rich, salty finish.

Combine the first 5 ingredients in a large bowl, stirring well with a whisk. Add the radicchio, frisée, and apple; toss well to coat. Place the salad on each of 4 salad plates. Top with the shaved cheese.

(serving size: about 1½ cups): CALORIES 126; **FAT** 9.4g (sat 2g, mono 4.9g, poly 0.8g); **PROTEIN** 3g; **CARB** 9g; **FIBER** 2g; **SUGARS** 6g (est. added sugars 1g); **CHOL** 8mg; **IRON** 0mg; **SODIUM** 199mg; **CALCIUM** 115mg

MAKING VINAIGRETTE

1. Vinaigrettes may seem easy enough to just stir together, but there's a method to their magic. They start with a base of oil, an acid (like vinegar or citrus juice), and salt to which an emulsifier (honey and mustard are common ones) is often added with other flavorings.

2. Adding an emulsifier keeps the vinaigrette from separating in the bottle and also keeps it clinging to the salad leaves, ensuring flavor in every forkful. You can add in fresh herbs, toasted spices, or finely minced shallots or onions to vary the flavor.

3. When properly emulsified, the ingredients will be suspended throughout the dressing, as shown on the right.

FENNEL AND RADICCHIO SALAD
WITH CITRUS VINAIGRETTE

HANDS-ON: **12 MINUTES**   TOTAL: **42 MINUTES**   SERVES **6**

1 navel orange
1 pink grapefruit
3 tablespoons extra-virgin olive oil
1 tablespoon white balsamic vinegar
1 tablespoon honey
4 cups thinly sliced fennel bulb
4 cups thinly sliced radicchio
½ cup thinly sliced red onion
½ teaspoon flaky sea salt (such as Maldon)

Let the salad stand at room temperature at least 30 minutes before serving. This allows the dressing to penetrate the vegetables and tenderize them a bit for a less aggressive crunch.

1. Peel and section the orange and grapefruit over a bowl; squeeze the membranes to extract the juice. Set the sections aside; reserve 3 tablespoons of juice. Discard the membranes.

2. Combine the juice, oil, vinegar, and honey in a large bowl. Add the fennel, radicchio, and onion; toss to coat. Cover and let stand 30 to 60 minutes. Top with the orange and grapefruit sections; sprinkle evenly with the salt.

(serving size: about 1 cup): CALORIES 132; FAT 7g (sat 1g, mono 4.9g, poly 0.8g); PROTEIN 2g; CARB 18g; FIBER 3g; SUGARS 10g (est. added sugars 3g); CHOL 0mg; IRON 1mg; SODIUM 231mg; CALCIUM 60mg

SECTIONING CITRUS

1. To section grapefruit and oranges, trim away the peel and bitter white pith.

2. Use a sharp paring knife to cut the sections between the membranes.

GRILLED LEEK AND RADICCHIO SALAD WITH CITRUS-WALNUT VINAIGRETTE

HANDS-ON: **20 MINUTES**   TOTAL: **30 MINUTES**   SERVES **8**

1 tablespoon grated orange rind

5 tablespoons fresh orange juice

½ teaspoon honey

3 tablespoons toasted walnut oil

3 heads radicchio, quartered (about 1½ pounds)

3 leeks, washed, trimmed, and halved lengthwise

Cooking spray

½ teaspoon kosher salt

¾ teaspoon freshly ground black pepper

1 ounce vegetarian Parmesan cheese, shaved (about ¼ cup)

¼ cup chopped walnuts, toasted

Bitter meets sweet in this warm salad filled with spring produce. Leeks gain caramelized sweetness when given a subtle char, and citrus spiked with a touch of honey counters the radicchio's bite. If April is still too cool for outdoor grilling where you live, you can also use a stovetop grill pan. Either way, it's important to let the vegetables sit for a bit after they're grilled to allow them to steam and become supple. You can leave the radicchio quartered instead of chopping it for a fork-and-knife salad.

1. Preheat the grill to high heat.

2. Combine the rind, juice, and honey in a large bowl; slowly whisk in the oil until combined.

3. Coat the radicchio and the leeks with cooking spray. Place on the grill rack coated with cooking spray. Grill 7 minutes, turning to brown on all sides. Remove to a cutting board; cool slightly. Coarsely chop the vegetables.

4. Add the chopped vegetables, salt, and pepper to the dressing; toss to coat. Top with Parmesan cheese and walnuts; serve immediately.

(serving size: ¾ cup): CALORIES 112; FAT 8.6g (sat 1.2g, mono 1.5g, poly 5g); **PROTEIN** 2g; CARB 7g; **FIBER** 1g; **SUGARS** 3g (est. added sugars 0g); **CHOL** 3mg; **IRON** 1mg; **SODIUM** 160mg; **CALCIUM** 71mg

SUMMER FIG AND WATERMELON SALAD WITH FETA

HANDS-ON: **15 MINUTES**   TOTAL: **15 MINUTES**   SERVES **4**

½ small watermelon, cut into wedges

½ cup thinly vertically sliced red onion

2 large fresh Calimyrna or other green-skinned figs, stemmed

2 large fresh Brown Turkey, Black Mission, or Striped Tiger figs, stemmed

1 ounce crumbled feta cheese (about ¼ cup)

1 tablespoon olive oil

1 teaspoon fresh lemon juice

1 teaspoon honey

1 tablespoon fresh mint sprigs

1 tablespoon fresh basil leaves

2 tablespoons balsamic glaze

¼ teaspoon coarse sea salt

¼ teaspoon freshly ground black pepper

Balsamic glaze is a syrup of concentrated, cooked-down, sweetened balsamic vinegar; it adds a sweet and tangy element to this refreshing salad. Look for it near the vinegar in the grocery store. You can also make your own: Pour balsamic vinegar into a saucepan and cook over medium heat until it's syrupy.

1. Arrange the watermelon on a serving platter; top evenly with the onion.

2. Halve the figs lengthwise; arrange the figs on the platter; sprinkle with the cheese.

3. Combine the oil, juice, and honey, stirring with a whisk. Drizzle over the salad; sprinkle with the mint and basil. Drizzle the balsamic glaze over the salad; sprinkle evenly with the salt and black pepper.

CALORIES 147; FAT 5.7g (sat 1.9g, mono 3g, poly 0.6g); PROTEIN 2g; CARB 23g; FIBER 2g; SUGARS 19g (est. added sugars 1g); CHOL 8mg; IRON 1mg; SODIUM 227mg; CALCIUM 80mg

when selecting figs, no matter the variety, choose those that are plump and heavy for their size and yield slightly when their skin is gently pressed. The skin should be smooth and the fruit fragrant.

BALSAMIC, BEET, AND BERRY SALAD

HANDS-ON: **10 MINUTES**   TOTAL: **10 MINUTES**   SERVES **1**

VINAIGRETTE*
- 3 tablespoons olive oil
- 1 tablespoon balsamic vinegar
- 1 teaspoon honey
- ¼ teaspoon kosher salt
- ¼ teaspoon freshly ground black pepper
- 1 teaspoon finely chopped fresh rosemary

SALAD
- 2 cups spinach
- ¼ cup quartered strawberries
- ¼ cup fresh blueberries and blackberries
- ½ cup thinly sliced raw Chioggia beets
- ¾ ounce goat cheese, crumbled (about 3 tablespoons)
- 1½ tablespoons chopped walnuts, toasted

Berries add a sweet-tart twist to classic salads. Strawberries, blueberries, and blackberries are called for in this recipe, but feel free to use any berries you like.

1. Make the vinaigrette: Combine the first 6 ingredients in a small bowl, stirring well with a whisk. Reserve 1 tablespoon of the vinaigrette.* Refrigerate the remaining vinaigrette in an airtight container for up to 1 week.

2. Make the salad: Combine the spinach, berries, and beets on a plate; sprinkle with the cheese and walnuts. Add the reserved 1 tablespoon vinaigrette; toss well.

*The vinaigrette makes about ⅓ cup, enough for 5 salads.

CALORIES 305; **FAT** 22.4g (sat 5.3g, mono 9.5g, poly 6.6g); **PROTEIN** 9g; **CARB** 21g; **FIBER** 6g; **SUGARS** 13g (est. added sugars 1g); **CHOL** 10mg; **IRON** 3mg; **SODIUM** 301mg; **CALCIUM** 122mg

salad toppings can often take salads from healthful to heavy, turning a nutrient-rich meal into a calorie bomb. To keep your salads light, add flavorful but calorie-dense crumbly cheeses (100 calories per ounce), chopped nuts (50 calories per tablespoon), and dried fruits (25 calories per tablespoon) in smart portions at the end so you can get a bit of each in every forkful. Serve your salad on a plate to keep all those tasty (and heavy) toppings from collecting in the bottom, as they might in a bowl.

ROASTED RED AND GOLDEN BEET SALAD

HANDS-ON: **15 MINUTES**   TOTAL: **1 HOUR, 35 MINUTES**   SERVES **6**

1 pound red beets (about 3 medium beets), trimmed

1 pound golden beets (about 3 medium beets), trimmed

2½ tablespoons extra-virgin olive oil

1 tablespoon red wine vinegar

1½ teaspoons honey

½ teaspoon minced fresh garlic

¼ teaspoon kosher salt

⅛ teaspoon freshly ground black pepper

4 cups chopped watercress

2 ounces goat cheese, crumbled (about ½ cup)

This composed two-toned beet salad is a show-stopping way to highlight the vegetable's natural beauty. We recommend dressing the red beets separately from the golden beets to preserve each one's rich jewel coloring (red beets aren't shy about spreading their natural beauty around). Use arugula as a substitute for the watercress.

1. Preheat the oven to 375°F.

2. Wrap the beets in foil. Bake at 375°F for 1 hour and 20 minutes or until tender. Remove the beets from the oven; remove from the foil. Cool.

3. Combine the oil, vinegar, honey, garlic, ⅛ teaspoon of the salt, and the pepper in a medium bowl, stirring with a whisk. Pour half of the oil mixture into a separate medium bowl. Spread the watercress over a large serving platter.

4. Remove the skin from the cooled beets; cut each beet into 8 wedges. Add the red beets to one bowl of the oil mixture; toss to combine. Add the yellow beets to other bowl of the oil mixture; toss to combine. Arrange the beet wedges over the watercress; sprinkle evenly with the remaining salt and cheese. Drizzle with any remaining vinaigrette from the bowl used to dress the golden beets.

(serving size: ⅔ cup watercress and about 8 beet wedges): **CALORIES** 149; **FAT** 7.9g (sat 2.2g, mono 4.6g, poly 0.7g); **PROTEIN** 5g; **CARB** 16g; **FIBER** 4g; **SUGARS** 12g (est. added sugars 1g); **CHOL** 4mg; **IRON** 2mg; **SODIUM** 242mg; **CALCIUM** 66mg

to revive wilting greens, soak them in ice water for a few minutes. The ice bath rehydrates their cells, perking them right up. Make sure you dry the greens well before using them, or the dressing won't stick to the leaves.

CILANTRO-KALE SALAD
WITH BUTTERMILK DRESSING

HANDS-ON: **10 MINUTES**   TOTAL: **10 MINUTES**   SERVES **4**

5 tablespoons low-fat
  buttermilk

¼ cup cilantro stems

3 tablespoons sour cream

½ teaspoon freshly ground
  black pepper

¼ teaspoon kosher salt

5 ounces baby kale

¼ cup chopped cilantro stems

4 radishes, thinly sliced

Often-discarded cilantro stems offer just as much flavor as the prettier leaves, plus an added bit of crunch when chopped and tossed into salads like this one.

Place the buttermilk, ¼ cup cilantro stems, sour cream, pepper, and salt in a mini food processor; process until combined. Combine the kale, ¼ cup chopped cilantro stems, and radishes in a bowl. Drizzle the salad with the dressing.

(serving size: about 2 cups salad): **CALORIES** 47; **FAT** 2.3g (sat 1.4g, mono 0.1g, poly 0g); **PROTEIN** 2g; **CARB** 4g; **FIBER** 1g; **SUGARS** 2g (est. added sugars 0g); **CHOL** 8mg; **IRON** 1mg; **SODIUM** 184mg; **CALCIUM** 98mg

add some variety to salad greens by tossing in fresh herbs like basil, tarragon, thyme, parsley, dill, and cilantro (used in this recipe). They add a new layer of flavor to your salads and can change with the seasons and your taste buds.

SUMMER VEGGIE SALAD

HANDS-ON: **18 MINUTES**   TOTAL: **28 MINUTES**   SERVES **4**

- 4 (4-inch) portobello mushroom caps
- 2 (½-inch-thick) slices red onion
- 2 ears shucked corn
- 1 large red bell pepper, quartered and seeded
- 1 medium zucchini, halved lengthwise
- 1 large yellow squash, halved lengthwise
- Cooking spray
- 2 tablespoons olive oil
- 2 teaspoons fresh lemon juice
- 1 teaspoon minced fresh thyme
- ½ teaspoon Dijon mustard
- ¼ teaspoon kosher salt
- ¼ teaspoon freshly ground black pepper
- 2 ounces vegetarian Manchego cheese, shaved (about ½ cup)
- 1 ounce pine nuts, toasted (about ¼ cup)

The beauty of this salad is its versatility: You can use whatever summer vegetables you like or have on hand. You can also swap in less-expensive walnuts for the pine nuts and vegetarian Parmesan for the Manchego.

1. Preheat the grill to medium-high heat.

2. Coat the mushrooms, onion, corn, bell pepper, zucchini, and yellow squash with cooking spray. Arrange the vegetables on the grill rack coated with cooking spray. Grill 5 minutes on each side or until tender.

3. Combine the oil and next 5 ingredients (through black pepper) in a large bowl, stirring with a whisk. Cut the kernels from the ears of the corn; add to the oil mixture. Cut the remaining vegetables into bite-sized pieces; add to the oil mixture. Toss gently to combine. Top with the cheese and pine nuts.

(serving size: about 1¼ cups): CALORIES 270; FAT 18.2g (sat 5.1g, mono 6.5g, poly 3.6g); PROTEIN 10g; CARB 22g; FIBER 5g; SUGARS 10g (est. added sugars 0g); CHOL 15mg; IRON 2mg; SODIUM 244mg; CALCIUM 213mg

TOMATO STACK WITH CORN AND AVOCADO

HANDS-ON: **20 MINUTES**   TOTAL: **20 MINUTES**   SERVES **4**

¼ cup low-fat buttermilk

1 tablespoon finely chopped fresh chives

1 tablespoon finely chopped fresh basil

2 tablespoons canola mayonnaise (such as Hellmann's)

2 teaspoons cider vinegar

1 garlic clove, minced

½ teaspoon freshly ground black pepper

2 ears shucked corn

Cooking spray

4 large beefsteak tomatoes, cut into 8 (½-inch-thick) slices total

2 globe tomatoes, cut into 8 (½-inch-thick) slices total

⅛ teaspoon kosher salt

½ ripe peeled avocado, thinly sliced

4 teaspoons extra-virgin olive oil

Capitalizing on the unrivaled flavor of in-season tomatoes, this side salad is the ultimate summer recipe. You can use a mix of whatever tomatoes you like, adding additional slices for a higher stack and even more tomato goodness. Keep the entrée simple, as this stack is the true star of the plate.

1. Preheat the grill to high heat.

2. Combine the buttermilk and the next 5 ingredients (through garlic), stirring with a whisk. Stir in ¼ teaspoon of the pepper.

3. Coat the corn with cooking spray. Place the corn on the grill rack; grill 8 minutes or until well marked, turning occasionally. Remove from the grill; cool slightly. Cut the corn kernels from the cobs.

4. Sprinkle the tomato slices evenly with the salt. Stack tomato and avocado slices on each of 4 plates. Scatter corn evenly onto plates. Drizzle each tomato stack with about 1½ tablespoons dressing and 1 teaspoon oil. Sprinkle remaining ¼ teaspoon black pepper evenly over salads.

(serving size: 1 stack): **CALORIES** 163; **FAT** 11g (sat 1.4g, mono 7.2g, poly 1.9g); **PROTEIN** 4g; **CARB** 15g; **FIBER** 4g; **SUGARS** 7g (est. added sugars 0g); **CHOL** 1mg; **IRON** 1mg; **SODIUM** 144mg; **CALCIUM** 40mg

FRIED EGG AND CRUNCHY BREADCRUMB BREAKFAST SALAD

HANDS-ON: **11 MINUTES**   TOTAL: **11 MINUTES**   SERVES 1

- 1 ounce whole-grain bread
- 1 tablespoon extra-virgin olive oil
- 1 large egg
- 1½ teaspoons white wine vinegar
- ⅛ teaspoon kosher salt
- ⅛ teaspoon freshly ground black pepper
- 1½ cups salad greens
- 4 radishes, halved

If you have access to whole-grain rye bread, definitely give it a try here; it's so flavorful on its own and adds a special lift to this salad. You can make the toasted breadcrumbs up to two days ahead; just store them in an airtight container or zip-top plastic bag until you're ready for them.

1. Tear the bread into small pieces. Heat a small skillet over medium-high heat. Add 1 teaspoon of the oil to the pan; swirl to coat the pan. Add the breadcrumbs to the pan; cook for 3 minutes or until toasted, stirring occasionally. Remove from the pan.
2. Reduce the heat to medium. Add ½ teaspoon of the oil to pan. Crack the egg into the pan; cover and cook for 1½ to 2 minutes or until desired degree of doneness.
3. Combine the remaining oil, vinegar, salt, and pepper in a bowl. Add the greens and radishes; toss to coat. Top with egg and breadcrumbs.

CALORIES 250; **FAT** 18.9g (sat 3.5g, mono 11.7g, poly 2.5g); **PROTEIN** 9g; **CARB** 14g; **FIBER** 5g; **SUGARS** 2g (est. added sugars 0g); **CHOL** 186mg; **IRON** 2mg; **SODIUM** 389mg; **CALCIUM** 163mg

a salad at breakfast? Yes! A well-made breakfast salad can deliver 20% of your daily protein, 2 to 3 servings of fruits and veggies, a serving of whole grains, and as much as 10 grams of fiber—all before 9 a.m. We do have some tips for building a great one: First, include protein and fat for satiety. The protein can come from an egg, a little cheese, nuts, canned beans, or whole grains. For fat, use unsaturated ones like olive and nut oils, avocado, or nuts, which are ideal for helping keep you satisfied until lunchtime. Second, pay attention to texture. Try to include something crispy-crunchy, creamy, juicy-fresh, and/or meaty-chewy. Lastly, vary the base. Go with greens on some days, and then try beans, whole grains, or roasted or raw vegetables on others.

MIXED GREENS WITH ROMESCO VINAIGRETTE

HANDS-ON: **30 MINUTES**   TOTAL: **1 HOUR, 19 MINUTES**   SERVES **10**

¼ cup Romesco Sauce

2 tablespoons hot water

1 tablespoon red wine vinegar

6 cups torn curly endive

1 (5-ounce) package gourmet salad greens

9 oil-cured ripe olives, pitted and halved

2 hard-cooked large eggs, quartered

Romesco refers to the type of chile used in the rich sauce. Since they can be difficult to find, we used smoky ancho chiles.

1. Combine the Romesco Sauce, 2 tablespoons hot water, and red wine vinegar in a small bowl, stirring well with a whisk.

2. Combine the endive and salad greens in a large bowl; toss gently to combine. Place the greens on each of 10 plates. Drizzle each serving with the vinaigrette; top with the olives and eggs. Serve immediately.

(serving size: about 1⅓ cups greens, about 2 teaspoons vinaigrette, about 1½ teaspoons olives, and about 1 tablespoon eggs): CALORIES 50; FAT 3.6g (sat 0.6g, mono 2.3g, poly 0.5g); PROTEIN 2g; CARB 3g; FIBER 2g; SUGARS 1g (est. added sugars 0g); CHOL 37mg; IRON 1mg; SODIUM 61mg; CALCIUM 27mg

ROMESCO SAUCE ▽

HANDS-ON: **15 MINUTES**   TOTAL: **1 HOUR, 4 MINUTES**   SERVES **40**

2 dried ancho chiles

2 small red bell peppers

½ cup hazelnuts

½ cup blanched almonds, toasted

4 garlic cloves, chopped

1 (1-ounce) slice bread, toasted

¼ cup red wine vinegar

2 tablespoons tomato paste

1 tablespoon plus 1 teaspoon sweet smoked paprika

¼ teaspoon ground red pepper

⅔ cup extra-virgin olive oil

¼ cup hot water

½ teaspoon salt

1. Place the ancho chiles in a small saucepan. Cover with water; bring to a boil. Remove from heat; cover and let stand 20 minutes. Drain well. Remove stems, seeds, and membranes; discard. Place chiles in a bowl.

2. Preheat the broiler to high.

3. Cut the bell peppers in half lengthwise; discard seeds and membranes. Place halves, skin sides up, on a foil-lined baking sheet; flatten. Broil 10 minutes or until blackened. Place in a paper bag; fold to close tightly. Let stand 15 minutes. Peel and cut into 2-inch pieces; add to the chiles.

4. Reduce the oven temperature to 350°F.

5. Arrange the hazelnuts in a single layer on a baking sheet. Bake at 350°F for 8 minutes or until toasted. Turn the nuts out onto a towel. Roll up the towel; rub off the skins. Place the hazelnuts in a food processor. Add the almonds, garlic, and bread to the food processor; process 1 minute or until finely ground. Add the chile mixture, vinegar, tomato paste, paprika, and ground red pepper; process 1 minute or until combined. With the processor on, slowly pour the oil through the food chute; process until well blended. Add ¼ cup hot water and the salt; process 10 seconds or until combined. Store in an airtight container in the refrigerator for up to 2 weeks.

(serving size: about 1 tablespoon): CALORIES 61; FAT 5.8g (sat 0.7g, mono 4.2g, poly 0.7g); PROTEIN 1g; CARB 2g; FIBER 1g; SUGARS 0g (est. added sugars 0g); CHOL 0mg; IRON 0mg; SODIUM 34mg; CALCIUM 9mg

LENTIL SALAD WITH SOFT-COOKED EGGS

HANDS-ON: **35 MINUTES**   TOTAL: **35 MINUTES**   SERVES **6**

1¼ cups dried petite green lentils

6 large eggs

3 tablespoons extra-virgin olive oil

3 tablespoons red wine vinegar

1 tablespoon Dijon mustard

2 teaspoons minced fresh garlic

¾ teaspoon kosher salt

⅜ teaspoon freshly ground black pepper

1¼ cups diced red bell pepper

½ cup chopped green onions

½ cup diced celery

8 cups baby arugula

Green lentils keep a firm texture even after cooking, a desirable trait for this hearty salad. The runny, creamy yolk of the soft-cooked eggs adds richness and doubles as a dressing.

1. Place the lentils in a medium saucepan. Cover with water to 3 inches above the lentils; bring to a boil. Reduce the heat, and simmer 20 minutes or until the lentils are tender. Drain and keep warm.

2. Add water to a large saucepan to a depth of 3 inches; bring to a boil. Add the eggs; boil 5 minutes and 30 seconds. Drain. Plunge the eggs into ice water; let stand 5 minutes. Drain and peel.

3. Combine the oil, vinegar, mustard, garlic, salt, and ¼ teaspoon of the black pepper in a medium bowl, stirring with a whisk. Set aside 2 tablespoons of the oil mixture. Add the lentils, bell pepper, onions, and celery to the remaining oil mixture; toss gently to coat. Place the reserved 2 tablespoons of oil mixture and the arugula in a large bowl; toss to coat.

4. Place the lentil mixture and the arugula mixture on each of 6 plates. Cut the eggs in half lengthwise; top each serving with egg halves. Sprinkle evenly with the remaining black pepper.

(serving size: about ¾ cup lentil mixture, about 1 cup arugula mixture, and 2 egg halves): CALORIES 286; FAT 12.9g (sat 2.6g, mono 7.2g, poly 1.7g); PROTEIN 16g; CARB 28g; FIBER 7g; SUGARS 3g (est. added sugars 0g); CHOL 186mg; IRON 4mg; SODIUM 394mg; CALCIUM 102mg

lentils are more like pasta than rice—they cook best in an abundance of liquid. Be sure to regularly taste your lentils as they simmer to make sure they're the consistency you want. For salads and if you're eating them on their own, pull them off the heat once they're tender but still on the firm side. If they get too soft, they can get mushy.

BUTTERNUT SQUASH
AND SMOKY BLACK BEAN SALAD

HANDS-ON: **47 MINUTES**   TOTAL: **47 MINUTES**   SERVES **4**

4 cups (½-inch) cubed peeled butternut squash

2 tablespoons plus 1 teaspoon extra-virgin olive oil

½ cup walnuts, chopped

Cooking spray

½ teaspoon kosher salt

2 tablespoons red wine vinegar

1 tablespoon Dijon mustard

1 tablespoon honey

1 tablespoon adobo sauce

2 garlic cloves, thinly sliced

¼ teaspoon freshly ground black pepper

1 (15-ounce) can no-salt-added black beans, rinsed and drained

1 (9-ounce) package baby arugula

2 ounces goat cheese, crumbled (about ½ cup)

You'll find chipotle chiles canned in adobo sauce on the international food aisle. Use just the sauce here, reserving the chiles for another use.

1. Preheat the oven to 425°F.

2. Combine the squash and 1 tablespoon of the oil; toss to coat. Arrange the squash on a jelly-roll pan. Bake at 425°F for 25 minutes or until tender.

3. Arrange the walnuts on the jelly-roll pan; coat with cooking spray. Sprinkle ⅛ teaspoon of the salt over the nuts; toss. Bake at 425°F for 10 minutes or until toasted, stirring once.

4. Combine 1 tablespoon of the oil and the vinegar, mustard, honey, and adobo sauce in a bowl, stirring with a whisk.

5. Heat a medium nonstick skillet over medium heat. Add the remaining 1 teaspoon oil to the pan; swirl to coat. Add the garlic; sauté 1 minute. Add the squash, the remaining salt, the pepper, and beans; cook 3 minutes or until heated through. Remove from the heat; stir in 3 tablespoons of the adobo dressing; toss to coat.

6. Combine the remaining dressing and the arugula in a bowl; toss to coat. Place the arugula mixture on each of 4 plates; top with the bean mixture. Sprinkle evenly with the nuts and cheese.

(serving size: 2 cups arugula, ¾ cup bean mixture, 2 tablespoons nuts, and 2 tablespoons cheese): CALORIES 369; FAT 20.1g (sat 4g, mono 7.1g, poly 7.8g); PROTEIN 11g; CARB 40g; FIBER 10g; SUGARS 8g (est. added sugars 4g); CHOL 10mg; IRON 5mg; SODIUM 544mg; CALCIUM 170mg

ROASTED ASPARAGUS AND TOMATO PENNE SALAD WITH GOAT CHEESE

HANDS-ON: **15 MINUTES**   TOTAL: **35 MINUTES**   SERVES **4**

2 cups uncooked penne or mostaccioli (tube-shaped pasta)

12 asparagus spears

12 cherry tomatoes

4 tablespoons extra-virgin olive oil

⅜ teaspoon kosher salt

½ teaspoon freshly ground black pepper

1 tablespoon minced shallots

2 tablespoons fresh lemon juice

1 tablespoon Dijon mustard

1 teaspoon dried herbes de Provence

1½ teaspoons honey

½ cup pitted kalamata olives, halved

2 cups baby arugula

2 ounces goat cheese, crumbled (about ½ cup)

The lemony vinaigrette makes this upscale pasta salad sing. Serve immediately or cover and chill for 2 hours for a cold pasta salad.

1. Preheat the oven to 400°F.

2. Cook the pasta according to the package directions, omitting the salt and fat; drain and set aside.

3. Place the asparagus and tomatoes on a jelly-roll pan. Drizzle with 1 tablespoon of the oil; sprinkle with ¼ teaspoon of the salt and ¼ teaspoon of the black pepper. Toss gently to coat; arrange the asparagus and tomato mixture in a single layer. Bake at 400°F for 6 minutes or until the asparagus is crisp-tender. Remove the asparagus from the pan. Place the pan back in the oven, and bake the tomatoes an additional 4 minutes. Remove the tomatoes from the pan; let the asparagus and tomatoes stand 10 minutes. Cut the asparagus into 1-inch lengths; halve the tomatoes.

4. Combine the shallots and the next 4 ingredients (through honey) in a small bowl, stirring with a whisk. Gradually add the remaining oil, stirring constantly with a whisk. Stir in the remaining salt and black pepper.

5. Place the pasta, asparagus, tomato, olives, and arugula in a large bowl; toss. Drizzle the juice mixture over the pasta mixture; toss. Sprinkle with the cheese.

(serving size: about 1¼ cups pasta mixture and 2 tablespoons cheese): **CALORIES** 408; **FAT** 22.3g (sat 5.5g, mono 13.7g, poly 2.1g); **PROTEIN** 11g; **CARB** 43g; **FIBER** 4g; **SUGARS** 6g (est. added sugars 2g); **CHOL** 11mg; **IRON** 4mg; **SODIUM** 584mg; **CALCIUM** 101mg

sandwiches

NOR-CAL VEGGIE SANDWICHES
WITH HAZELNUT BUTTER

HANDS-ON: **43 MINUTES**   TOTAL: **43 MINUTES**   SERVES **4**

1 large garlic clove

½ cup hazelnuts, toasted

2 tablespoons canola mayonnaise (such as Hellmann's)

2 tablespoons water

¼ teaspoon salt

6 cups water

3 tablespoons fresh lemon juice

4 trimmed fresh globe artichoke hearts, halved crosswise

2 teaspoons olive oil

1½ cups arugula

8 (1-ounce) slices whole-grain sunflower bread, toasted (such as Ezekiel)

1 ounce radish sprouts

1 peeled ripe avocado, thinly sliced

This sandwich leans on nutty artichoke hearts and avocado for richness. Peppery radish sprouts and arugula add crisp crunch. But, the secret sandwich weapon is the umami-rich puree of hazelnuts slathered over seed-studded whole-grain bread. You can use any sprouts you like in place of radish sprouts. Finish it with a sprinkling of freshly ground pepper.

1. Place the garlic in the bowl of a mini food processor; process until finely chopped. Add the nuts; process until a coarse butter forms. Add the mayonnaise, 2 tablespoons water, and ⅛ teaspoon salt; process until smooth.

2. Combine 6 cups water and 2½ tablespoons juice in a medium saucepan. Bring to a boil. Add the artichoke hearts to the pan; cook 6 minutes or until tender. Drain; dry with a paper towel.

3. Heat a large skillet over medium-high heat. Add the oil to the pan; swirl to coat. Add the artichokes. Sprinkle with the remaining ⅛ teaspoon salt; cook 2 minutes on each side or until well browned.

4. Combine the remaining juice and the arugula; toss to coat.

5. Spread 2 tablespoons of the hazelnut butter on 1 side of each of 4 bread slices. Top hazelnut butter with 2 artichoke pieces, about ⅓ cup arugula mixture, ¼ ounce sprouts, about 4 avocado slices, and 1 bread slice.

(serving size: 1 sandwich): CALORIES 359; **FAT** 22.4g (sat 2g, mono 14.6g, poly 4.1g); **PROTEIN** 10g; **CARB** 35g; **FIBER** 9g; **SUGARS** 3g (est. added sugars 0g); **CHOL** 0mg; **IRON** 2mg; **SODIUM** 417mg; **CALCIUM** 66mg

the best way to toast nuts is to spread them in a single layer on a baking sheet so they'll cook evenly, and then cook in a 325°F oven until the nuts smell toasty. To save time on future meals, toast a lot of nuts and freeze the extras. There's no need to thaw them before using.

AVOCADO, SPROUT, AND CASHEW SPREAD SANDWICH

HANDS-ON: **20 MINUTES**   TOTAL: **20 MINUTES**   SERVES **1**

CASHEW SPREAD

⅓ cup cashews, toasted

¼ teaspoon kosher salt

1 garlic clove

1 tablespoon water

1 tablespoon canola mayonnaise (such as Hellmann's)

SANDWICH

2 (1-ounce) slices whole-wheat bread, toasted

¼ cup baby radish sprouts

3 radishes, very thinly sliced

¼ peeled ripe avocado, sliced

¼ cup arugula

1 teaspoon lemon fresh juice

⅛ teaspoon freshly ground black pepper

This spread uses cashews as its base but adds in mayonnaise to make it creamier and easier to slather on the bread.

1. Make the cashew spread: Place the first 3 ingredients in a mini food processor; pulse until coarsely ground. Add 1 tablespoon water and the mayonnaise; process until smooth. Reserve 2 tablespoons of the cashew spread for another use.

2. Make the sandwich: Spread 1 tablespoon of the remaining cashew spread over each bread slice. Top 1 slice with the sprouts, radishes, avocado, arugula, juice, pepper, and the remaining bread slice. Cut in half.

CALORIES 356; **FAT** 19.8g (sat 3.3g, mono 11.6g, poly 3.5g); **PROTEIN** 12g; **CARB** 36g; **FIBER** 7g; **SUGARS** 5g (est. added sugars 0g); **CHOL** 0mg; **IRON** 3mg; **SODIUM** 571mg; **CALCIUM** 88mg

variation

APPLE AND CASHEW SPREAD SANDWICH

Spread 1 tablespoon of the cashew spread over each of 2 (1-ounce) slices toasted whole-wheat bread. Top 1 slice with ½ sliced Fuji apple, 1 teaspoon fresh lemon juice, ⅛ teaspoon freshly ground black pepper, and the remaining bread slice. Cut in half. Serves 1

CALORIES 324; **FAT** 14.4g (sat 2.5g, mono 8.3g, poly 2.8g); **PROTEIN** 11g; **CARB** 40g; **FIBER** 5g; **SUGARS** 11g (est. added sugars 0g); **CHOL** 0mg; **IRON** 3mg; **SODIUM** 563mg; **CALCIUM** 77mg

AVOCADO-EGG SALAD SANDWICHES
WITH PICKLED CELERY

HANDS-ON: **20 MINUTES**   TOTAL: **25 MINUTES**   SERVES **4**

6 large eggs

3 tablespoons water

3 tablespoons cider vinegar

2 teaspoons sugar

¼ cup finely chopped celery

¼ cup mashed ripe avocado

1 tablespoon canola mayonnaise (such as Hellmann's)

1 teaspoon fresh lemon juice

¾ teaspoon Dijon mustard

½ teaspoon freshly ground black pepper

⅜ teaspoon kosher salt

2 tablespoons dry-roasted salted sunflower seeds

8 (1-ounce) slices whole-grain sunflower bread, toasted (such as Ezekiel)

1 cup baby arugula

4 heirloom tomato slices

To prevent the avocado from browning in any leftover egg salad, place the remaining salad in a bowl and place plastic wrap directly on the surface of the salad. Then cover the entire bowl tightly with plastic wrap. You can omit the mayo and add an additional tablespoon of mashed avocado, if you like.

1. Add water to a large saucepan to a depth of 1 inch; set a large vegetable steamer in the pan. Bring the water to a boil over medium-high heat. Add the eggs to the steamer. Cover and steam the eggs 16 minutes. Remove from the heat. Place the eggs in a large ice water-filled bowl.

2. While the eggs cook, combine 3 tablespoons water, vinegar, and sugar in a medium microwave-safe bowl; microwave at HIGH 2 minutes or until boiling. Add the celery; let stand 15 minutes. Drain.

3. Meanwhile, combine the avocado, mayonnaise, juice, mustard, pepper, and salt in a medium bowl, stirring well until smooth.

4. Peel the eggs; discard the shells. Slice the eggs in half lengthwise; reserve 2 yolks for another use. Chop the remaining egg yolks and egg whites. Gently stir the eggs, celery, and sunflower seeds into the avocado mixture. Top 4 bread slices with about ½ cup egg mixture, ¼ cup arugula, 1 tomato slice, and remaining 4 bread slices.

(serving size: 1 sandwich): **CALORIES** 304; **FAT** 12.3g (sat 2.6g, mono 4.6g, poly 4g); **PROTEIN** 17g; **CARB** 31g; **FIBER** 6g; **SUGARS** 7g (est. added sugars 2g); **CHOL** 186mg; **IRON** 3mg; **SODIUM** 591mg; **CALCIUM** 107mg

quick pickling is a fast trick to tenderize vegetables (celery, in this recipe) and enhance their flavor. Using a mix of water and vinegar in the brine helps tone down the sharpness of the vinegar.

GRILLED EGGPLANT BANH MI SANDWICH ⍌

HANDS-ON: **25 MINUTES**   TOTAL: **25 MINUTES**   SERVES **5**

½ cup rice wine vinegar

1½ tablespoons sugar

¼ teaspoon salt

2 cups julienne-cut peeled carrot (about 4 medium)

1¼ pounds eggplant

1½ tablespoons canola oil

⅓ cup creamy peanut butter

¼ cup minced green onions

1 tablespoon minced peeled fresh ginger

2 teaspoons yellow miso (soybean paste)

1½ teaspoons fresh lime juice

1 (16-ounce) French bread baguette, cut in half horizontally

1 cup thinly sliced cucumber

1 cup cilantro leaves

Thinly sliced jalapeño pepper (optional)

Hollowing out the bread is certainly a way of saving some calories, but it also creates the perfect ratio of bread to fillings in this Vietnamese-style sandwich.

1. Preheat the oven to 375°F.

2. Combine the vinegar, sugar, and salt in a bowl, stirring until the sugar dissolves. Add the carrot; let stand 15 minutes, stirring occasionally. Drain.

3. Heat a grill pan over medium-high heat. Cut off the eggplant stem. Cut the eggplant lengthwise into ¼-inch-thick slices; brush with the oil. Grill 7 minutes or until tender, turning once.

4. Combine the peanut butter, onions, ginger, miso, and juice in a bowl; stir well.

5. Hollow out the top and bottom halves of the bread, leaving a 1-inch-thick shell; reserve the torn bread for another use. Place the bread on a baking sheet, cut sides up. Bake at 375°F for 5 minutes or until golden brown. Spread the bottom half of the bread with the peanut butter mixture. Arrange the eggplant evenly over the peanut butter mixture. Arrange the carrot mixture and cucumber evenly over the eggplant; top with the cilantro and jalapeño, if desired. Place the top half of the bread on the sandwich. Cut into 5 equal pieces.

(serving size: 1 piece): CALORIES 392; FAT 14.6g (sat 2.5g, mono 7.1g, poly 4.4g); PROTEIN 14g; CARB 55g; FIBER 8g; SUGARS 9g (est. added sugars 0g); CHOL 0mg; IRON 3mg; SODIUM 575mg; CALCIUM 70mg

eggplant is spongy and plain when raw, but once it's roasted, sautéed, grilled, or stir-fried, the flesh becomes creamy and tender. Choose eggplant that has firm, glossy skin and that is free of soft or brown spots. Eggplant is a little delicate and can't withstand temperatures below 45°F without becoming damaged, so keep it in your vegetable bin or the warmest part of your refrigerator.

OPEN-FACED EGGPLANT SANDWICHES

HANDS-ON: **20 MINUTES**   TOTAL: **20 MINUTES**   SERVES 4

Cooking spray

½ cup lower-sodium
  marinara sauce

⅓ cup all-purpose flour

2 large eggs, lightly beaten

1 cup panko (Japanese
  breadcrumbs)

1 medium eggplant,
  cut crosswise into
  8 (½-inch-thick) slices

¼ teaspoon kosher salt

4 (1-ounce) slices country
  wheat bread, toasted

12 large basil leaves

4 ounces fresh mozzarella
  cheese, shredded

Here's the key to a speedy dinner: While the eggplant broils, toast your bread slices in a toaster oven.

1. Preheat the broiler to high. Coat a baking sheet with cooking spray.

2. Place the marinara in a microwave-safe measuring cup. Microwave at HIGH for 2 minutes or until hot; keep warm.

3. Place the flour in a shallow dish. Place the eggs in another dish. Place the panko in another. Sprinkle the eggplant evenly with the salt. Dredge both sides of the eggplant slices in the flour; dip in the egg, and dredge in the panko. Place the breaded eggplant slices on the prepared baking sheet. Broil the eggplant 3 minutes on each side or until lightly browned. Transfer the eggplant slices to a plate. Place the bread slices on the baking sheet; top each slice with 1 basil leaf. Place 1 eggplant slice over each leaf; top eggplant with 1 basil leaf and ½ ounce cheese. Top the cheese with the remaining slices of eggplant; finish with ½ ounce of cheese over each eggplant slice. Broil eggplant stacks 3 minutes or until the cheese is lightly browned and bubbly. Spoon 2 tablespoons marinara over each serving. Top with the remaining basil leaves.

(serving size: 1 sandwich): **CALORIES** 326; **FAT** 11.6g (sat 5.5g, mono 2.8g, poly 0.8g); **PROTEIN** 14g; **CARB** 41g; **FIBER** 6g; **SUGARS** 8g (est. added sugars 0g); **CHOL** 118mg; **IRON** mg; **SODIUM** 415mg; **CALCIUM** 231mg

PORTOBELLO SANDWICHES WITH RED PEPPER SAUCE

HANDS-ON: **30 MINUTES**   TOTAL: **30 MINUTES**   SERVES **4**

4 (4-inch) portobello mushroom caps

2 tablespoons extra-virgin olive oil

2 garlic cloves, minced

2 (½-inch-thick) slices red onion

¼ teaspoon kosher salt

8 (1.25-ounce) slices ciabatta bread

½ cup bottled roasted red bell peppers, rinsed and drained

1 tablespoon dry-roasted almonds, coarsely chopped

1 teaspoon red wine vinegar

2 ounces goat cheese, crumbled (about ½ cup)

1 cup fresh spinach

12 basil leaves

When using thick, hearty portobellos in a sandwich, pair them with a sturdy bread. Ciabatta is an excellent bread partner for them, but you could also use focaccia.

1. Preheat the broiler to high.

2. Heat a grill pan over medium-high heat. Remove the gills from the mushrooms using a spoon; discard the gills. Combine 1½ tablespoons of the oil and half of the garlic; brush over the mushrooms and onion slices. Place the mushrooms and onion slices in the pan, and cook for 5 minutes on each side or until tender. Remove from the heat. Sprinkle the mushrooms with ⅛ teaspoon of the salt. Separate the onion slices into rings.

3. Place the bread slices on a baking sheet, and broil for 1 minute on each side or until toasted.

4. Place the remaining ½ tablespoon oil, remaining garlic, remaining ⅛ teaspoon salt, bell peppers, almonds, and vinegar in a food processor, and process until smooth. Spread the red pepper sauce evenly over 1 side of each bread slice; top 4 bread slices evenly with cheese, 1 mushroom, onion rings, spinach, and basil. Top with the remaining 4 bread slices, sauce side down.

(serving size: 1 sandwich): **CALORIES** 362; **FAT** 15.4g (sat 4.4g, mono 9.2g, poly 1.3g); **PROTEIN** 12g; **CARB** 47g; **FIBER** 4g; **SUGARS** 4g (est. added sugars 0g); **CHOL** 11mg; **IRON** 3mg; **SODIUM** 711mg; **CALCIUM** 67mg

when storing portobellos, place them in a paper bag or wrap them in paper towels before storing in the refrigerator. Plastic bags will lock in moisture, making the mushrooms slimy.

MUSTARD GREEN PESTO AND EGG OPEN-FACED SANDWICHES

HANDS-ON: **18 MINUTES**   TOTAL: **18 MINUTES**   SERVES **4**

2 cups chopped mustard greens

¼ cup toasted walnut oil

2 tablespoons apple cider vinegar

¾ teaspoon freshly ground black pepper

¼ teaspoon kosher salt

6 ounces frozen green peas, thawed

1½ ounces vegetarian Parmesan cheese, grated (about 6 tablespoons)

1 tablespoon olive oil

4 large eggs

4 (1½-ounce) slices multigrain bread, toasted

This pesto works with any hearty greens, so feel free to try turnip greens, kale, or Swiss chard. Any extra pesto will keep in the refrigerator for up to 4 days and in the freezer for up to a month.

1. Place the mustard greens, walnut oil, vinegar, ½ teaspoon of the pepper, salt, peas, and cheese in a food processor; process until smooth.

2. Heat a large nonstick skillet over medium-high heat. Add the olive oil to the pan; swirl to coat. Crack the eggs into the pan. Reduce the heat to medium; cook 4 minutes or until the whites are set. Sprinkle the eggs with the remaining ¼ teaspoon pepper. Top each bread slice with about ¼ cup pesto and 1 egg.

(serving size: 1 sandwich): CALORIES 386; **FAT** 23.4g (sat 4.4g, mono 5.8g, poly 11.1g); **PROTEIN** 16g; **CARB** 28g; **FIBER** 4g; **SUGARS** 8g (est. added sugars 0g); **CHOL** 195mg; **IRON** 3mg; **SODIUM** 508mg; **CALCIUM** 272mg

GRILLED MARGHERITA SANDWICHES

HANDS-ON: **12 MINUTES**   TOTAL: **12 MINUTES**   SERVES **4**

¼ cup lower-sodium marinara

8 (1-ounce) slices whole-grain bread

4 ounces fresh mozzarella cheese, thinly sliced

1 large tomato, cut into 8 thin slices

½ teaspoon freshly ground black pepper

¼ teaspoon kosher salt

12 large basil leaves

Cooking spray

1 tablespoon olive oil

This quick five-ingredient entrée transforms a favorite pizza combo into a melty grilled sandwich. To thinly slice fresh mozzarella with ease, freeze the cheese for about 30 minutes before cutting.

1. Spread 1 tablespoon of the marinara over 1 side of each of 4 bread slices. Top evenly with the cheese and tomatoes. Sprinkle the tomatoes evenly with the pepper and salt. Top the tomatoes with the basil and the remaining bread slices. Lightly coat the sandwiches with cooking spray.

2. Heat a large skillet over medium-low heat. Add 1½ teaspoons of the oil to the pan; swirl to coat. Add the sandwiches to the pan; cook 2½ minutes or until browned. Brush the tops evenly with the remaining oil. Turn the sandwiches over; cook 2 minutes or until browned. Serve immediately.

(serving size: 1 sandwich): **CALORIES** 284; **FAT** 13g (sat 4.9g, mono 2.9g, poly 1.5g); **PROTEIN** 13g; **CARB** 29g; **FIBER** 5g; **SUGARS** 6g (est. added sugars 0g); **CHOL** 23mg; **IRON** 2mg; **SODIUM** 410mg; **CALCIUM** 69mg

GRIDDLED BANANA, MANGO, AND JALAPEÑO SANDWICHES

HANDS-ON: **20 MINUTES**   TOTAL: **20 MINUTES**   SERVES **2**

2 teaspoons grapeseed or canola oil

4 (1-ounce) slices dense multigrain bread, thinly sliced

2 tablespoons natural peanut butter

1 small (½ cup) banana (ripe, coarsely fork-smashed) or very ripe plantain

4 ounces very ripe mango, peeled and thinly sliced

1 large jalapeño pepper, sliced paper thin

3 tablespoons cotija or feta cheese, finely crumbled

¼ teaspoon kosher salt

1½ teaspoons powdered sugar

⅛ teaspoon ground red pepper

Be sure to coarsely mash the banana; you want to keep some texture there. If you're serving this to kids (or adults!) with sensitive palates, leave off the jalapeño; the sandwiches will still be great. Be sure to keep the heat on medium-low as you cook the sandwiches. At that level, the fillings will have time to warm while the bread evenly browns.

1. Heat a large nonstick skillet over medium-low heat.

2. Brush oil on 1 side of each bread slice. (This will be the pan-contact side.) Lay out all 4 bread slices, oil side down, on foil or parchment paper (as a work surface).

3. Spread 1 tablespoon peanut butter evenly onto each of 2 bread slices. Evenly distribute the banana over the peanut butter. Layer the mango evenly over the banana. Scatter the jalapeño over the mango. Sprinkle evenly with the cheese and salt. Close the sandwiches. Press gently to adhere all the ingredients.

4. Place the sandwiches in the skillet. Cook the sandwiches for 4 to 6 minutes on each side, pressing gently to ensure that all the surface area of the bread is in contact with the pan. Be patient, and let it cook without peeking (you'll get a more even toast that way).

5. Combine the powdered sugar and red pepper. Cut the sandwiches in half, and dust with the powdered sugar mixture.

(serving size: 1 sandwich): **CALORIES** 411; **FAT** 17.8g (sat 3.5g, mono 5.5g, poly 7g); **PROTEIN** 13g; **CARB** 54g; **FIBER** 7g; **SUGARS** 22g (est. added sugars 2g); **CHOL** 11mg; **IRON** 2mg; **SODIUM** 673mg; **CALCIUM** 336mg

grapeseed oil, with its high smoke point, is ideal for toasting sandwiches as well as cooking methods like sautéing and stir-frying that require high heat. It has a neutral flavor that allows the flavor of the ingredients being cooked to shine.

GRILLED CHEESE AND GREEN CHILE SANDWICHES

HANDS-ON: **10 MINUTES**   TOTAL: **35 MINUTES**   SERVES **4**

2 mild green chiles
(such as Anaheim)

2 poblano chiles

¼ teaspoon kosher salt

3 ounces cheddar cheese,
shredded (about ¾ cup)

1½ ounces part-skim
mozzarella cheese,
shredded (about ⅓ cup)

8 (1-ounce) slices whole-
wheat bread

Cooking spray

We love the mix of mild green chiles (with their distinct vegetal flavors) and spicy poblanos. For fun, cut the sandwiches into strips and serve with gazpacho.

1. Preheat the broiler to high.

2. Place the chiles on a foil-lined baking sheet; broil 10 minutes or until blackened, turning once. Wrap in foil; let stand 10 minutes. Peel the chiles; cut in half lengthwise. Discard the seeds and membranes. Cut the chiles into strips; place in a bowl. Add the salt; toss.

3. Sprinkle half of the cheeses evenly over 4 bread slices; top with the chiles, remaining cheese, and remaining bread slices.

4. Heat a large cast-iron skillet over medium heat. Coat both sides of 2 sandwiches with cooking spray; place in the pan. Cook 4 minutes or until golden brown and crisp. Turn over; cover and cook 3 minutes or until the cheese melts. Remove from the pan. Repeat the procedure with the remaining 2 sandwiches and cooking spray.

(serving size: 1 sandwich): **CALORIES** 269; **FAT** 10.7g (sat 6g, mono 3.4g, poly 0.6g); **PROTEIN** 16g; **CARB** 28g; **FIBER** 4g; **SUGARS** 6g (est. added sugars 0g); **CHOL** 29mg; **IRON** 2mg; **SODIUM** 585mg; **CALCIUM** 304mg

cast-iron skillets are fantastic all-purpose pans, helping to create lovely crisp crusts on fish, meats, and breads; bake brownies; and cook a wide array of other foods. What makes them so amazing is their consistent heat distribution that cooks food evenly. They can also handle high heat and can easily go from stovetop to oven.

LEMONY ZUCCHINI PITAS
WITH QUICK PICKLED DILL CARROTS

HANDS-ON: **30 MINUTES**   TOTAL: **1 HOUR**   SERVES **4**

½ cup sugar

½ cup white vinegar

¼ cup water

1 dill sprig

½ teaspoon kosher salt

2 cups matchstick carrots

1 tablespoon olive oil

2 medium zucchini, spiralized or cut into thin strips with a vegetable peeler or mandoline (about 2 cups)

1 small red onion, cut vertically into thin slices (about 1 cup)

1 medium-sized yellow bell pepper, cut into thin strips (about 1 cup)

1 medium-sized red bell pepper, cut into thin strips (about 1 cup)

2 teaspoons lemon rind

1 tablespoon fresh lemon juice

¼ teaspoon freshly ground black pepper

¼ cup canola mayonnaise (such as Hellmann's)

2 teaspoons chopped fresh dill

4 (6-inch) whole-wheat pita rounds, halved

8 Bibb lettuce leaves

These veggie-packed pitas capitalize on the fresh flavors of spring and summer vegetables. Feel free to use whatever vegetables you prefer in this sandwich. The quick-pickled carrots add freshness and an acidic bite.

1. Combine the sugar, vinegar, water, dill sprig, and ¼ teaspoon of the salt in a small saucepan. Bring to a simmer over medium. Place the carrots in a heatproof bowl, and pour the hot sugar mixture over the carrots. Cover and let stand at least 30 minutes or overnight. Drain; discard the dill sprig.

2. Heat a large nonstick skillet over medium-high heat. Add the olive oil to the pan; swirl to coat. Add the zucchini, onion, bell peppers, 1 teaspoon of the rind, lemon juice, and black pepper. Cook, stirring occasionally, until the vegetables are softened, 4 to 5 minutes. Stir in the remaining ¼ teaspoon salt. Set aside.

3. Stir together the mayonnaise, chopped dill, and remaining 1 teaspoon rind in a small bowl. Spread about 2 teaspoons mayonnaise mixture on the inside of each pita half. Place 1 lettuce leaf, ½ cup zucchini mixture, and 2 tablespoons pickled carrots in each pita half.

(serving size: 2 pita halves): CALORIES 329; FAT 9.5g (sat 0.9g, mono 5.1g, poly 2.8g); PROTEIN 9g; CARB 56g; FIBER 9g; SUGARS 15g (est. added sugars 6g); CHOL 0mg; IRON 3mg; SODIUM 500mg; CALCIUM 62mg

FRIED CHICKPEA AND ARUGULA
PITA SANDWICHES WITH LIME TZATZIKI

HANDS-ON: **23 MINUTES**   TOTAL: **23 MINUTES**   SERVES **6**

1 cup plain 2% reduced-fat Greek yogurt

3 tablespoons chopped fresh mint

2 teaspoons fresh lime juice

⅝ teaspoon kosher salt

2 garlic cloves, minced

1 cucumber (about 8 ounces), peeled, seeded, and shredded

6 (6-inch) whole-wheat pitas, halved

2 (15-ounce) cans organic chickpeas (garbanzo beans), rinsed and drained

3 tablespoons extra-virgin olive oil

2 teaspoons ground cumin

2 teaspoons Spanish smoked paprika

¼ teaspoon ground red pepper

1 tablespoon fresh lemon juice

¼ teaspoon freshly ground black pepper

8 cups loosely packed arugula

12 (¼-inch-thick) slices tomato

This sandwich offers flavors reminiscent of a falafel, but it takes less work, making it an easy weeknight meal to put together.

1. Preheat the oven to 350°F.

2. Combine the yogurt, mint, lime juice, ⅛ teaspoon of the salt, garlic, and cucumber in a small bowl.

3. Wrap the pitas in foil; bake at 350°F for 10 minutes or until warm.

4. Place the chickpeas in a single layer on paper towels. Cover with additional paper towels; pat dry. Heat a large skillet over medium-high heat. Add 2 tablespoons of the oil to the pan; swirl to coat. Add the chickpeas to the pan; sauté 10 minutes or until lightly browned and crispy, stirring frequently. Remove the chickpeas from the pan using a slotted spoon; drain on paper towels. Combine the remaining salt, chickpeas, cumin, paprika, and red pepper in a medium bowl; toss well to coat.

5. Combine the remaining olive oil, lemon juice, and black pepper in a small bowl, stirring well with a whisk. Add the arugula; toss gently to coat. Add the chickpea mixture; toss to coat. Fill each pita half with about ⅔ cup chickpea mixture, 1 tomato slice, and 2 tablespoons sauce. Serve immediately.

(serving size: 2 pita halves): CALORIES 370; **FAT** 10.4g (sat 1.8g, mono 5.2g, poly 2g); **PROTEIN** 16g; **CARB** 57g; **FIBER** 10g; **SUGARS** 5g (est. added sugars 0g); **CHOL** 3mg; **IRON** 4mg; **SODIUM** 586mg; **CALCIUM** 131mg

HUMMUS "CHEESESTEAK" HOAGIES

HANDS-ON: **18 MINUTES**   TOTAL: **18 MINUTES**   SERVES **4**

4 (3-ounce) hoagie rolls, split
1 tablespoon olive oil
1 cup vertically sliced yellow onion
1 cup thinly sliced red bell pepper
1 cup thinly sliced poblano chile
3 garlic cloves, thinly sliced
¼ teaspoon crushed red pepper
¼ teaspoon freshly ground black pepper
1 (8-ounce) container plain hummus
4 (½-ounce) slices provolone cheese

These hoagies are a great option for a quick weeknight supper. Made with yellow onion, red bell pepper, poblano chile, and provolone cheese, they're hearty and filling. Use whatever variety of hummus you like.

1. Preheat the broiler to high.

2. Hollow out the top and bottom halves of the rolls, leaving a ½-inch-thick shell; reserve the torn bread for another use. Place the rolls, cut sides up, on a baking sheet. Broil 1 minute or until toasted.

3. Heat a large skillet over medium-high heat. Add the oil to the pan; swirl to coat. Add the onion and next 5 ingredients (through black pepper); sauté 5 minutes or until the vegetables are tender.

4. Spread about ¼ cup hummus over the bottom half of each roll; top with ½ cup of the onion mixture and 1 cheese slice. Broil 2 minutes or until the cheese melts. Top the hoagies with the top halves of the rolls.

(serving size: 1 sandwich): **CALORIES** 410; **FAT** 20.3g (sat 3.3g, mono 12.1g, poly 3.6g); **PROTEIN** 14g; **CARB** 50g; **FIBER** 5g; **SUGARS** 2g (est. added sugars 0g); **CHOL** 10mg; **IRON** 4mg; **SODIUM** 807mg; **CALCIUM** 161mg

MEXICAN-STYLE GRILLED VEGETABLE SANDWICH

HANDS-ON: **33 MINUTES**   TOTAL: **33 MINUTES**   SERVES **4**

1 large red bell pepper

2 tablespoons fresh lime juice

1 tablespoon minced fresh oregano

1 tablespoon olive oil

½ teaspoon ground cumin

½ teaspoon freshly ground black pepper

¼ teaspoon ground red pepper

1 (15-ounce) can unsalted black beans, rinsed and drained

Cooking spray

1 large zucchini, cut lengthwise into (¼-inch-thick) slices

1 small red onion, cut into (¼-inch-thick) slices

1 (12-ounce) ciabatta bread loaf, halved horizontally

¼ teaspoon kosher salt

2 ounces reduced-fat pepper-Jack cheese, shredded (about ½ cup)

This classic Mexican sandwich, or **torta,** *swaps the usual meat for colorful grilled summer vegetables. The traditional black bean spread adds protein and acts as a moisture barrier so the bread stays extra crispy. We opted for ciabatta bread since it has a great crust that's perfect for pressed sandwiches, but you could also use French bread or Cuban bread.*

1. Preheat the broiler to high.

2. Cut the bell pepper in half lengthwise; discard the seeds and membranes. Place the pepper halves, skin sides up, on a foil-lined baking sheet; flatten with hand. Broil 11 minutes or until blackened. Wrap the pepper halves in foil. Let stand 5 minutes; peel. Cut into strips.

3. Place the juice, oregano, oil, cumin, ¼ teaspoon of the black pepper, ground red pepper, and beans in a food processor; pulse 5 times or until coarsely chopped.

4. Heat a grill pan over high heat. Coat the pan with cooking spray. Arrange the zucchini and onion slices on the pan; grill 5 minutes on each side.

5. Hollow out the top and bottom halves of the bread, leaving a 1-inch-thick shell; reserve the torn bread for another use. Spread the black bean mixture over the bottom half of the bread; top with the zucchini, onion, and bell pepper. Sprinkle with the remaining black pepper, salt, and cheese. Top with the top half of the bread. Coat both sides of the sandwich with cooking spray. Place the sandwich on the grill pan; top with a heavy skillet. Grill 3 minutes on each side or until the cheese melts. Remove the sandwich from the pan; cut into quarters.

(serving size: 1 sandwich quarter): **CALORIES** 360; **FAT** 10.1g (sat 2.8g, mono 4.8g, poly 0.8g); **PROTEIN** 15g; **CARB** 55g; **FIBER** 6g; **SUGARS** 4g (est. added sugars 0g); **CHOL** 7mg; **IRON** 4mg; **SODIUM** 722mg; **CALCIUM** 69mg

WHOLE-WHEAT ROASTED VEGETABLE BURRITOS

HANDS-ON: **40 MINUTES**   TOTAL: **40 MINUTES**   SERVES **4**

1 cup broccoli florets

2 medium carrots, peeled and cut into ¼-inch slices (about 1½ cups)

1 medium-sized red bell pepper, cut into strips (about 1 cup)

1 small yellow squash, cut into ¼-inch-thick half moons (about 1 cup)

¼ red onion, sliced vertically

Cooking spray

¼ teaspoon salt

1½ tablespoons fresh lime juice

1 tablespoon ground cumin

½ cup farmer's cheese (about 2 ounces)

1½ teaspoons lime rind

4 (8-inch) whole-wheat tortillas

1 (15-ounce) can unsalted black beans, rinsed and drained

1 ripe avocado, sliced

¼ cup chopped fresh cilantro

Pico de gallo (optional)

Zesty farmer's cheese is a tasty contrast to the caramelized sweetness of the roasted vegetables in these hearty burritos.

1. Preheat the oven to 375°F. Line a rimmed baking sheet with aluminum foil.

2. Place the broccoli, carrots, bell pepper, squash, and onion on prepared baking sheet. Spray the vegetables liberally with cooking spray, and toss to coat. Sprinkle evenly with the salt, lime juice, and ½ tablespoon of the cumin; toss to coat. Bake at 375°F for 20 minutes, or until the vegetables are crisp-tender and lightly browned, stirring after 10 minutes.

3. Stir together the farmer's cheese, lime rind, and remaining ½ tablespoon cumin. Place the tortillas on a work surface. Spread 2 tablespoons of cheese mixture on each tortilla, leaving a 1-inch border.

4. Place the black beans in a medium bowl, and lightly mash with a fork, leaving some beans whole. Spread the beans evenly on the cheese.

5. Divide the roasted vegetables evenly among the tortillas, placing on top of the cheese. Top with the avocado slices and cilantro. Fold one side of the tortilla over the filling, and fold in the sides. Roll the burrito to enclose the filling. Serve with pico de gallo, if desired.

(serving size: 1 burrito): **CALORIES** 380; **FAT** 12.7g (sat 2.7g, mono 5.7g, poly 2.1g); **PROTEIN** 16g; **CARB** 54g; **FIBER** 14g; **SUGARS** 7g (est. added sugars 0g); **CHOL** 10mg; **IRON** 3mg; **SODIUM** 574mg; **CALCIUM** 181mg

SPINACH SALAD MULTIGRAIN WRAPS ♥

HANDS-ON: **30 MINUTES**   TOTAL: **30 MINUTES**   SERVES **4**

- 3 tablespoons canola oil
- 2 (8-ounce) containers presliced cremini mushrooms
- 1 garlic clove, finely chopped
- 1 teaspoon Dijon mustard
- 2 tablespoons apple cider vinegar
- 1 pint cherry tomatoes, halved
- 1 (5-ounce) package baby spinach
- ¼ cup toasted sunflower seeds
- 2 medium carrots, peeled and cut into ribbons
- 4 vegan bacon slices (such as LightLife Smart Bacon), crumbled
- 4 (10-inch) round multigrain wraps (such as Flatout Flatbread Wraps)

These wraps are ideal for lunch or a light supper with soup. Look for the vegan tofu bacon in the produce section of the grocery store near the tofu and tempeh. You can use baby kale or arugula in place of the spinach.

1. Heat a large nonstick skillet over medium-high heat. Add 2 tablespoons of the oil to the pan. Swirl to coat. Add the mushrooms, and cook, stirring occasionally, until browned and moisture is mostly evaporated, about 10 minutes. Add the garlic, and cook, stirring often, until fragrant, about 1 minute. Remove from the heat; stir in the mustard and 1 tablespoon of the vinegar.

2. Place the tomatoes, spinach, sunflower seeds, carrots, and crumbled vegan bacon in a large bowl. Add the mushroom mixture and the remaining 1 tablespoon each of the oil and vinegar; toss to combine. Divide the mixture evenly among the wraps. Fold one side of the wrap over the filling; fold in the sides. Roll to enclose the filling.

(serving size: 1 wrap): CALORIES 340; FAT 20.5g (sat 2g, mono 7.7g, poly 5.4g); PROTEIN 17g; CARB 32g; FIBER 12g; SUGARS 6g (est. added sugars 0g); CHOL 0mg; IRON 3mg; SODIUM 589mg; CALCIUM 108mg

TEMPEH GREEK SALAD WRAPS

HANDS-ON: **20 MINUTES**   TOTAL: **25 MINUTES**   SERVES **4**

2 tablespoons olive oil

1 (8-ounce) package tempeh, cut into 24 pieces

1 cup water

3 tablespoons fresh lemon juice

2 tablespoons plain low-fat yogurt

1½ teaspoons dried Italian seasoning

1 teaspoon grated lemon rind

½ teaspoon paprika

¼ teaspoon salt

1 garlic clove, minced

2 cups baby spinach

1 cup shredded romaine lettuce

⅔ cup sliced cherry tomatoes

⅔ cup sliced English cucumber

1 ounce feta cheese, crumbled (about ¼ cup)

¼ teaspoon freshly ground black pepper

4 (8-inch) whole-wheat tortillas

Searing the tempeh creates a nice, toasty crust. Serve with pita chips.

1. Heat a 10-inch skillet over medium-high heat. Add 1 tablespoon of the oil to the pan; swirl to coat. Add the tempeh; sauté 4 minutes or until lightly browned, turning once. Add 1 cup water and 2 tablespoons of the juice to the pan; reduce the heat to medium, and simmer 10 minutes, turning once.

2. Combine the yogurt, ½ teaspoon of the Italian seasoning, and the next 4 ingredients (through garlic) in a small bowl.

3. Combine the remaining 1 tablespoon olive oil, remaining 1 tablespoon lemon juice, remaining 1 teaspoon Italian seasoning, spinach, and the next 5 ingredients (through black pepper) in a bowl.

4. Warm the tortillas according to the package directions. Spread 2 teaspoons of the yogurt mixture over each tortilla. Top each tortilla with ¾ cup spinach mixture and 6 pieces tempeh; roll up.

(serving size: 1 wrap): **CALORIES** 319; **FAT** 16.2g (sat 3.7g, mono 7.1g, poly 3g); **PROTEIN** 16g; **CARB** 30g; **FIBER** 2g; **SUGARS** 3g (est. added sugars 0g); **CHOL** 9mg; **IRON** 3mg; **SODIUM** 468mg; **CALCIUM** 194mg

TEMPEH REUBENS

HANDS-ON: **20 MINUTES**   TOTAL: **40 MINUTES**   SERVES **4**

⅓ cup plain 2% reduced-fat Greek yogurt

1½ tablespoons ketchup

¾ cup plus 2 tablespoons refrigerated sauerkraut (such as Bubbies), drained

1 teaspoon Dijon mustard

1 (8-ounce) package tempeh

1 tablespoon olive oil

1 cup chopped onion

2 garlic cloves, thinly sliced

1 tablespoon cider vinegar

1 tablespoon lower-sodium soy sauce

½ teaspoon dried dill

½ teaspoon caraway seeds

1¼ cups water

8 (1-ounce) slices whole-grain rye bread, toasted

2 ounces Swiss cheese, shredded (about ½ cup)

The fermentation process used to make tempeh helps to keep your digestive track healthy by providing good-for-you bacteria and by keeping harmful bacteria at bay. While braising may destroy some of the good bacteria that are found on the surface of the tempeh, as long as the internal temp doesn't get too high, most of the probiotics will survive.

1. Place the Greek yogurt, ketchup, 2 tablespoons of the sauerkraut, and mustard in a mini food processor; process until smooth.

2. Cut the tempeh in half horizontally; cut each half into 4 slices, forming 8 pieces. Heat a large skillet over medium heat. Add the oil to the pan; swirl to coat. Add the onion; cook 5 minutes or until tender. Add the garlic; cook 1 minute, stirring constantly. Add the vinegar, soy sauce, dill, and caraway, stirring constantly. Add the tempeh; cook 1 minute on each side. Add 1¼ cups water; bring to a boil. Reduce the heat; simmer, uncovered, 10 minutes or until the water evaporates, turning the tempeh occasionally.

3. Preheat the broiler to high. Place 4 bread slices in a single layer on a heavy baking sheet. Divide the cheese evenly among the bread slices. Broil 1 minute or until the cheese melts. Top the cheese with about 1 tablespoon of the yogurt mixture, 1½ tablespoons of the onion mixture, 2 pieces of the tempeh, and about 3 tablespoons of the remaining sauerkraut. Spread the remaining yogurt mixture evenly over 1 side of the remaining 4 bread slices. Place the bread, yogurt side down, on top of the sauerkraut.

(serving size: 1 sandwich): **CALORIES** 382; **FAT** 16.6g (sat 4.5g, mono 5.2g, poly 2.7g); **PROTEIN** 22g; **CARB** 41g; **FIBER** 10g; **SUGAR** 6g (est. added sugar 2g); **CHOL** 14mg; **IRON** 4mg; **SODIUM** 740mg; **CALC** 285mg

BLACK BEAN–QUINOA BURGERS

HANDS-ON: **30 MINUTES**   TOTAL: **45 MINUTES**   SERVES **4**

1 (15-ounce) can unsalted black beans, rinsed and drained

4 teaspoons olive oil

2 tablespoons finely chopped shallots

5 tablespoons uncooked quinoa, rinsed and drained

6 tablespoons water

4 ounces cremini mushrooms

2 garlic cloves

2 tablespoons chopped fresh cilantro

2 teaspoons seeded minced serrano chile

1 teaspoon ground cumin

⅝ teaspoon kosher salt

¼ teaspoon ancho chile powder

1 large egg

½ cup chopped peeled ripe avocado

1 tablespoon fresh lime juice

1 small tomatillo, finely chopped

4 (1.5-ounce) whole-grain bakery-style hamburger buns, toasted

4 (¼-inch-thick) slices tomato

4 (¼-inch-thick) slices red onion

The whole-grain quinoa in these burgers has double the fiber and protein of breadcrumbs, which are traditionally used to bind vegetable burgers. Here, some of the quinoa is cooked until fluffy, acting as both a binder and a filler, while the rest is left uncooked for added texture and crunch. Folding the beans in whole adds texture and helps prevent the patty from becoming mushy.

1. Preheat the oven to 350°F.

2. Spread half of the beans in a single layer on a foil-lined baking sheet. Bake at 350°F for 20 minutes. Place the toasted beans in a large bowl.

3. Heat a small saucepan over medium heat. Add 1 teaspoon of the oil to the pan; swirl to coat. Add the shallots; sauté 2 minutes or until tender. Add 3 tablespoons of the quinoa; cook 2 minutes or until toasted, stirring frequently. Add 6 tablespoons water; bring to a boil. Cover, reduce heat, and simmer 10 minutes or until the liquid is absorbed.

4. Place the remaining 2 tablespoons uncooked quinoa, mushrooms, garlic, and remaining (untoasted) beans in a food processor; pulse until coarsely chopped. Add the cooked quinoa mixture, cilantro, serrano, cumin, ½ teaspoon salt, chile powder, and egg; pulse until combined. Add the mixture to the toasted beans; stir well to combine. Divide the mixture into 4 equal portions; shape each portion into a ½-inch-thick patty.

5. Heat a large cast-iron skillet over medium heat. Add the remaining 1 tablespoon oil to the pan; swirl to coat. Add the patties; cook 10 minutes, gently turning once.

6. Combine the chopped avocado, lime juice, tomatillo, and the remaining ⅛ teaspoon salt in a small bowl; mash to desired consistency.

7. Place 1 patty on the bottom half of each bun. Top each patty with 1 tomato slice, 1 onion slice, and about 2 tablespoons avocado mixture. Top with the top halves of the buns.

(serving size: 1 burger): **CALORIES** 352; **FAT** 11.6g (sat 1.9g, mono 6.4g, poly 2.6g); **PROTEIN** 15g; **CARB** 51g; **FIBER** 11g; **SUGARS** 6g (est. added sugars 0g); **CHOL** 47mg; **IRON** 4mg; **SODIUM** 511mg; **CALCIUM** 124mg

store-bought buns and bread nearly always contain artificial preservatives to help maintain freshness. Instead, buy whole-grain buns from your local bakery, where ingredients are kept clean and simple.

OPEN-FACED FALAFEL BURGERS ∇

HANDS-ON: **29 MINUTES**   TOTAL: **29 MINUTES**   SERVES **6**

SAUCE

1 cup hot water

¼ cup tahini (sesame seed paste)

3 tablespoons fresh lemon juice

⅛ teaspoon salt

2 garlic cloves, minced

PATTIES

1 cup chopped red onion

½ cup chopped fresh parsley

2 tablespoons fresh lemon juice

1 teaspoon ground cumin

1 teaspoon ground coriander

¼ teaspoon salt

2 (15-ounce) cans chickpeas (garbanzo beans), rinsed and drained

4 garlic cloves, minced

½ cup dry breadcrumbs

1 tablespoon plus 1 teaspoon olive oil

REMAINING INGREDIENTS

6 mini pitas (about 5 inches wide)

3 cups chopped romaine lettuce

2 cups chopped tomato

2 cups sliced peeled cucumber

½ cup finely chopped red onion

These burgers are a delicious spin on the Middle Eastern sandwich typically stuffed in a pita, but our version offers a more eye-catching presentation.

1. Make the sauce: Place the first 5 ingredients in a blender, and process until smooth.

2. Make the patties: Place 1 cup onion and the next 7 ingredients (through 4 garlic cloves) in a food processor; process until smooth, scraping sides of bowl occasionally. Place the bean mixture in a large bowl; stir in ¼ cup of the breadcrumbs. Divide the bean mixture into 6 equal portions, shaping each into a ½-inch-thick patty. Place the remaining breadcrumbs in a shallow dish. Dredge the patties in the breadcrumbs.

3. Heat a large nonstick skillet over medium-high heat. Add 2 teaspoons of the oil to the pan; swirl to coat. Add 3 patties to the pan; cook 3 minutes on each side or until browned. Repeat procedure with the remaining oil and patties.

4. Warm the mini pitas according to package directions. Top each pita with ½ cup lettuce, ⅓ cup tomato, ⅓ cup cucumber, and 4 teaspoons onion. Drizzle each serving with about 3 tablespoons of the sauce; top with 1 patty.

(serving size: 1 burger): **CALORIES** 404; **FAT** 11.8g (sat 1.7g, mono 4g, poly 4.6g); **PROTEIN** 15g; **CARB** 62g; **FIBER** 9g; **SUGARS** 6g (est. added sugars 0g); **CHOL** 0mg; **IRON** 5mg; **SODIUM** 789mg; **CALCIUM** 166mg

BERKELEY VEGGIE BURGER

HANDS-ON: **42 MINUTES** TOTAL: **42 MINUTES** SERVES **6**

6 (1½-ounce) artisanal sandwich rolls

Cooking spray

3 cups grated cooked golden beet (about 3 medium)

⅓ cup chopped walnuts, toasted

⅓ cup panko (Japanese breadcrumbs)

3 tablespoons grated fresh horseradish

3 tablespoons minced fresh chives

¼ teaspoon freshly ground black pepper

1 (8.8-ounce) package precooked brown rice

2 teaspoons Dijon mustard

2 large eggs

1 large egg white

⅜ teaspoon kosher salt

2 tablespoons canola oil

¼ cup canola mayonnaise (such as Hellmann's)

1 teaspoon fresh lemon juice

2 ounces blue cheese, crumbled (about ½ cup)

1½ cups arugula

A mix of golden beets and chewy whole-grain brown rice makes up this veggie burger. Chopped toasted walnuts and blue cheese add subtle crunch and rich flavor.

1. Preheat the broiler to high.

2. Place the rolls, cut sides up, on a baking sheet; coat with cooking spray. Broil 2 minutes or until toasted. Set aside.

3. Reduce oven temperature to 400°F; place a baking sheet in the oven.

4. Combine the beet and next 6 ingredients (through rice) in a large bowl. Combine the mustard, eggs, and egg white. Add ¼ teaspoon of the salt and the mustard mixture to the beet mixture; stir well. Spoon about ⅔ cup rice mixture into a 4-inch round biscuit cutter; pack the mixture down. Remove the mold; repeat 5 times to form 6 patties.

5. Heat a large skillet over medium-high heat. Add 1 tablespoon of the oil to the pan; swirl to coat. Carefully add 3 patties to the pan; cook 3 minutes. Carefully transfer the patties to the preheated baking sheet coated with cooking spray, turning patties over. Repeat procedure with the remaining oil and 3 patties. Return the baking sheet to the oven; bake the patties at 400°F for 12 minutes.

6. Combine the mayonnaise, juice, cheese, and remaining ⅛ teaspoon salt. Place the bottom half of each roll on a plate. Divide the mayonnaise mixture among the roll bottoms; top each with 1 patty. Arrange ¼ cup arugula on each patty; top with the roll tops.

(serving size: 1 burger): CALORIES 384; FAT 17.8g (sat 3.4g, mono 6.9g, poly 6.3g); PROTEIN 13g; CARB 43g; FIBER 4g; SUGARS 5g (est. added sugars 0g); CHOL 69mg; IRON 3mg; SODIUM 649mg; CALCIUM 111mg

soups, stews
& chilis

DOUBLE BARLEY POSOLE

HANDS-ON: **45 MINUTES**   TOTAL: **1 HOUR, 10 MINUTES**   SERVES **4**

- 2 tablespoons olive oil
- 8 ounces cremini mushrooms, quartered
- 1 cup chopped red bell pepper (from 1 bell pepper)
- ½ cup chopped yellow onion
- 1 tablespoon minced fresh garlic
- 1 tablespoon chopped fresh thyme
- 1 tablespoon all-purpose flour
- 1 (12-ounce) bottle Pilsner beer
- 3½ cups unsalted vegetable stock
- ¾ cup chopped peeled butternut squash (about 4½ ounces)
- ½ cup uncooked pearl barley
- 1 teaspoon freshly ground black pepper
- ⅛ teaspoon kosher salt
- 1 (15-ounce) can white hominy, rinsed and drained
- ½ cup chopped zucchini
- 1 ripe peeled avocado, diced
- ¼ cup packed cilantro leaves
- ¼ cup reduced-fat sour cream
- 4 lime wedges

This hearty soup gets its name from the pearl barley used in the soup and the barley used to produce the beer that's added. Hominy is a hallmark of posole, but if you have trouble finding it, you can substitute fresh corn instead. The lime juice adds a bright note at the end, but you could also use hot sauce.

1. Heat the oil in a Dutch oven over medium-high heat. Add the mushrooms; cook, stirring occasionally, until the mushrooms begin to release their liquid, about 5 minutes. Add the bell pepper and onion; cook, stirring occasionally, until the onion is translucent, about 4 minutes. Add the garlic, thyme, and flour; cook, stirring often, 1 minute. Stir in the beer; cook until the liquid is reduced and is glossy, about 7 minutes. Stir in the stock, squash, barley, black pepper, and salt; bring to a boil. Reduce the heat to medium-low; cover and cook until the barley is tender, about 40 minutes. Stir in the hominy and zucchini; simmer until the zucchini is tender but still bright green, about 5 minutes.

2. Ladle the soup into each of 4 bowls; top evenly with avocado, cilantro, sour cream, and lime wedges.

(serving size: 1½ cups): CALORIES 417; **FAT** 17.5g (sat 3.4g, mono 10.2g, poly 2.3g); **PROTEIN** 11g; **CARB** 58g; **FIBER** 13g; **SUGARS** 8g (est. added sugars 0g); **CHOL** 8mg; **IRON** 3mg; **SODIUM** 662mg; **CALCIUM** 92mg

hominy is a dried form of corn that has been soaked in a lye or lime solution. This process removes the tough outer hull and germ and plumps the kernels to two or three times their original size. The resulting kernels can be ground into masa (the base ingredient of corn tortillas or tamales), added whole to soups or stews (use it as you would beans), or served on its own. It has a mild corn flavor and a slightly chewy texture. You can find it canned in the canned vegetable aisle or the international aisle of most supermarkets.

SMOKY FARRO AND CHICKPEA SOUP

HANDS-ON: **15 MINUTES**   TOTAL: **25 MINUTES**   SERVES **6**

2 tablespoons extra-virgin olive oil

2 cups finely chopped onion

½ cup finely chopped celery

½ cup chopped fresh parsley

1 teaspoon chopped fresh rosemary

2 garlic cloves, chopped

1 bay leaf

3 cups unsalted vegetable stock

3 cups water

1½ teaspoons Spanish smoked paprika

½ teaspoon freshly ground black pepper

¼ teaspoon kosher salt

1 (15-ounce) can unsalted chickpeas (garbanzo beans), rinsed and drained

1 (14.5-ounce) can unsalted, fire-roasted diced tomatoes, undrained

4 cups chopped Swiss chard

3 cups cooked farro

½ cup sliced green onions

1½ ounces vegetarian Parmesan cheese, shaved (about 6 tablespoons)

This one-pot meal couldn't be easier, and it makes for simple cleanup. To save time, you can use pouches of precooked farro. You'll find it either on the grain aisle or in the frozen food section of your supermarket. Much of the farro you'll find in grocery stores is pearled. It cooks fast but it isn't whole grain.

Heat a large Dutch oven over medium heat. Add the oil to the pan; swirl to coat. Add the onion and the next 5 ingredients (through bay leaf). Cook 7 minutes or until the onion is tender, stirring frequently. Stir in the stock and the next 6 ingredients (through tomatoes); bring to a boil. Stir in the Swiss chard and farro; cook 2 minutes or until the chard wilts. Stir in the green onions. Remove and discard the bay leaf. Ladle the soup into each of 6 bowls. Top with the cheese.

(serving size: 1½ cups soup and about 2½ teaspoons cheese): CALORIES 279; FAT 8g (sat 1.7g, mono 3.6g, poly 0.5g); PROTEIN 12g; CARB 47g; FIBER 8g; SUGARS 6g (est. added sugars 0g); CHOL 6mg; IRON 2mg; SODIUM 496mg; CALCIUM 163mg

COOKING FARRO

1. The best way to prepare farro is pasta-style, i.e. in lots of water that lets the grains circulate as they cook. Bring the water to a full rolling boil over high heat. Add the grain, reduce the heat, and simmer for 25 to 60 minutes.

2. The cook times vary among brands based on how the farro is produced, so follow the package directions. Drain the cooked grain through a fine-mesh sieve, and shake it well to remove the excess water.

SWEET PEA SOUP
WITH YOGURT AND PINE NUTS

HANDS-ON: **15 MINUTES**   TOTAL: **15 MINUTES**   SERVES **6**

3 cups shelled fresh green peas

1 cup coarsely chopped pea shoots or baby spinach leaves

2 tablespoons chopped fresh mint

2 garlic cloves

1 cup unsalted vegetable stock

½ teaspoon kosher salt

2 tablespoons pine nuts, toasted

1 teaspoon extra-virgin olive oil

1 teaspoon chopped fresh dill

2 tablespoons plain 2% reduced-fat Greek yogurt

We love this dish at room temp, though you can also serve it chilled. Frozen green peas can also work—just be sure to thaw them first in cold water.

1. Bring a large pot of water to a boil. Add the peas; cook 15 seconds. Add the pea shoots, mint, and garlic; cook 15 seconds. Drain; plunge the pea mixture into ice water. Drain well.

2. Place the pea mixture, stock, and salt in a blender; process until very smooth.

3. Combine the nuts, oil, and dill in a small bowl. Ladle the soup into each of 6 shallow bowls. Drizzle with the yogurt; top with the nut mixture.

(serving size: about ⅔ cup soup, 1 teaspoon yogurt, and about 2 teaspoons nut mixture): **CALORIES** 88; **FAT** 3.1g (sat 0.4g, mono 1.2g, poly 1.2g); **PROTEIN** 5g; **CARB** 11g; **FIBER** 3g; **SUGARS** 4g (est. added sugars 0g); **CHOL** 0mg; **IRON** 1mg; **SODIUM** 281mg; **CALCIUM** 24mg

RUSTIC TOMATO SOUP
WITH CHEESE TOASTS

HANDS-ON: **23 MINUTES**   TOTAL: **23 MINUTES**   SERVES **4**

½ cup coarsely chopped carrot

½ cup coarsely chopped onion

½ cup coarsely chopped fennel bulb

1 celery stalk, coarsely chopped

1 tablespoon olive oil

1 (26.46-ounce) box unsalted chopped tomatoes (such as Pomì), undrained

1 cup unsalted vegetable stock

¾ teaspoon freshly ground black pepper

⅝ teaspoon salt

1 tablespoon butter

8 celery leaves

4 (1.5-ounce) slices diagonally cut whole-grain bread

3 ounces vegetarian Gruyère cheese, shredded (about ¾ cup)

The food processor speeds prep by finely chopping the vegetables quickly—much faster than even cooks with masterful knife skills—giving the soup a rustic, crisp-tender texture. If you want a smoother texture, process the vegetables longer.

1. Preheat the broiler to high.

2. Place the first 4 ingredients in a food processor; process until finely chopped. Heat a large saucepan over medium-high heat. Add the oil to the pan; swirl to coat. Add the vegetable mixture to the pan; cook 5 minutes or until crisp-tender, stirring occasionally. Add the tomatoes to the food processor; pulse until finely chopped. Add the tomatoes, stock, ½ teaspoon of the pepper, and salt to pan; bring to a simmer. Reduce the heat to low; simmer 10 minutes. Stir in the butter; sprinkle with the celery leaves.

3. Place the bread on a baking sheet. Broil 2 minutes. Turn the bread slices over; sprinkle evenly with the cheese. Broil 2 minutes or until the cheese is lightly browned. Sprinkle with the remaining ¼ teaspoon black pepper. Ladle the soup into each of 4 bowls. Serve with the cheese toasts.

(serving size: about 1 cup soup and 1 cheese toast): **CALORIES** 292; **FAT** 13.9g (sat 6.3g, mono 5.4g, poly 0.9g); **PROTEIN** 11g; **CARB** 34g; **FIBER** 11g; **SUGARS** 3g (est. added sugars 0g); **CHOL** 31mg; **IRON** 2mg; **SODIUM** 661mg; **CALCIUM** 362mg

SUMMER MINESTRONE SOUP

HANDS-ON: **50 MINUTES**   TOTAL: **1 HOUR, 5 MINUTES**   SERVES **8**

2 tablespoons olive oil

2 cups thinly sliced leek, white and light green parts only (about 2 leeks)

1 cup thinly sliced carrot

1 cup thinly sliced celery

2 large garlic cloves, minced

2 tablespoons tomato paste

8 cups unsalted vegetable stock

1 (14.5-ounce) can unsalted diced tomatoes, undrained

1 (14.5-ounce) can unsalted cannellini beans, rinsed and drained

2 cups chopped yellow squash

2 cups chopped zucchini

1 cup chopped red bell pepper

1 cup fresh green beans, cut into 1-inch pieces

½ cup uncooked ditalini pasta

½ teaspoon salt

½ teaspoon freshly ground black pepper

5 ounces Lacinato kale, stemmed and chopped

¼ cup homemade or refrigerated pesto

2 ounces vegetarian Parmesan cheese, grated (about ½ cup)

A gentle simmer keeps the vegetables in the soup slightly firm, so they maintain a nice texture, which is also a plus if you're freezing some for later.

1. Heat a large Dutch oven over medium heat. Add the oil to the pan; swirl to coat. Add the leek, carrot, celery, and garlic; cover and cook 5 minutes, stirring occasionally (do not brown). Add the tomato paste; cook 2 minutes, stirring constantly. Add the stock and tomatoes; bring to a boil. Reduce the heat to low, and simmer 15 minutes.

2. Place 1 cup of the cannellini beans in a small bowl; mash with a fork. Add the mashed beans, remaining cannellini beans, the squashes, bell pepper, green beans, pasta, salt, and black pepper to the pan. Increase the heat to medium; cook 10 minutes. Stir in the kale; cook 2 minutes. Ladle the soup into each of 8 bowls. Top with the pesto and the Parmesan cheese.

(serving size: 2 cups soup, 1½ teaspoons pesto, and 1 tablespoon Parmesan cheese): CALORIES 243; FAT 9.5g (sat 2.2g, mono 5.6g, poly 1g); PROTEIN 11g; CARB 31g; FIBER 5g; SUGARS 8g (est. added sugars 0g); CHOL 9mg; IRON 3mg; SODIUM 584mg; CALCIUM 190mg

to freeze soups and stews, cool them completely. Then, ladle them into a large zip-top plastic freezer bag and freeze flat for up to 2 months. To thaw, microwave in the bag at MEDIUM (50% power) for 5 minutes or until pliable. To reheat, pour into a large Dutch oven, and cook over medium heat, partially covered, for 20 minutes or until thoroughly heated.

SWEET AND SPICY CARROT SOUP ♈

HANDS-ON: **15 MINUTES**   TOTAL: **55 MINUTES**   SERVES **4**

1 tablespoon olive oil

⅓ cup sliced green onions

¾ pound carrots, cut into
¼-inch-thick slices

2 teaspoons minced peeled
fresh ginger

2 teaspoons chopped Fresno
chile

1½ cups unsalted vegetable
stock

1½ cups water

Stems from 1 bunch cilantro,
tied with kitchen twine

½ cup light coconut milk

1 tablespoon brown sugar

1½ teaspoons fresh lime juice

¼ teaspoon kosher salt

Sliced Fresno chile

Sliced green onions

Cilantro leaves

*The combination of carrots, Fresno chile, brown sugar, fresh
ginger, and green onions gives this soup its sweet and spicy flavor.*

1. Heat a saucepan over medium heat. Add the olive oil to the pan;
swirl to coat. Add ⅓ cup sliced green onions; cook 3 minutes. Stir
in the carrot, ginger, and 2 teaspoons chopped Fresno chile; cook
2 minutes. Add the stock, 1½ cups water, and the cilantro stems to the
pan; simmer 30 minutes or until the carrots are soft. Cool 10 minutes;
discard the cilantro stems.

2. Place the carrot mixture, coconut milk, brown sugar, lime juice, and
salt in a blender; process until smooth. Return to the pan; heat over
medium-low until warm. Serve with the sliced Fresno chile, the sliced
green onions, and the cilantro leaves.

(serving size: about 1 cup): CALORIES 96; **FAT** 3.9g (sat 0.8g, mono 2.5g, poly 0.5g);
PROTEIN 2g; **CARB** 15g; **FIBER** 3g; **SUGARS** 8g (est. added sugars 3g); **CHOL** 0mg;
IRON 1mg; **SODIUM** 276mg; **CALCIUM** 42mg

WHITE CHEDDAR AND CHIVE POTATO SOUP

HANDS-ON: **25 MINUTES**   TOTAL: **35 MINUTES**   SERVES **4**

1 tablespoon canola oil

⅓ cup chopped shallots

2 garlic cloves, minced

2 tablespoons all-purpose flour

3½ cups chopped Yukon gold potatoes (about 1 pound)

1¾ cups 1% low-fat milk

1½ cups organic vegetable broth (such as Swanson)

⅜ teaspoon kosher salt

¼ teaspoon freshly ground black pepper

2 ounces sharp white cheddar cheese, shredded (about ½ cup)

⅓ cup fat-free sour cream

Freshly ground black pepper

2 tablespoons minced fresh chives

This luscious, creamy potato soup uses just one pan, making it ideal for fast weeknight comfort food and even faster cleanup. We love the look and tang of sharp white cheddar in this soup.

1. Heat a large saucepan over medium-high heat. Add the oil to the pan; swirl to coat. Add the shallots and garlic; sauté 1½ minutes or until tender. Sprinkle the flour over the vegetables; cook 1 minute, stirring constantly with a whisk.

2. Add the potatoes, milk, broth, salt, and pepper to the pan; bring to a boil. Cover, reduce the heat, and simmer 10 minutes or until the potatoes are tender. Remove the pan from the heat. Mash the potato mixture with a potato masher to the desired consistency. Stir in the cheese until melted. Stir in 1 tablespoon of the sour cream. Ladle the soup into each of 4 bowls. Top with the remaining sour cream, the freshly ground black pepper, and the minced chives.

(serving size: 1 cup soup, about 1 tablespoon sour cream, and 1½ teaspoons chives): **CALORIES** 263; **FAT** 9.6g (sat 4.2g, mono 2.5g, poly 1.1g); **PROTEIN** 11g; **CARB** 34g; **FIBER** 3g; **SUGARS** 9g (est. added sugars 0g); **CHOL** 20mg; **IRON** 1mg; **SODIUM** 562mg; **CALCIUM** 286mg

CREAMY BROCCOLI-CHEESE SOUP

HANDS-ON: **45 MINUTES**   TOTAL: **45 MINUTES**   SERVES **6**

- 4 cups unsalted vegetable stock
- ½ cup uncooked instant brown rice
- 1 cup 1% low-fat milk
- 2 teaspoons extra-virgin olive oil
- 1 cup chopped onion
- 3 garlic cloves, minced
- 1¼ pounds broccoli florets, coarsely chopped
- ¾ teaspoon kosher salt
- ½ teaspoon freshly ground black pepper
- 5 ounces extra-sharp cheddar cheese, shredded (about 1¼ cups)

We like our version extra chunky, so we only puree about a third of the broccoli mixture in step 3. For a thinner, smoother consistency, add more soup to the blender.

1. Combine 2 cups of the stock and the rice in a small saucepan over medium-high heat; bring to a boil. Cover, reduce the heat, and simmer 25 minutes. Remove from the heat; let stand 5 minutes. Place the rice mixture and milk in a blender. Remove center piece of blender lid (to allow the steam to escape); secure the blender lid on the blender. Place a clean towel over the opening in the blender lid (to avoid splatters). Blend until smooth.

2. Heat a large saucepan over medium heat. Add the oil to the pan; swirl to coat. Add the onion; sauté 4 minutes, stirring occasionally. Add the garlic; cook 30 seconds. Add the broccoli and salt; cook 5 minutes, stirring frequently. Add the remaining 2 cups stock; bring to a boil. Reduce the heat, and simmer 5 minutes or just until the broccoli is tender. Add the rice mixture; simmer 2 minutes, stirring occasionally.

3. Place 2 cups of the soup in the blender; process until smooth. Return the pureed soup to the pan. Add the pepper and 4 ounces of the cheese; stir until the cheese melts. Ladle the soup into each of 6 bowls. Sprinkle with the remaining cheese.

(serving size: about 1 cup and 2 teaspoons cheese): **CALORIES** 208; **FAT** 10.4g (sat 5.5g, mono 3.6g, poly 0.5g); **PROTEIN** 12g; **CARB** 19g; **FIBER** 4g; **SUGARS** 3g (est. added sugars 0g); **CHOL** 27mg; **IRON** 1mg; **SODIUM** 593mg; **CALCIUM** 276mg

instant brown rice is the trick to making this broccoli-cheese soup as comforting and creamy as the original without all the saturated fat. When overcooked in stock, the rice becomes silky, savory, and soft. That texture isn't ideal as a side at dinner, but it's perfect for a puree when blended with low-fat milk. The result is a thick, nutty, whole-grain "cream" that eliminates the need for heavy cream, butter, or refined white flour.

ONE-POT GREEN CURRY STEW
WITH POTATOES AND CAULIFLOWER

HANDS-ON: **25 MINUTES**   TOTAL: **25 MINUTES**   SERVES **8**

1½ tablespoons butter

1 (8-ounce) package prechopped onion

2 garlic cloves, minced

3 tablespoons green curry paste (such as Thai Kitchen)

1 tablespoon minced peeled fresh ginger

1 teaspoon ground cumin

1½ tablespoons lower-sodium soy sauce

2 (14-ounce) cans light coconut milk

1 (12-ounce) package trimmed green beans, cut into 1-inch pieces

2 (10-ounce) packages fresh cauliflower florets

1 (20-ounce) package refrigerated diced potatoes with onions (such as Simply Potatoes)

2 (15-ounce) cans unsalted chickpeas, rinsed and drained

½ teaspoon kosher salt

¾ cup torn basil leaves

1 cup plain 2% reduced-fat Greek yogurt

8 lime wedges

Layer the vegetables in the pan rather than stirring them in so they steam to the right doneness. Add red pepper for extra kick. You can make this stew ahead and freeze it until ready to serve. See page 107 for tips on freezing, thawing, and reheating soups and stews.

Melt the butter in a large Dutch oven over medium-high heat. Add the onion and garlic; sauté 4 minutes. Stir in the curry paste, ginger, and cumin; cook 1 minute. Stir in the soy sauce and coconut milk; bring to a boil. Layer the beans, cauliflower, potatoes, and chickpeas in the pan; bring to a boil. Cover; reduce the heat, and simmer for 10 minutes. Stir in the salt and basil. Ladle the stew into each of 8 bowls. Top with the yogurt and the lime wedges.

(serving size: 1¾ cups stew, 2 tablespoons yogurt, and 1 lime wedge): CALORIES 237; FAT 4.8g (sat 2.9g, mono 0.6g, poly 0.2g); PROTEIN 11g; CARB 40g; FIBER 8g; SUGARS 6g (est. added sugars 0g); CHOL 8mg; IRON 2mg; SODIUM 533mg; CALCIUM 103mg

coconut milk, a staple of Thai, Chinese, Indian, and Caribbean cuisine, has a rich, mildly sweet flavor and creamy texture. It's vegan and can also be used as a dairy replacement. To store leftover coconut milk, transfer it to an airtight container and keep it in the refrigerator for up to 3 days.

QUICK WHITE BEAN, ASPARAGUS, AND MUSHROOM CASSOULET

HANDS-ON: **26 MINUTES**   TOTAL: **38 MINUTES**   SERVES **4**

5 cups water

3 cups (2-inch) slices asparagus (about 1 pound)

2 tablespoons extra-virgin olive oil

3 cups sliced chanterelle or oyster mushrooms (about 10 ounces)

⅓ cup finely chopped shallots

6 garlic cloves, minced

¼ cup dry white wine

1½ cups organic vegetable broth (such as Swanson)

½ teaspoon dried marjoram or dried oregano

2 (15-ounce) cans no-salt-added cannellini beans, rinsed and drained

¼ teaspoon freshly ground black pepper

2 ounces French bread, cut into 1-inch cubes

1 tablespoon butter, cut into small pieces

2 ounces vegetarian Parmesan cheese, grated (about ½ cup)

Cassoulet—a rich, slow-cooked bean stew with meat—is reinvented here as a quick-cooking vegetarian dish, starting with canned beans and using mushrooms to lend a meaty mouthfeel and earthy flavor.

1. Bring 5 cups of water to a boil in a large ovenproof skillet, and add the asparagus to the pan. Cover and cook 2 minutes; drain. Rinse the asparagus with cold water; drain well.

2. Return the pan to medium-high heat. Add 1 tablespoon of the oil to the pan; swirl to coat. Add the mushrooms, shallots, and garlic; sauté 8 minutes or until the mushrooms are tender. Add the wine; cook 3 minutes or until the liquid evaporates. Stir in the broth, marjoram, and beans; bring to a simmer. Reduce the heat to medium, and cook for 12 minutes or until thick and the beans are very tender. Stir in the black pepper.

3. Preheat the broiler to high.

4. Place the French bread and butter in a food processor; pulse until coarse crumbs form. Add the remaining 1 tablespoon oil and cheese to the coarse breadcrumbs; pulse until combined. Stir the asparagus into the bean mixture; sprinkle the coarse breadcrumb mixture evenly over the bean mixture. Broil for 3 minutes or until the crumbs are golden brown.

(serving size: about 1¾ cups): **CALORIES** 362; **FAT** 15.4g (sat 4.9g, mono 6.5g, poly 1g); **PROTEIN** 18g; **CARB** 39g; **FIBER** 10g; **SUGARS** 5g (est. added sugars 0g); **CHOL** 20mg; **IRON** 6mg; **SODIUM** 507mg; **CALCIUM** 273mg

BLACK BEAN, HOMINY, AND KALE STEW

HANDS-ON: **25 MINUTES**   TOTAL: **35 MINUTES**   SERVES **6**

2 poblano chiles

8 ounces tomatillos, husks removed and halved (about 4)

2 teaspoons olive oil

1½ cups chopped onion

1 jalapeño, seeded and minced

2 garlic cloves, minced

2 teaspoons ground cumin

3 cups organic vegetable broth (such as Swanson)

¼ teaspoon salt

⅛ teaspoon ground red pepper

2 (15.5-ounce) cans unsalted black beans, rinsed and drained

1 (8-ounce) bunch kale, stemmed and chopped (about 4 packed cups)

1 (15-ounce) can hominy, rinsed and drained

6 tablespoons reduced-fat sour cream

2 ounces sharp white cheddar cheese, shredded (about ½ cup)

¼ cup chopped fresh cilantro

You can use whatever leafy greens you like in this hearty, stick-to-your-ribs stew.

1. Preheat the broiler to high.

2. Place the poblano chiles on a foil-lined baking sheet. Broil 7 minutes on each side or until blackened and charred. Place in a zip-top plastic or paper bag; fold to close tightly. Let stand 15 minutes. Peel the chiles; cut in half lengthwise. Discard the seeds and membranes; coarsely chop.

3. While the poblano chiles roast, place the tomatillos in a food processor; process until smooth.

4. Heat a Dutch oven over medium heat. Add the oil to the pan; swirl to coat. Add the onion and jalapeño; sauté 5 minutes or until tender, stirring occasionally. Add the garlic and cumin; sauté 1 minute, stirring constantly. Add the tomatillos, broth, and next 4 ingredients (through kale); bring to a boil. Cover, reduce the heat, and simmer for 10 minutes or until the vegetables are tender. Add the roasted poblanos and hominy; cook 2 minutes or until heated through. Ladle the stew into each of 4 shallow bowls. Top with the sour cream and the cheese. Sprinkle evenly with the cilantro.

(serving size: 1¼ cups stew, 1 tablespoon sour cream, and about 1 tablespoon cheese): **CALORIES** 240; **FAT** 7.7g (sat 3.5g, mono 2.7g, poly 0.8g); **PROTEIN** 11g; **CARB** 33g; **FIBER** 8g; **SUGARS** 5g (est. added sugars 0g); **CHOL** 16mg; **IRON** 3mg; **SODIUM** 573mg; **CALCIUM** 210mg

BROILING CHILE PEPPERS

1. Broiling chiles gives them a soft, silky texture and deep smoky flavor. Place the chiles on a foil-lined baking sheet for easy cleanup and broil until they're blackened and charred.

2. Placing the charred peppers in a zip-top plastic bag or paper bag lets them steam, loosening the blackened skin so you can easily peel it off.

WINTER SQUASH STEW
WITH CILANTRO-AVOCADO SALSA

HANDS-ON: **24 MINUTES**   TOTAL: **35 MINUTES**   SERVES **4**

STEW

- 1 tablespoon olive oil
- 2 cups (½-inch) cubed peeled butternut squash
- 1 cup diced onion
- 1 teaspoon dried oregano
- 1 dried red New Mexican or guajillo chile, seeded and crumbled
- 1 teaspoon smoked paprika
- ¼ teaspoon kosher salt
- ¼ teaspoon ground red pepper (optional)
- 2 (15-ounce) cans hominy, undrained

SALSA

- ⅔ cup diced avocado
- ½ cup minced fresh cilantro
- 1 tablespoon plus 1 teaspoon diced jalapeño pepper
- 1 teaspoon olive oil
- 1½ teaspoons grated lime rind
- 1½ tablespoons fresh lime juice
- 1 ounce Monterey Jack cheese, shredded (about ¼ cup)
- ¼ cup plain 2% reduced-fat Greek yogurt

Winter greens would also make a lovely addition to this filling stew; simply toss a few handfuls in when the squash is almost tender, and stir until the greens begin to wilt. For more about hominy, see page 99.

1. Make the stew: Heat a 3-quart saucepan over medium-high heat. Add 1 tablespoon oil to the pan; swirl to coat. Add the squash, onion, oregano, and chile; cook 10 minutes or until the onion and squash begin to brown, stirring frequently. Add the paprika, salt, red pepper (if desired), and hominy; bring to a boil. Cover, reduce the heat, and simmer 10 minutes or until the squash is tender.

2. Make the salsa: Combine the avocado, cilantro, jalapeño, and 1 teaspoon oil in a small bowl. Stir in the rind and juice. Ladle the hominy mixture into each of 4 bowls. Top with the salsa, cheese, and yogurt. Serve immediately.

(serving size: about 1¼ cups stew, about ¼ cup salsa, about 1 tablespoon cheese, and 1 tablespoon yogurt): **CALORIES** 330; **FAT** 12.8g (sat 3g, mono 6.9g, poly 2g); **PROTEIN** 8g; **CARB** 48g; **FIBER** 10g; **SUGARS** 9g (est. added sugars 0g); **CHOL** 7mg; **IRON** 2mg; **SODIUM** 632mg; **CALCIUM** 138mg

STEWED BULGUR AND BROCCOLI RABE
WITH POACHED EGGS

HANDS-ON: **20 MINUTES**   TOTAL: **40 MINUTES**   SERVES **6**

2 teaspoons extra-virgin olive oil

1½ cups chopped onion

½ teaspoon crushed red pepper

4 garlic cloves, minced

3 cups organic vegetable broth (such as Swanson)

1 cup water

¾ cup uncooked bulgur

¼ teaspoon salt

1 bunch broccoli rabe (rapini), cut into 2-inch-long pieces (about 1 pound)

1 tablespoon fresh lemon juice

1 tablespoon white vinegar

6 large eggs

1½ ounces vegetarian Parmesan cheese, shredded (about 6 tablespoons)

¼ teaspoon freshly ground black pepper

For less cleanup, you can poach the eggs directly in the stew once the broccoli rabe is tender. See page 261 for more tips about poaching eggs.

1. Heat a large Dutch oven over medium heat. Add the oil to the pan; swirl to coat. Add the onion; sauté 10 minutes or until browned. Stir in the red pepper and garlic; cook 1 minute. Add the broth and 1 cup water; bring to a boil. Stir in the bulgur and salt. Cover and simmer 10 minutes. Add the broccoli rabe. Cover and simmer 12 minutes or until the broccoli rabe is tender; stir in the lemon juice. Ladle the stew into each of 6 shallow bowls.

2. Add water to a large skillet, filling two-thirds full; bring to a boil. Reduce the heat; simmer. Add the vinegar. Break each egg into a custard cup, and pour each gently into the pan; cook 3 minutes or until the desired degree of doneness. Carefully remove the eggs from the pan using a slotted spoon; place the eggs on each serving of stew. Sprinkle with the cheese and black pepper.

(serving size: about 1 cup stew, 1 egg, and 1 tablespoon cheese): CALORIES 226; FAT 8.6g (sat 3.1g, mono 3.6g, poly 1.3g); PROTEIN 14g; CARB 24g; FIBER 4g; SUGARS 3g (est. added sugars 0g); CHOL 192mg; IRON 2mg; SODIUM 579mg; CALCIUM 162mg

BUTTERNUT-CHICKPEA CHILI ♈

HANDS-ON: **22 MINUTES**   TOTAL: **10 HOURS, 22 MINUTES**   SERVES **8**

1 cup dried chickpeas

2 quarts boiling water

2 tablespoons olive oil

1½ cups chopped onion

5 garlic cloves, minced

1 tablespoon tomato paste

1½ teaspoons ground cumin

1 teaspoon kosher salt

½ teaspoon ground red pepper

½ teaspoon ground cinnamon

¼ teaspoon ground turmeric

2½ cups organic vegetable broth (such as Swanson)

½ cup water

⅔ cup sliced pimiento-stuffed olives

½ cup golden raisins

1 (28-ounce) can whole tomatoes, undrained and crushed

4 cups chopped peeled butternut squash

1 cup frozen green peas, thawed

¼ cup chopped fresh cilantro

6 cups hot cooked couscous

8 lime wedges

Add this tasty chili dish to your winter meal plans. It's loaded with fiery flavors. Serve it over couscous with lime wedges and a sprinkling of cilantro.

1. Place the chickpeas in a saucepan; add 2 quarts of boiling water. Cover and let stand 1 hour; drain. Place the beans in a 6-quart slow cooker.

2. Heat a large skillet over medium-high heat. Add 1 tablespoon of the oil to the pan; swirl to coat. Add the onion; sauté 4 minutes, stirring occasionally. Add the garlic; sauté 1 minute, stirring constantly. Stir in the tomato paste and the next 5 ingredients (through turmeric); sauté 30 seconds, stirring constantly. Add the onion mixture to the slow cooker. Add the broth and the next 4 ingredients (through tomatoes) to the slow cooker; cover and cook on HIGH 8 hours.

3. Heat a large skillet over medium-high heat. Add the remaining 1 tablespoon oil; swirl to coat. Add the squash; sauté 5 minutes. Add the squash to the slow cooker. Cover and cook on HIGH 1 hour; stir in the peas. Sprinkle with the cilantro. Spoon the couscous into each of 8 bowls. Ladle the chili over each serving. Serve with the lime wedges.

(serving size: ¾ cup couscous, 1 cup chili, and 1 lime wedge): **CALORIES** 386; **FAT** 6.9g (sat 0.6g, mono 3.6g, poly 1.9g); **PROTEIN** 12g; **CARB** 71g; **FIBER** 8g; **SUGARS** 15g (est. added sugars 0g); **CHOL** 0mg; **IRON** 4mg; **SODIUM** 656mg; **CALCIUM** 125mg

SMOKY TWO-BEAN VEGETARIAN CHILI ⱴ

HANDS-ON: **15 MINUTES**   TOTAL: **28 MINUTES**   SERVES **4**

1 tablespoon olive oil

4 garlic cloves, finely chopped

1 small onion, finely chopped (about 1 cup)

1 small green bell pepper, chopped (about 1 cup)

1 teaspoon ground cumin

1 cup water

2 teaspoons finely chopped chipotle chiles, canned in adobo sauce

1 teaspoon salt

½ teaspoon freshly ground black pepper

2 (15-ounce) cans unsalted black beans, rinsed and drained

1 (15-ounce) can unsalted pinto beans, rinsed and drained

1 (14.5-ounce) can unsalted petite diced tomatoes, undrained

A wee bit of canned chipotle chiles goes a long way in infusing this hearty chili with rich, smoky flavor and a hint of heat. To vary the flavor, you can use any type of bean you like—kidney beans, chickpeas (garbanzo beans), or red beans would all be tasty. Or, swap in one can of hominy or a cup of frozen corn in place of one can of beans.

1. Heat a Dutch oven or a large saucepan over medium-high heat. Add the oil to the pan; swirl to coat. Add the garlic, onion, and bell pepper; sauté 4 minutes. Add the cumin; sauté 30 seconds. Stir in 1 cup water, the chipotle chiles, and the remaining ingredients. Bring to a boil; cover, reduce the heat, and simmer 5 minutes.

2. Remove 1 cup of the bean mixture from the pan with a slotted spoon; place in a bowl. Mash the beans with a fork. Stir the mashed beans into the chili. Simmer 5 minutes.

(serving size: about 1½ cups): **CALORIES** 233; **FAT** 3.6g (sat 0.5g, mono 2.5g, poly 0.4g); **PROTEIN** 12g; **CARB** 38g; **FIBER** 11g; **SUGARS** 5g (est. added sugars 0g); **CHOL** 0mg; **IRON** 4mg; **SODIUM** 655mg; **CALCIUM** 128mg

CAN'T-BELIEVE-IT'S-VEGAN CHILI ⓥ

HANDS-ON: **25 MINUTES**   TOTAL: **35 MINUTES**   SERVES **10**

2 tablespoons olive oil

1 cup chopped onion

1 cup chopped red bell pepper

1 tablespoon chopped fresh garlic

1 (12.95-ounce) package vegan sausage, chopped (such as Field Roast Mexican Chipotle)

2 cups chopped tomato

½ cup white wine

2 teaspoons freshly ground black pepper

1 teaspoon salt

1 teaspoon dried ground sage

1 teaspoon crushed red pepper

6 cups unsalted vegetable stock

3 (15-ounce) cans unsalted cannellini beans, rinsed and drained

2 (15-ounce) cans unsalted kidney beans, rinsed and drained

2 cups chopped kale

2 tablespoons fresh oregano leaves

This dish is sure to make it into your regular rotation. It's completely satisfying and cooks in a fraction of the time it takes to make traditional meat chili. This recipe makes plenty, and you can freeze leftovers for up to three months. Vegan sausage varies widely in taste and texture; we liked the meatiness and mild heat of the Field Roast brand, Mexican Chipotle flavor, but use whatever brand you like best.

1. Heat a large Dutch oven over medium-high heat. Add the oil to the pan; swirl to coat. Add the onion and next 3 ingredients (through sausage); sauté 4 minutes. Add the tomato and next 5 ingredients (through red pepper). Bring to a boil; cook until the liquid is reduced by half (about 1 minute). Stir in the stock.

2. Combine 2 cans of the cannellini beans and 1 can of the kidney beans in a medium bowl; mash with a potato masher. Add the bean mixture and the remaining beans to the pan. Bring to a simmer; cook 5 minutes. Add the kale; cover and simmer 5 minutes. Top with the oregano.

(serving size: 1½ cups): **CALORIES** 235; **FAT** 5g (sat 0.4g, mono 3.2g, poly 1.3g); **PROTEIN** 18g; **CARB** 34g; **FIBER** 8g; **SUGARS** 4g (est. added sugars 0g); **CHOL** 0mg; **IRON** 3mg; **SODIUM** 544mg; **CALCIUM** 87mg

pasta & noodles

SQUASH RIBBON PASTA WITH HERB CREAM SAUCE

HANDS-ON: **19 MINUTES**   TOTAL: **25 MINUTES**   SERVES **4**

1 medium zucchini (about 8 ounces)

1 medium summer squash (about 8 ounces)

8 ounces uncooked fettuccine

½ cup thinly sliced red onion

1 cup 2% reduced-fat milk

1½ tablespoons all-purpose flour

⅓ cup heavy cream

½ cup chopped fresh tarragon, basil, or parsley

¾ teaspoon kosher salt

½ teaspoon freshly ground black pepper

Adding the red onion to the pasta in the last 2 minutes of cooking removes its harsh bite. The pasta gets a big, herbaceous hit from lots of fresh tarragon. Feel free to substitute fresh basil or parsley.

1. Shave the squashes into thin strips using a vegetable peeler; place in a colander. Bring a large saucepan filled with water to a boil. Add the pasta; cook 6 minutes. Add the red onion; cook 2 minutes. Drain the pasta mixture over the squash in the colander.

2. Return the pan to medium-high heat. Add the milk and flour; bring to a boil. Cook 1 minute or until slightly thickened, stirring constantly. Stir in the cream; cook for 1 minute. Add the pasta mixture, stirring to coat. Stir in the tarragon, salt, and pepper. Serve immediately.

(serving size: about 1½ cups): **CALORIES** 378; **FAT** 10g (sat 5.7g, mono 2.5g, poly 0.5g); **PROTEIN** 13g; **CARB** 60g; **FIBER** 4g; **SUGARS** 9g (est. added sugars 0g); **CHOL** 32mg; **IRON** 3mg; **SODIUM** 407mg; **CALCIUM** 142mg

MAKING SQUASH "PASTA"

1. Thinly slicing the squash with a vegetable peeler mimics thickness of the fettuccine.

2. Draining the hot cooked pasta over the squash ribbons softens the vegetables just enough to keep their fresh texture and combine well with the pasta.

VEGETABLE BOLOGNESE OVER SPAGHETTI SQUASH

HANDS-ON: **55 MINUTES**   TOTAL: **1 HOUR, 30 MINUTES**   SERVES **8**

4 (1½-pound) spaghetti squash

¼ cup olive oil

Cooking spray

2 cups chopped yellow onion (from 1 large onion)

2 cups chopped butternut squash (about 10 ounces)

1 cup chopped celery (3 stalks)

1 cup chopped carrot (about 5 ounces)

1 (15-ounce) can unsalted chickpeas (garbanzo beans), rinsed and drained

8 ounces cremini mushrooms, roughly chopped

8 ounces white mushrooms, roughly chopped

5 garlic cloves

3 tablespoons unsalted tomato paste

2 teaspoons dried oregano

1 (28-ounce) jar lower-sodium marinara sauce

½ cup unsalted vegetable stock

1¼ teaspoons kosher salt

1 teaspoon freshly ground black pepper

¼ cup chopped fresh flat-leaf parsley

2 ounces vegetarian Parmesan cheese, shaved (about ½ cup)

The sauce makes a large batch. It can easily be halved to serve four or you can freeze the extra for later meals. To simplify the sauce, you can use just one type of mushroom if you'd like.

1. Preheat the oven to 425°F. Cut each spaghetti squash in half lengthwise; remove and discard the seeds. Brush 2 tablespoons of the oil over the cut sides of the squash. Place the squash, cut sides down, on a baking sheet coated with cooking spray. Bake at 425°F for 25 to 30 minutes or until tender. Cool until ready to use.

2. Place the onion, butternut squash, celery, carrot, chickpeas, mushrooms, and garlic, in 2 batches, in a food processor; process until finely ground. Heat a large skillet over medium-high heat. Add the the remaining 2 tablespoons oil to the pan; swirl to coat. Add the processed vegetable mixture to the pan, and cook, stirring often, until tender and lightly browned, about 12 minutes. Add the tomato paste and oregano; cook, stirring constantly, until fully incorporated and beginning to brown, about 2 minutes. Stir in the marinara and stock. Bring to a boil, reduce the heat to medium, and simmer until the mixture thickens and deepens in color, about 20 minutes. Stir in the salt, pepper, and 3 tablespoons of the parsley.

3. Scrape the inside of the squash with a fork to remove spaghetti-like strands. Place the squash strands onto each of 8 plates. Top with the Bolognese sauce, and sprinkle with the cheese and the remaining 1 tablespoon parsley.

(serving size: 1 cup spaghetti squash and 1 cup sauce): CALORIES 438; FAT 12.7g (sat 2.6g, mono 5.7g, poly 1.8g); PROTEIN 18g; CARB 68g; FIBER 14g; SUGARS 17g (est. added sugars 0g); CHOL 5mg; IRON 4mg; SODIUM 617mg; CALCIUM 275mg

SPRING VEGGIE PASTA

HANDS-ON: **18 MINUTES**   TOTAL: **18 MINUTES**   SERVES **4**

2 teaspoons butter

5 ounces thinly diagonally sliced baby carrots (about 1 cup)

1 cup unsalted vegetable stock

¾ teaspoon kosher salt

1 cup fresh asparagus tips

½ cup frozen petite green peas, thawed

2 teaspoons finely shredded lemon rind

5 ounces ⅓-less-fat cream cheese

¼ teaspoon freshly ground black pepper

10 ounces fresh lasagna noodles, cut into ½-inch-wide strips

¼ cup chopped fresh dill, mint, or parsley

If peas and carrots bring back memories of that dreaded cafeteria side dish, this simple, fresh pasta will change your mind. Any soft herb (chervil, dill, chives, mint, parsley) would be perfect for this delicate dish. Use a zester to get long curls of lemon rind, or grate with a Microplane grater.

1. Heat the butter in a large skillet over medium-high heat; swirl until foamy. Add the carrots; sauté 1 minute. Add the stock and ½ teaspoon of the salt; simmer 4 minutes. Add the asparagus, peas, and 1 teaspoon of the lemon rind; simmer 3 minutes or until the liquid is reduced to ½ cup and the vegetables are crisp-tender. Reduce the heat to medium-low. Add the remaining ¼ teaspoon salt, cream cheese, and pepper to the vegetable mixture, stirring with a whisk until smooth.

2. Cook the pasta according to the package directions, omitting the salt and fat. Drain in a colander over a bowl, reserving ½ cup of the pasta cooking liquid.

3. Add the noodles to the vegetable mixture; toss to coat. Stir in ¼ cup of the pasta cooking liquid; add additional cooking liquid as needed to thin the sauce. Sprinkle the remaining 1 teaspoon rind and the dill over the pasta mixture. Place the pasta mixture into each of 4 shallow bowls. Serve immediately.

(serving size: 1½ cups): **CALORIES** 349; **FAT** 11.8g (sat 6g, mono 2.8g, poly 1.2g); **PROTEIN** 14g; **CARB** 48g; **FIBER** 5g; **SUGARS** 4g (est. added sugars 0g); **CHOL** 83mg; **IRON** 4mg; **SODIUM** 615mg; **CALCIUM** 78mg

PASTA GIARDINIERA

HANDS-ON: **29 MINUTES**   TOTAL: **45 MINUTES**   SERVES **4**

1 large red bell pepper

10 cups water

10 baby carrots with tops, trimmed (do not peel)

4 ounces red pearl onions

3 ounces sugar snap peas, trimmed

¼ cup extra-virgin olive oil

3½ ounces shiitake mushroom caps, halved

1 fennel bulb, trimmed and vertically sliced

½ teaspoon salt

2 tablespoons champagne vinegar

6 ounces fresh lasagna noodles, cut into 1¼ x 5-inch ribbons

1 tablespoon capers, drained

½ teaspoon crushed red pepper

3 ounces (¼-inch) cubed fresh mozzarella cheese (about ¾ cup)

1 tablespoon thyme leaves

Fresh lasagna noodles offer silky texture without the work of making your own pasta. Here, we cut the sheets into thick noodles. Sub pappardelle or fettuccine, if necessary.

1. Preheat the broiler to high.

2. Cut the bell pepper in half lengthwise; discard the seeds and membranes. Place the pepper halves, skin sides up, on a foil-lined baking sheet; flatten with your hand. Broil 8 minutes or until blackened. Place in a paper bag; fold to close tightly. Let stand 10 minutes. Peel and cut into strips.

3. While the bell pepper broils, bring 10 cups water to a boil in a Dutch oven. Add the carrots and onions; cook 2 minutes. Add the peas; cook 2 minutes. Drain; rinse with cold water. Drain. Remove the carrot skins by rubbing gently with a clean, dry paper towel. Remove the stem ends from the onions; peel.

4. Heat a large nonstick skillet over medium-high heat. Add 2 tablespoons of the olive oil to the pan; swirl to coat. Add the onions, mushrooms, and fennel; sauté for 2 minutes, stirring occasionally. Add ¼ teaspoon of the salt; reduce the heat to medium, and sauté for 3 minutes, stirring occasionally. Add the bell pepper, carrots, and vinegar; cook 2 minutes or until the liquid almost evaporates.

5. Cook the pasta in boiling water 2 minutes; drain. Combine the pasta, the remaining 2 tablespoons oil, the remaining ¼ teaspoon salt, the fennel mixture, capers, and crushed red pepper in a large bowl; toss to combine. Add the mozzarella; sprinkle with the thyme.

(serving size: 1¼ cups): **CALORIES** 392; **FAT** 19.6g (sat 4.8g, mono 11.4g, poly 2.1g); **PROTEIN** 12g; **CARB** 44g; **FIBER** 7g; **SUGARS** 6g (est. added sugars 0g); **CHOL** 48mg; **IRON** 3mg; **SODIUM** 569mg; **CALCIUM** 178mg

ONE-PAN PASTA
WITH RICOTTA AND ARTICHOKES

HANDS-ON: **10 MINUTES**   TOTAL: **20 MINUTES**   SERVES **4**

1 tablespoon olive oil

1 cup chopped onion

8 ounces presliced mushrooms

4 garlic cloves, sliced

2½ cups unsalted vegetable stock

1½ cups frozen artichoke quarters, thawed

¾ teaspoon kosher salt

½ teaspoon freshly ground black pepper

1 (14.5-ounce) can unsalted fire-roasted tomatoes

1 (9-ounce) package refrigerated fresh fettuccine

½ cup part-skim ricotta cheese

3 ounces fresh mozzarella cheese, torn into small pieces

¼ cup fresh basil leaves

This recipe uses one skillet from start to finish—you can't beat that on a busy weeknight. The ricotta adds rich creaminess, while fresh mozzarella creates that ooey-gooey baked pasta feel.

1. Preheat the broiler to high.

2. Heat a large ovenproof skillet over medium-high heat. Add the oil to the pan; swirl to coat. Add the onion, mushrooms, and garlic to the pan; cook 7 minutes, stirring occasionally. Add the stock, artichokes, salt, pepper, tomatoes, and pasta to the pan, and bring to a boil. Stir to combine. Cover; reduce the heat, and simmer 8 minutes or until the pasta is tender. Dot the pasta mixture evenly with the ricotta and mozzarella cheeses.

3. Place the pan under the broiler. Broil the mixture 2 minutes or until the cheese melts. Sprinkle evenly with the basil.

(serving size: 1¼ cups): **CALORIES** 407; **FAT** 13g (sat 5.2g, mono 3.4g, poly 1.2g); **PROTEIN** 20g; **CARB** 54g; **FIBER** 7g; **SUGARS** 6g (est. added sugars 0g); **CHOL** 73mg; **IRON** 3mg; **SODIUM** 623mg; **CALCIUM** 136mg

fresh pasta is an excellent option when you just don't have the time or inclination to spend 12 minutes cooking dried pasta. Fresh pasta is done in 2 to 3 minutes. The texture is deliciously different; it's more delicate, with a slightly springy bounce yet it's not too refined for bold seasonings or a creamy sauce.

SPAGHETTI WITH SPINACH-AVOCADO SAUCE ⊽

HANDS-ON: **12 MINUTES**   TOTAL: **20 MINUTES**   SERVES **4**

8 ounces uncooked whole-wheat spaghetti

1 cup baby spinach leaves

¼ cup rinsed and drained unsalted cannellini beans

¼ cup basil leaves

2 tablespoons extra-virgin olive oil

2 teaspoons grated lemon rind

1 tablespoon fresh lemon juice

1 teaspoon kosher salt

2 garlic cloves

1 ripe peeled avocado

¼ cup cherry tomatoes, halved

2 tablespoons sliced almonds, toasted

Move over, pesto. You're not the only sauce worth going green for. Pureed avocado makes this dish positively irresistible. Garnish with extra basil leaves, if desired.

1. Prepare the pasta according to the package directions, omitting the salt and fat. Reserve ½ cup of the cooking liquid. Drain the pasta.
2. Place the reserved ½ cup cooking liquid, the spinach, and the next 8 ingredients (through avocado) in a food processor; process until smooth. Combine the pasta and spinach mixture; toss to coat. Sprinkle with the tomato and almonds.

(serving size: about 1 cup): **CALORIES** 374; **FAT** 15.2g (sat 2g, mono 10.1g, poly 2.1g); **PROTEIN** 10g; **CARB** 50g; **FIBER** 6g; **SUGARS** 2g (est. added sugars 0g); **CHOL** 0mg; **IRON** 3mg; **SODIUM** 502mg; **CALCIUM** 46mg

whole-wheat pastas are thirsty. They absorb a lot more liquid than traditional white pasta, so the longer they sit, the more sauce they'll soak in. One quick trick to check the quality of the pasta is to look for white spots. More spots on uncooked pasta means it was dried too quickly and will likely fall apart more easily in your sauce.

ROASTED CAULIFLOWER AND CHICKPEA
WHOLE-WHEAT SPAGHETTI BOWL ♥

HANDS-ON: **35 MINUTES**   TOTAL: **35 MINUTES**   SERVES **4**

1 small head cauliflower, broken into 1-inch florets (about 3½ cups)

1 (15-ounce) can unsalted chickpeas (garbanzo beans), rinsed and drained

2 tablespoons olive oil

½ teaspoon freshly ground black pepper

¼ teaspoon kosher salt

¼ cup water

3 tablespoons white miso paste

2 tablespoons tahini

1 tablespoon fresh lemon juice

1 garlic clove

6 ounces uncooked whole-wheat spaghetti

½ cup firmly packed parsley leaves

1 red chile pepper, thinly sliced

This one-bowl meal is an ideal option for healthy meals on the go: It comes together quickly and can be made ahead. It gets wonderful texture from the chickpeas and cauliflower, nuttiness from the whole-wheat pasta, and rich umami flavor from the miso and tahini. You'll find the miso paste in the refrigerated produce section and tahini in the international aisle.

1. Preheat the oven to 425°F. Combine the cauliflower, chickpeas, oil, black pepper, and salt in a large bowl. Spread the mixture in a single layer on a baking sheet; bake at 425°F for 20 minutes or until the cauliflower is tender and lightly browned.

2. Place ¼ cup water, miso, tahini, lemon juice, and garlic in a mini food processor; process until smooth.

3. Prepare the pasta according to the package directions, omitting the fat and salt. Drain. Divide the noodles evenly among 4 bowls. Top evenly with the cauliflower mixture. Drizzle evenly with the miso dressing; top evenly with the parsley and sliced chile.

(serving size: 2 cups): CALORIES 411; FAT 13.2g (sat 1.8g, mono 5.1g, poly 1.3g); PROTEIN 18g; CARB 61g; FIBER 13g; SUGARS 7g (est. added sugars 0g); CHOL 0mg; IRON 5mg; SODIUM 581mg; CALCIUM 98mg

GOLDEN BEET PASTA
WITH BASIL-ALMOND PESTO

HANDS-ON: **29 MINUTES**   TOTAL: **29 MINUTES**   SERVES **4**

- 8 ounces uncooked whole-wheat penne (tube-shaped pasta)
- 2 (8-ounce) golden beets with greens
- 2 tablespoons extra-virgin olive oil
- ¾ cup water
- ⅓ cup organic vegetable broth
- ½ teaspoon kosher salt
- ½ teaspoon freshly ground black pepper
- 2 cups loosely packed basil leaves
- ¼ cup dry-roasted unsalted almonds
- 3 garlic cloves, chopped
- 2 ounces grated vegetarian Parmesan cheese (about ½ cup)
- 1 tablespoon fresh lemon juice

This bright, earthy springtime dish uses the entire beet—stems, leaves, and all.

1. Cook the pasta according to the package directions, omitting the salt and fat. Drain.

2. Remove the greens and stems from the beets; rinse and drain. Coarsely chop the greens and stems to measure 4 cups. Peel the beets, cut in half vertically, and cut into ⅛-inch slices.

3. Heat a large skillet over medium-high heat. Add 1 tablespoon of the oil to the pan; swirl to coat. Add the beets; sauté 3 minutes. Add the beet greens and stems, ½ cup of the water, broth, salt, and pepper; cover. Reduce heat to medium; simmer 8 minutes or until the beets are tender.

4. Place the remaining 1 tablespoon oil, basil, almonds, and garlic in a food processor; process until smooth. Add the cheese and the remaining ¼ cup water; process until blended. Add the pasta, pesto, and lemon juice to the beet mixture; toss to combine.

(serving size: 1½ cups): **CALORIES** 431; **FAT** 16.7g (sat 3.4g, mono 7.8g, poly 2g); **PROTEIN** 17g; **CARB** 55g; **FIBER** 10g; **SUGARS** 8g (est. added sugars 0g); **CHOL** 13mg; **IRON** 4mg; **SODIUM** 573mg; **CALCIUM** 320mg

beet greens look and taste similar to Swiss chard and can be used in much the same way as you would any greens—added to soups and stews, as the base of a salad, or as the star of a sauté for a quick side. Some of the larger stems can be tough, so you'll want to remove those before cooking.

TRIPLE-PEPPER PASTA

HANDS-ON: **30 MINUTES**   TOTAL: **1 HOUR, 30 MINUTES**   SERVES **6**

¼ cup balsamic vinegar

¼ cup water

1 medium-sized red onion, peeled and cut into wedges

1½ teaspoons kosher salt

1 teaspoon sugar

2 Fresno chiles, thinly sliced

12 ounces uncooked whole-wheat rotini

12 ounces red bell peppers (about 2 large)

Cooking spray

3 tablespoons olive oil

2 tablespoons sherry vinegar

¼ teaspoon ground red pepper

2 large garlic cloves

1 pound multicolored mini baby bell peppers

6 ounces fresh mozzarella cheese, cubed

¼ cup small oregano leaves

1 tablespoon Aleppo pepper or sweet paprika

This dish is an exposition of sweet peppers. Here, they're charred and pureed for a sauce, roasted and stirred into the pasta, and quick-cured for a pretty topper. Mild Aleppo pepper and spicy ground red pepper actually make this a five-pepper pasta.

1. Preheat the oven to 400°F.

2. Place the balsamic vinegar, ¼ cup water, and onion in an 11 x 7-inch glass or ceramic baking dish; cover tightly with foil. Bake at 400°F for 45 minutes. Uncover and bake 10 minutes or until the liquid evaporates. Cool.

3. Combine ¼ teaspoon of the salt, the sugar, and Fresno chiles in a bowl. Let stand 20 minutes.

4. While the chiles stand, cook the pasta according to the package directions, omitting the salt and fat. Drain. Rinse with cold water; drain.

5. Preheat the broiler to high.

6. Place the large bell peppers on a baking sheet. Coat with cooking spray. Broil 15 minutes or until charred, turning occasionally. Place the peppers in a bowl; cover tightly with plastic wrap. Cool. Peel and seed the large bell peppers over a bowl, reserving the juices. Place the peeled peppers and their juices in a blender with ½ teaspoon of the salt, oil, sherry vinegar, ground red pepper, and garlic; blend until smooth.

7. Add the baby bell peppers to the baking sheet. Coat with cooking spray. Broil 10 minutes or until lightly charred, stirring once after 5 minutes. Place the baby bell peppers in a bowl; tightly cover with plastic wrap. Cool. Remove the stems and seeds; coarsely chop the peppers. Place the onion mixture, the remaining ¾ teaspoon salt, pureed pepper mixture, pasta, baby bell peppers, and half of the mozzarella in a large bowl; toss to combine. Top with the Fresno chile mixture, the remaining mozzarella, oregano, and Aleppo pepper.

(serving size: 1½ cups): **CALORIES** 415; **FAT** 13.6g (sat 4.3g, mono 6.9g, poly 1g); **PROTEIN** 12g; **CARB** 57g; **FIBER** 5g; **SUGARS** 12g (est. added sugars 1g); **CHOL** 20mg; **IRON** 3mg; **SODIUM** 538mg; **CALCIUM** 194mg

PASTA WITH LEMON CREAM SAUCE, ASPARAGUS, AND PEAS

HANDS-ON: **13 MINUTES**   TOTAL: **20 MINUTES**   SERVES **4**

8 ounces uncooked rotini

1¾ cups (1½-inch) slices asparagus (about ½ pound)

1 cup frozen green peas, thawed

1 tablespoon butter

1 garlic clove, minced

1 cup organic vegetable broth

1 teaspoon cornstarch

⅓ cup heavy cream

3 tablespoons fresh lemon juice (about 1 lemon)

½ teaspoon salt

¼ teaspoon freshly ground black pepper

Dash of ground red pepper

Coarsely ground black pepper (optional)

Lemon slices (optional)

Citrus flavors and fresh asparagus brighten this pasta. Another perk: Leftovers pack nicely for work or school.

1. Cook the pasta according to the package directions, omitting the salt and fat. Add the asparagus during last minute of cooking time. Place the peas in a colander. Drain the pasta mixture over the peas.
2. Melt the butter in a skillet over medium-high heat. Add the garlic to the pan; sauté 1 minute. Combine the broth and cornstarch in a small bowl; stir until well blended. Add the broth mixture to the pan; bring to a boil. Cook 1 minute or until thick, stirring constantly. Remove from the heat. Stir in the cream, juice, salt, ¼ teaspoon black pepper, and red pepper. Add the pasta mixture to the broth mixture; toss gently to coat. Garnish with coarsely ground black pepper and lemon slices, if desired. Serve immediately.

(serving size: about 1½ cups): **CALORIES** 352; **FAT** 11.2g (sat 6.7g, mono 2.9g, poly 0.5g); **PROTEIN** 12g; **CARB** 53g; **FIBER** 5g; **SUGARS** 6g (est. added sugars 0g); **CHOL** 35mg; **IRON** 4mg; **SODIUM** 471mg; **CALCIUM** 49mg

FARFALLE WITH BUTTERNUT SQUASH

HANDS-ON: **20 MINUTES**   TOTAL: **25 MINUTES**   SERVES **6**

3 cups cubed peeled
   butternut squash (about
   1 pound)
2 tablespoons extra-virgin
   olive oil
¼ teaspoon kosher salt
¼ teaspoon freshly ground
   black pepper
½ cup walnut halves
8 ounces uncooked farfalle
   (bow tie pasta)
1½ cups organic vegetable
   stock
1½ tablespoons white
   balsamic vinegar
1 garlic clove, minced
¼ cup flat-leaf parsley leaves
1 tablespoon minced
   fresh sage
2 ounces shaved vegetarian
   Parmesan cheese (about
   ½ cup)

A tasty bow tie recipe makes for a quick and easy weeknight meal. Packed with protein and fiber in the form of walnuts and butternut squash, this heart-healthy pasta dish can be on your table in under 30 minutes.

1. Preheat the oven to 400°F.
2. Combine the squash, 1 tablespoon of the olive oil, salt, and pepper on a baking sheet; arrange in a single layer. Bake at 400°F for 15 minutes or until tender. Add the walnuts to the baking sheet; bake at 400°F for 5 minutes or until toasted. Cool slightly; coarsely chop the walnuts.
3. While the squash roasts, cook the pasta according to the package directions, omitting the salt and fat. Drain.
4. While the pasta cooks, combine the remaining 1 tablespoon olive oil, stock, vinegar, and garlic in a large skillet over medium-high heat; simmer 8 minutes or until reduced to ½ cup. Combine the pasta, squash mixture, walnuts, stock mixture, parsley, and sage in a large bowl; toss to coat. Sprinkle with the cheese.

(serving size: about 1 cup): CALORIES 317; FAT 13.3g (sat 2.9g, mono 4.8g, poly 4.6g); PROTEIN 11g; CARB 41g; FIBER 3g; SUGARS 4g (est. added sugars 0g); CHOL 8mg; IRON 2mg; SODIUM 292mg; CALCIUM 164mg

EGG NOODLE STIR-FRY WITH BROCCOLI

HANDS-ON: **35 MINUTES**   TOTAL: **35 MINUTES**   SERVES **4**

2 tablespoons dark sesame oil

1 (3.5-ounce) package shiitake mushrooms

½ cup diagonally cut carrot (about 2 ounces)

4 Thai red chile peppers, halved

3 garlic cloves, minced

1 (1-inch) piece fresh ginger, peeled and thinly sliced

2 cups unsalted vegetable stock

2 tablespoons lower-sodium soy sauce

2 teaspoons honey

7 ounces broccoli florets (about 3 cups)

4 baby bok choy, quartered (about 10 ounces)

1 (16-ounce) package refrigerated cooked Chinese egg noodles (such as Twin Marquis)

2 teaspoons canola oil

4 large eggs

1 tablespoon rice vinegar

Freshly ground black pepper

The red chiles add vibrant color and deep, fruity heat. If you can't find them, substitute ¼ cup thinly sliced Fresno peppers (which are much milder). Look for very young ginger; it will have thinner skin and a less fibrous interior.

1. Heat a medium saucepan over medium-high heat. Add 1 tablespoon of the sesame oil to the pan; swirl to coat. Thinly slice the mushroom caps. Add the mushrooms and carrot to the pan; sauté 5 minutes or until tender. Add the peppers, garlic, and ginger; cook 30 seconds, stirring constantly. Add the stock; bring to a boil, scraping the pan to loosen the browned bits. Cover and simmer 10 minutes. Remove from the heat; stir in the soy sauce and honey. Keep warm.

2. Heat a wok or large skillet over high heat. Add the remaining 1 tablespoon sesame oil to the pan; swirl to coat. Add the broccoli; stir-fry 3 minutes. Add the bok choy; stir-fry 1 minute.

3. Place the noodles in a colander; rinse under hot water to separate the noodles. Drain; divide the noodles evenly among 4 bowls. Top evenly with the broccoli, bok choy, and stock mixture.

4. Heat a large nonstick skillet over medium heat. Add the canola oil to the pan; swirl to coat. Crack the eggs into the pan; cook 4 minutes or until the whites are just set. Top each bowl with 1 egg. Drizzle the servings evenly with rice vinegar and sprinkle with black pepper.

(serving size: 1 bowl): **CALORIES** 467; **FAT** 22g (sat 3.2g, mono 11g, poly 6.8g); **PROTEIN** 18g; **CARB** 53g; **FIBER** 4g; **SUGARS** 5g (est. added sugars 3g); **CHOL** 214mg; **IRON** 5mg; **SODIUM** 768mg; **CALCIUM** 136mg

STIR-FRIED CHINESE EGG NOODLES

HANDS-ON: **27 MINUTES**   TOTAL: **27 MINUTES**   SERVES **4**

8 ounces fresh or frozen Chinese egg noodles, thawed

1 tablespoon canola oil

1 cup sliced cremini mushrooms

5 garlic cloves, minced

3 green onions, diagonally sliced

¼ cup lower-sodium soy sauce

1 tablespoon brown sugar

1½ tablespoons fresh lime juice

1 tablespoon dark sesame oil

1 tablespoon ketchup

1 tablespoon chile paste (such as sambal oelek)

2 large eggs

2 cups spinach, trimmed

Though the chewy texture of Chinese egg noodles is fantastic, you can substitute rice sticks or linguine. Omit or decrease the amount of chile paste if serving to kids.

1. Cook the egg noodles according to the package directions, omitting the salt and fat. Drain.

2. Heat a large skillet over medium-high heat. Add the canola oil to the pan; swirl to coat. Add the mushrooms; sauté 4 minutes, stirring occasionally. Add the garlic and green onions; sauté for 1 minute, stirring constantly. Combine the soy sauce and the next 5 ingredients (through chile paste), stirring well. Stir the soy sauce mixture into the mushroom mixture; bring to a boil.

3. Add the noodles to the pan; toss to coat. Add the eggs; cook 2 minutes or until the eggs are set, tossing well. Remove from the heat; stir in the spinach.

(serving size: 1 cup): CALORIES 298; FAT 10.1g (sat 1.8g, mono 4.5g, poly 2.9g); PROTEIN 13g; CARB 39g; FIBER 2g; SUGARS 5g (est. added sugars 3g); CHOL 93mg; IRON 2mg; SODIUM 648mg; CALCIUM 55mg

fresh Chinese egg noodles are located in the refrigerated section of most Asian markets. Like other fresh pastas, they should be stored in their package in the refrigerator until you're ready to cook them. Unopened, they'll last for about a week, but once opened, they should be used within 2 to 3 days.

CHINESE NOODLE SALAD
WITH SESAME DRESSING

HANDS-ON: **20 MINUTES** TOTAL: **25 MINUTES** SERVES **4**

- 1 (8-ounce) package uncooked dried Chinese-style flat noodles
- 1 cup sugar snap peas, trimmed
- 2 teaspoons peanut oil
- 1 cup cubed firm water-packed tofu (about 6 ounces)
- 1 cup cherry tomatoes, halved
- ½ cup drained sliced water chestnuts
- ½ cup thinly sliced green onions
- 3 tablespoons seasoned rice vinegar
- 1 tablespoon lower-sodium soy sauce
- 2 teaspoons dark sesame oil
- 2 teaspoons chile paste (such as sambal oelek)
- ⅛ teaspoon kosher salt
- 1 tablespoon sesame seeds, toasted

The sweetness of the tomatoes and sugar snap peas balances the heat of the chile paste.

1. Cook the noodles according to the package directions, omitting the salt and fat. Add the peas during the last minute of cooking. Drain; rinse with cold water.

2. Heat a large nonstick skillet over medium-high heat. Add the peanut oil to the pan; swirl to coat. Add the tofu to the pan; cook 5 minutes or until browned, stirring frequently.

3. Combine the noodle mixture, tofu, tomatoes, water chestnuts, and onions in a large bowl. Combine the vinegar and the next 4 ingredients (through salt) in a small bowl, stirring with a whisk. Add the vinegar mixture to the noodle mixture, tossing gently to coat. Add 1½ teaspoons of the sesame seeds; toss to combine. Sprinkle with the remaining 1½ teaspoons sesame seeds.

(serving size: 2 cups): **CALORIES** 293; **FAT** 8.6g (sat 1.2g, mono 2g, poly 1.7g); **PROTEIN** 14g; **CARB** 39g; **FIBER** 3g; **SUGARS** 6g (est. added sugars 0g); **CHOL** 0mg; **IRON** 5mg; **SODIUM** 704mg; **CALCIUM** 111mg

MOCK CHAM NOODLE BOWL ▽

HANDS-ON: **30 MINUTES**   TOTAL: **30 MINUTES**   SERVES **4**

SAUCE

- ¼ cup water
- 3 tablespoons fresh lime juice
- 3 tablespoons liquid aminos or lower-sodium soy sauce
- 2 tablespoons light brown sugar
- 1 teaspoon rice vinegar
- 1 Thai chile sliced
- 1 garlic clove, grated

NOODLE BOWLS

- 3 shallots, cut crosswise into ¼-inch-thick slices and separated into rings
- 1 tablespoon cornstarch
- 2 tablespoons canola oil
- 6 ounces uncooked rice noodles
- 16 ounces firm tofu, drained and cut into thin strips
- ½ medium cucumber, cut into thin strips
- 1 cup matchstick carrots
- 1 cup thinly sliced red bell pepper (from 1 bell pepper)
- 1 cup bean sprouts
- ¼ cup torn mint leaves
- ¼ cup torn basil leaves
- ¼ cup firmly packed cilantro leaves
- ¼ cup dry-roasted unsalted cashews

Sliced green onions (optional)

The sauce in this dish is a variation of Vietnamese nouc cham, which is a dipping sauce that includes fish sauce. Here, we've substituted liquid aminos, which is exactly what it sounds like: liquid amino acids. This umami-rich sauce made from soybeans and water is a vegetarian (and gluten-free) protein source that tastes a lot like soy sauce. You'll find it at most grocery stores. The sauce can be made ahead and refrigerated for up to 5 days.

1. Make the sauce: Combine ¼ cup water, lime juice, liquid aminos, brown sugar, vinegar, chile, and garlic in a small bowl; set aside.

2. Make the noodle bowls: Combine the shallots and cornstarch. Let stand 10 minutes. Heat a large skillet over medium-high heat. Add the oil to the pan; swirl to coat. Add the shallots; cook until browned and crisp, about 5 minutes. Drain on a paper towel.

3. Cook the rice noodles according to the package directions. Rinse with cold water; drain well. Divide the noodles evenly among 4 bowls; top evenly with the shallots, tofu, cucumber, carrots, bell pepper, and bean sprouts. Sprinkle with the mint, basil, cilantro, and cashews; drizzle 3 tablespoons of the sauce over each serving. Garnish with sliced green onions, if desired. Serve immediately.

(serving size: 1 bowl): **CALORIES** 411; **FAT** 14.4g (sat 1.8g, mono 7.4g, poly 4.5g); **PROTEIN** 10g; **CARB** 65g; **FIBER** 4g; **SUGARS** 15g (est. added sugars 7g); **CHOL** 0mg; **IRON** 4mg; **SODIUM** 534mg; **CALCIUM** 99mg

CURRIED PEANUT SAUCE
AND RAMEN NOODLE PIZZA ▼

HANDS-ON: **30 MINUTES**   TOTAL: **30 MINUTES**   SERVES **4**

2 (3-ounce) packages ramen noodle soup mix

2 tablespoons olive oil

¾ teaspoon kosher salt

¼ cup coconut milk

2 tablespoons creamy peanut butter

2 teaspoons rice vinegar

1 teaspoon curry powder

1 teaspoon light brown sugar

1 teaspoon Sriracha chili sauce

1 teaspoon minced peeled fresh ginger

1 garlic clove, coarsely chopped

2 teaspoons water

8 ounces extra-firm tofu, drained and cut into ½-inch cubes

1 cup fresh Broccolini florets (from 1 [8-ounce] bunch)

½ red bell pepper, thinly sliced

2 tablespoons dry-roasted unsalted peanuts, chopped

¼ cup firmly packed cilantro leaves

This is not your typical pizza. Crisped up ramen noodles stand in for the traditional dough–based crust for a delicious textural difference. Ramen noodles come in a variety of flavors, but you can use any of them since the seasoning packet is reserved for another use.

1. Preheat the oven to 450°F.

2. Cook the noodles according to the package directions, reserving the seasoning packets for another use. Drain the noodles, and spread on a towel; press lightly to remove the moisture.

3. Heat a 12-inch cast-iron skillet or ovenproof nonstick skillet over medium-high heat. Add the oil to the pan; swirl to coat. Add the noodles to the pan. Press and flatten the noodles in the bottom of the pan; sprinkle with ½ teaspoon of the salt. Cook until the bottom browns and the noodles feel firm, about 6 minutes. Remove the pan from the heat.

4. Place the coconut milk, peanut butter, vinegar, curry powder, brown sugar, Sriracha, ginger, garlic, 1 teaspoon of the water, and remaining ¼ teaspoon salt in a food processor; process until smooth, about 1 minute, stopping to scrape sides as necessary. Remove 2 tablespoons of the curry sauce to a medium bowl; stir in the remaining 1 teaspoon water. Add the tofu; toss to coat. Spread the remaining curry sauce over the noodles. Top with the Broccolini, tofu mixture, and bell pepper. Bake at 450°F for 15 minutes or until the vegetables are tender and beginning to brown. Sprinkle the peanuts and cilantro leaves over the top. Cut into 8 wedges.

(serving size: 2 wedges): CALORIES 385; **FAT** 20.1g (sat 5.4g, mono 8.8g, poly 4.6g); **PROTEIN** 14g; **CARB** 40g; **FIBER** 5g; **SUGARS** 4g (est. added sugars 1g); **CHOL** 0mg; **IRON** 2mg; **SODIUM** 608mg; **CALCIUM** 63mg

GRILLED VEGETABLE LASAGNA

HANDS-ON: 25 MINUTES   TOTAL: 1 HOUR, 40 MINUTES   SERVES 10

3 eggplants, cut lengthwise into ¼-inch slices (about 3 pounds)

3 zucchini, cut lengthwise into ⅛-inch slices (about 1¼ pounds)

Cooking spray

1 teaspoon salt

¾ teaspoon freshly ground black pepper

2 red bell peppers, quartered and seeded

1 (15-ounce) container fat-free ricotta cheese

1 large egg

3 ounces grated vegetarian Parmesan cheese (about ¾ cup)

¼ cup minced fresh basil

¼ cup minced fresh parsley

9 lasagna noodles

1 (26-ounce) jar tomato-basil pasta sauce (such as Muir Glen)

¾ cup shredded part-skim mozzarella cheese (about 3 ounces)

¼ cup pesto

Basil leaves

Grilling the vegetables deepens their flavors for this vegetable-focused lasagna. To speed preparation, use no-boil lasagna noodles; the baking time remains the same.

1. Preheat the grill to medium-high heat.

2. Coat the eggplants and zucchini with cooking spray. Sprinkle with ½ teaspoon of the salt and ¼ teaspoon of the black pepper. Grill the eggplant and zucchini 1½ minutes on each side or just until tender. Cool; combine in a large bowl.

3. Place the bell peppers on the grill, skin sides down; grill 3 minutes or until tender. Cut into (1-inch-wide) strips. Add the bell peppers to the eggplant mixture.

4. Combine the ricotta cheese, egg, ½ cup of the Parmesan cheese, basil, parsley, the remaining ½ teaspoon salt, and the remaining ½ teaspoon black pepper.

5. Cook the lasagna noodles according to the package directions, omitting the salt and fat. Drain.

6. Preheat the oven to 375°F.

7. Spread ½ cup of the pasta sauce in the bottom of a 13 x 9-inch baking dish coated with cooking spray. Arrange 3 noodles over the tomato sauce. Top with half of the eggplant mixture. Spread half of the ricotta cheese mixture over the eggplant mixture; sprinkle with ¼ cup of the mozzarella cheese.

8. Arrange 3 noodles and 1 cup of the pasta sauce over the cheese; cover with the remaining eggplant mixture. Top with the remaining ricotta mixture. Spread the pesto over the ricotta; sprinkle with ¼ cup of the mozzarella cheese. Cover with the remaining 3 noodles.

9. Spoon 1 cup of the pasta sauce over the noodles. Sprinkle with the remaining ¼ cup Parmesan cheese and the remaining ¼ cup mozzarella cheese. Bake at 375°F for 1 hour. Let stand 15 minutes before serving. Top with the basil leaves.

CALORIES 298; FAT 9.7g (sat 3.2g, mono 2.4g, poly 0.7g); PROTEIN 16g; CARB 36g; FIBER 8g; SUGARS 13g (est. added sugars 0g); CHOL 40mg; IRON 2mg; SODIUM 748mg; CALCIUM 325mg

SWEET POTATO AND PESTO LASAGNA

HANDS-ON: **1 HOUR**   TOTAL: **1 HOUR, 20 MINUTES**   SERVES **6**

2 pounds sweet potatoes, peeled

2 tablespoons water

¼ cup olive oil

1 cup chopped yellow onion (from 1 onion)

8 ounces cremini mushrooms, chopped

½ cup chopped red bell pepper (from 1 bell pepper)

1 tablespoon chopped fresh garlic

9 cups baby spinach (about 9 ounces)

¾ teaspoon kosher salt

8 ounces firm tofu, drained and finely chopped

1 cup fat-free ricotta cheese

1 large egg

1 large egg yolk

2 tablespoons chopped fresh flat-leaf parsley

2 teaspoons chopped fresh oregano

1 cup firmly packed basil leaves

¼ cup pine nuts, toasted

2½ ounces vegetarian Parmesan cheese, grated (about ½ cup plus 2 tablespoons)

Cooking spray

2 ounces reduced-fat mozzarella cheese, shredded (about ½ cup)

This veggie–packed lasagna gets a flavor boost from using pesto instead of traditional tomato sauce. You can substitute Swiss chard, kale, or other dark leafy greens for the spinach, if you like. Garnish with fresh basil leaves.

1. Cut the potatoes crosswise into ¼-inch-thick slices. Place the potatoes and 2 tablespoons water in a microwave-safe dish; cover with plastic wrap, and poke several holes to vent. Microwave at HIGH until tender-crisp, about 5 minutes. Drain water; let stand 10 minutes.

2. Heat a large skillet over medium-high heat. Add 1 tablespoon of the oil to the pan; swirl to coat. Add the onion and mushrooms; cook, stirring occasionally, until tender, about 8 minutes. Add the bell pepper and garlic; cook until the pepper is slightly browned, about 3 minutes. Add 8 cups of the spinach; cook, stirring constantly, until the spinach wilts, about 2 minutes. Remove from the heat. Stir in the salt, and set aside.

3. Preheat the oven to 375°F. Stir together the tofu, ricotta, egg, egg yolk, parsley, and oregano in a bowl until well combined.

4. Place the basil, pine nuts, ¼ cup of the Parmesan cheese, and remaining 1 cup spinach in a food processor; process until finely ground. With the processor running, pour the remaining 3 tablespoons oil through the food chute in a slow, steady stream, processing until smooth.

5. To assemble the lasagna, coat a broiler-safe 8-inch square glass or ceramic baking dish generously with cooking spray. Layer one-third of the potato slices in the bottom of prepared dish. Top with half of the vegetable mixture. Spread half of the ricotta mixture over the vegetables. Swirl half of the pesto over the ricotta. Repeat the layers once. Top with the remaining potato slices, mozzarella, and Parmesan. Loosely cover with aluminum foil. Bake at 375°F for 15 minutes or until bubbly.

6. Preheat the broiler to high. (Keep lasagna covered in oven.)

7. Uncover the lasagna, and broil until the cheese is golden brown, about 2 minutes. Remove from the oven; let stand 10 minutes before slicing.

(serving size: about 1 cup): CALORIES 406; **FAT** 21.3g (sat 5g, mono 9.3g, poly 4.6g); **PROTEIN** 21g; **CARB** 33g; **FIBER** 6g; **SUGARS** 9g (est. added sugars 0g); **CHOL** 82mg; **IRON** 4mg; **SODIUM** 578mg; **CALCIUM** 530mg

rice, grains
& risotto

BROWN RICE AND
STIR-FRIED VEGETABLE BOWL

HANDS-ON: **20 MINUTES**   TOTAL: **55 MINUTES**   SERVES **4**

6 cups water

1 cup uncooked brown rice

3 tablespoons toasted
sesame oil

8 ounces extra-firm tofu,
drained, cut into ½-inch
cubes, patted dry

8 ounces cremini mushrooms,
halved

1 red bell pepper (about
6 ounces), thinly sliced
(about 1½ cups)

1½ cups fresh broccoli florets
(about 3¼ ounces)

5 garlic cloves, thinly sliced

¾ cup unsalted vegetable
stock

1 tablespoon cornstarch

1½ teaspoons light brown
sugar

3 tablespoons lower-
sodium soy sauce

¼ cup unsalted roasted
peanuts, roughly chopped

*This one-bowl meal is the perfect weeknight stir-fry. There's
enough sauce to coat the crispy tofu and crisp-tender vegetables
with extra to soak into the rice.*

1. Bring 6 cups water to a boil in a medium saucepan over high heat.
Add the rice, reduce the heat to medium-low, and simmer 45 minutes
or until cooked through. Remove from the heat. Drain any remaining
liquid; cover to keep warm.

2. Heat a large skillet over high heat. Add 1½ tablespoons of the
sesame oil to the pan; swirl to coat. Add the tofu, and cook, stirring
often, 4 minutes or until browned on all sides. Remove from the
pan. Add the remaining 1½ tablespoons oil to the pan; swirl to
coat. Add the mushrooms to the pan; cook, stirring constantly,
4 minutes. Add the bell pepper, broccoli, and garlic; cook, stirring
constantly, 3 minutes. Whisk together the stock, cornstarch, and
brown sugar until smooth. Add the stock mixture and soy sauce to
pan. Cook, stirring constantly, 1 minute or until thickened. Stir in
the tofu. Place the rice into each of 4 bowls. Top with the tofu mixture,
and sprinkle with the peanuts.

(serving size: ¾ cup rice, 1 cup tofu mixture, 1 tablespoon peanuts): **CALORIES** 428;
FAT 19.3g (sat 2.9g, mono 7.7g, poly 7.5g); **PROTEIN** 15g; **CARB** 51g; **FIBER** 5g; **SUGARS** 5g
(est. added sugars 2g); **CHOL** 0mg; **IRON** 2mg; **SODIUM** 507mg; **CALCIUM** 99mg

SUMMER VEGGIE RICE BOWL

HANDS-ON: **12 MINUTES**   TOTAL: **1 HOUR, 15 MINUTES**   SERVES **4**

1⅓ cups cooked brown rice, cooled to room temperature

1 cup frozen shelled edamame (green soybeans), thawed

1 cup grape tomatoes, halved

½ cup torn fresh basil

¼ cup pine nuts, toasted

2 teaspoons grated lemon rind

3 tablespoons fresh lemon juice

1 teaspoon kosher salt

¼ teaspoon freshly ground black pepper

3 tablespoons olive oil

2 cups chopped zucchini

½ ounce vegetarian Parmesan cheese, shaved (about 2 tablespoons)

Basil leaves (optional)

Fresh tomatoes, zucchini, basil, and toasted pine nuts bring this rice salad to life. Serve it with roasted fresh green beans on the side.

Combine the first 9 ingredients in a large bowl, and toss until well blended. Heat a medium skillet over medium-high heat. Add 1 tablespoon of the olive oil to the pan; swirl to coat. Add the zucchini; sauté 4 minutes, stirring occasionally. Add the zucchini and the remaining 2 tablespoons oil to the rice mixture; toss. Top with the cheese. Garnish with basil leaves, if desired.

(serving size: about 1 cup): **CALORIES** 305; **FAT** 19.1g (sat 2.5g, mono 9.5g, poly 4.3g); **PROTEIN** 10g; **CARB** 25g; **FIBER** 5g; **SUGARS** 4g (est. added sugars 0g); **CHOL** 3mg; **IRON** 2mg; **SODIUM** 539mg; **CALCIUM** 111mg

creating a great bowl is all about mixing flavors and textures. Start with a base of hearty whole grains—they add volume and fiber and will absorb the sauces and seasonings you add in. Then, pile on a mix of beans and vegetables, which can change with the seasons or with your cravings. Vary the sauces and seasonings you add (this can include vinaigrettes, relishes, and pickles) to keep the flavors fresh, and then top it with nuts or seeds for some added crunch.

BROWN RICE BOWL WITH MISO, POACHED EGG, AND KALE-RADISH SLAW

HANDS-ON: **20 MINUTES**   TOTAL: **20 MINUTES**   SERVES **4**

8 teaspoons rice wine vinegar

2 tablespoons white miso paste

¼ cup plus 5 teaspoons water

4 teaspoons toasted sesame oil

2 teaspoons lower-sodium soy sauce

2 teaspoons brown sugar

3 cups trimmed and thinly sliced Lacinato kale

2 cups thinly sliced radishes

¼ cup thinly sliced green onions

2 teaspoons butter

2 teaspoons minced fresh garlic

2 (8.8-ounce) packages precooked brown rice

4 large eggs

2 teaspoons toasted sesame seeds

Nutrient-rich kale has a mild flavor and becomes tender very quickly, making it a snap to add to speedy meals like this one.

1. Combine 2 teaspoons of the vinegar, miso, and 5 teaspoons of the water in a small bowl, stirring with a whisk.

2. Combine the remaining 2 tablespoons vinegar, 2 teaspoons of the oil, soy sauce, and sugar in a large bowl. Add the kale, radishes, and green onions to the bowl; toss to coat.

3. Heat a large nonstick skillet over medium-high heat. Add the butter and the remaining 2 teaspoons oil to the pan; swirl to coat. Add the garlic; sauté 30 seconds. Add the rice; sauté 5 minutes or until lightly browned. Stir in the kale mixture; remove the pan from the heat. Remove the kale mixture from the pan; keep warm. Wipe the pan with paper towels.

4. Return the pan to medium-high heat. Gently break the eggs into the pan. Pour the remaining ¼ cup water around the eggs; cover and cook 3 minutes or until the desired degree of doneness. Place the kale mixture in each of 4 shallow bowls. Top with the eggs and miso mixture. Sprinkle with the sesame seeds.

(serving size: about 1¼ cups kale mixture, 1 egg, about 1 tablespoon miso mixture, and ½ teaspoon sesame seeds): CALORIES 370; FAT 15g (sat 3.6g, mono 4.4g, poly 3.4g); PROTEIN 15g; CARB 49g; FIBER 7g; SUGARS 5g (est. added sugars 2g); CHOL 191mg; IRON 4mg; SODIUM 490mg; CALCIUM 123mg

WARM BROWN RICE AND CHICKPEA SALAD
WITH CHERRIES AND GOAT CHEESE

HANDS-ON: **10 MINUTES**   TOTAL: **10 MINUTES**   SERVES **4**

1 (8.8-ounce) package precooked brown rice (such as Uncle Ben's)

¼ cup chopped green onions

¼ cup chopped fresh basil

3 tablespoons extra-virgin olive oil

2 tablespoons white balsamic vinegar

½ teaspoon salt

¼ teaspoon freshly ground black pepper

32 cherries, pitted and quartered

1 (15-ounce) can unsalted chickpeas, rinsed and drained

2 ounces goat cheese, crumbled (about ½ cup)

Fresh cherries add a meaty bite and tart-sweet flavor to this salad. If you can't find fresh cherries, add 2 tablespoons boiling water to ¼ cup unsweetened dried cherries, and let them stand for 10 minutes. Then, just drain and chop them.

Heat the rice according to the package directions. Place the rice in a medium bowl. Stir in the onions and the next 7 ingredients (through chickpeas). Sprinkle evenly with the goat cheese.

(serving size: 1 cup): CALORIES 348; **FAT** 16.4g (sat 4.4g, mono 8.4g, poly 1.2g); **PROTEIN** 10g; **CARB** 43g; **FIBER** 6g; **SUGARS** 11g (est. added sugars 0g); **CHOL** 11mg; **IRON** 2mg; **SODIUM** 394mg; **CALCIUM** 102mg

precooked brown rice is an easy— and fast—way to work more whole grains into your meals. Traditional brown rice can take up to an hour to cook, but precooked brown rice takes just a couple minutes to warm before serving or combining with other ingredients.

SOUTHWEST BROWN-RICE SKILLET DINNER ⓥ

2 tablespoons olive oil

2 cups chopped yellow onion (about 1 large onion)

2 poblano chiles, chopped (about 1½ cups)

2 teaspoons ground cumin

1 teaspoon ancho chile powder

¾ teaspoon kosher salt

3½ cups unsalted vegetable stock

3 medium tomatillos, chopped (about 2 cups)

¾ cup uncooked brown rice

1 (15.5-ounce) can no-salt-added black beans, rinsed and drained

1 cup diced tomato (about 1 medium tomato)

⅓ cup chopped fresh cilantro

This boldly flavored bowl is hearty and filling. It gets some smokiness from the ancho chile powder and acidity from the tomatillos. Serve with tortilla chips.

1. Preheat the oven to 400°F.

2. Heat a 10-inch cast-iron or other ovenproof skillet over high heat. Add the oil to the pan; swirl to coat. Add the onion and poblanos; cook, stirring occasionally, 6 minutes or until softened and lightly charred. Add the cumin, chile powder, and salt; cook, stirring constantly, 1 minute. Add the stock and tomatillos; bring to a boil, stirring occasionally. Add the rice and beans; return to a boil, and cook, stirring occasionally, 3 minutes.

3. Transfer the pan to the oven, and bake at 400°F for 50 minutes or until the rice is tender. (Some liquid will remain.) Top with the tomato and cilantro.

(serving size: about 2 cups): **CALORIES** 390; **FAT** 8.3g (sat 1.2g, mono 5.4g, poly 1.2g); **PROTEIN** 13g; **CARB** 66g; **FIBER** 13g; **SUGARS** 6g (est. added sugars 0g); **CHOL** 0mg; **IRON** 4mg; **SODIUM** 730mg; **CALCIUM** 99mg

CRISPY CAULIFLOWER, MUSHROOMS, AND HAZELNUTS OVER POLENTA

HANDS-ON: **1 HOUR, 10 MINUTES**   TOTAL: **1 HOUR, 10 MINUTES**   SERVES **4**

1 cup plus 2 teaspoons water

¾ cup plus 2 tablespoons unsalted vegetable stock

½ cup 2% reduced-fat milk

½ teaspoon kosher salt

½ cup stone-ground polenta

2 teaspoons unsalted butter

¼ teaspoon freshly ground black pepper

1½ ounces vegetarian Parmesan cheese, finely grated (about 6 tablespoons)

Cooking spray

1 teaspoon grated lemon rind

½ teaspoon onion powder

¼ teaspoon ground red pepper

1 large egg, lightly beaten

5 cups (1-inch) cauliflower florets

2 tablespoons chopped fresh flat-leaf parsley

1½ tablespoons fresh lemon juice

2 teaspoons olive oil

2 cups shiitake mushroom caps, quartered

1 tablespoon white wine vinegar

2 tablespoons chopped hazelnuts, toasted

Use a Microplane grater to get fine shreds of Parmesan that melt evenly into the polenta. Stone-ground polenta will be a little coarser compared to instant varieties, which have a smooth texture.

1. Bring 1 cup of the water, ¾ cup of the stock, 6 tablespoons of the milk, and ¼ teaspoon of the salt to a boil in a large saucepan. Reduce the heat to medium-low; stir in the polenta. Cook 20 minutes or until thick, stirring frequently. Stir in the remaining 2 tablespoons milk, butter, black pepper, and 2 tablespoons of the Parmesan cheese; keep warm.

2. Preheat the oven to 450°F.

3. Coat a jelly-roll pan with cooking spray. Combine the remaining Parmesan, rind, onion powder, and ground red pepper in a dish. Combine the remaining 2 teaspoons water and egg in a dish. Dip the cauliflower in the egg mixture; dredge in the Parmesan mixture. Arrange the cauliflower on the prepared pan; coat with cooking spray. Bake at 450°F for 15 minutes, stirring after 6 minutes. Place the cauliflower, parsley, juice, and remaining ¼ teaspoon salt in a bowl; toss.

4. Heat a large skillet over medium heat. Add the oil to the pan; swirl to coat. Add the mushrooms; sauté 7 minutes. Add the remaining 2 tablespoons stock and vinegar to the pan; cook 2 minutes. Place the polenta in each of 4 bowls; top with the cauliflower mixture, mushroom mixture, and hazelnuts.

(serving size: ½ cup polenta, 1 cup cauliflower mixture, ¼ cup mushroom mixture, and ½ tablespoon hazelnuts): CALORIES 266; FAT 11.6g (sat 4.2g, mono 4.5g, poly 1g); PROTEIN 13g; CARB 30g; FIBER 6g; SUGARS 5g (est. added sugars 0g); CHOL 64mg; IRON 2mg; SODIUM 467mg; CALCIUM 217mg

ASIAN STIR-FRY QUINOA BOWL

HANDS-ON: **28 MINUTES** TOTAL: **28 MINUTES** SERVES **4**

- **8 ounces extra-firm tofu**
- **2 tablespoons toasted sesame oil**
- **1 cup (1-inch) slices green onions**
- **1 tablespoon minced peeled fresh ginger**
- **5 ounces thinly sliced shiitake mushroom caps**
- **5 garlic cloves, thinly sliced**
- **1 red bell pepper, thinly sliced**
- **3 tablespoons lower-sodium soy sauce**
- **2 tablespoons rice vinegar**
- **¼ teaspoon kosher salt**
- **2 cups cooked quinoa**
- **2 cups thinly sliced napa cabbage**
- **¼ cup chopped fresh cilantro**
- **½ teaspoon sugar**

This quinoa bowl is brimming with fresh veggies and tofu, making it a healthy replacement for the days you just can't kick the craving for takeout.

1. Arrange the tofu on several layers of heavy-duty paper towels. Cover with additional paper towels; let stand 15 minutes. Cut into ½-inch-thick cubes.

2. Heat a large nonstick skillet over medium-high heat. Add 1 tablespoon of the oil to the pan; swirl to coat. Add the tofu; sauté 4 minutes or until browned. Place the tofu in a bowl. Return the pan to medium-high heat. Add the remaining 1 tablespoon oil to the pan. Add the onions and the next 4 ingredients (through bell pepper); stir-fry 4 minutes or just until tender. Add 2 tablespoons of the soy sauce, 1 tablespoon of the vinegar, and salt; cook 30 seconds. Add the mushroom mixture to the tofu.

3. Stir in the remaining 1 tablespoon soy sauce, remaining 1 tablespoon vinegar, quinoa, cabbage, cilantro, and sugar. Toss well to combine.

(serving size: 1¼ cups): CALORIES 283; **FAT** 12.5g (sat 1.7g, mono 3.7g, poly 5.1g); **PROTEIN** 12g; **CARB** 32g; **FIBER** 5g; **SUGARS** 5g (est. added sugars 1g); **CHOL** 0mg; **IRON** 3mg; **SODIUM** 540mg; **CALCIUM** 99mg

COOKING QUINOA

1. You'll need to rinse quinoa thoroughly before cooking to remove the protective coating called saponin. If you don't rinse quinoa well, it can taste bitter. Often packages don't specify if the quinoa has been rinsed. If not, just rinse it. It won't affect the quinoa or the cooking process.

2. Quinoa cooks more like rice than pasta, which means it's essential to add the right amount of water. Use a ratio of 1 cup of uncooked quinoa to 1¼ cups of water. Bring it to a boil, cover, reduce the heat, and simmer for 12 to 14 minutes or until the liquid is absorbed and the quinoa is tender.

3. You'll know the quinoa is ready when it appears as if each grain has "popped" open. Remove the pan from the heat and fluff the quinoa with a fork. This amount will yield about 3 cups of cooked quinoa.

SPICED QUINOA BOWL
WITH ROASTED FALL VEGETABLES

HANDS-ON: **15 MINUTES**   TOTAL: **55 MINUTES**   SERVES **4**

2 cups water

½ cup dry white wine

2 cups uncooked quinoa

½ teaspoon dry mustard

¼ teaspoon ground allspice

¼ teaspoon ground ginger

1¼ teaspoons kosher salt

1 medium-sized sweet potato (about 12 ounces), cubed (about 2½ cups)

2 parsnips (about 8 ounces), peeled and cut diagonally into 2-inch pieces

2 carrots (about 5 ounces), peeled and cut diagonally into 2-inch pieces

2 tablespoons olive oil

¾ teaspoon freshly ground black pepper

½ cup chopped fresh dill

Cooking spray

1 Winesap or Honeycrisp apple (about 8 ounces), cut into 12 wedges

¼ cup light sour cream

Quinoa recipes are everywhere these days, but this is an interesting new way to eat it with a wonderfully unexpected combination of big, bold flavors. The quinoa gets cooked with a bit of wine and spices to perk it up.

1. Preheat the oven to 400°F.

2. Bring 2 cups water and the wine to a boil over high heat in a medium saucepan. Add the quinoa, dry mustard, allspice, ginger, and ¾ teaspoon of the salt. Return to a boil; cover and reduce the heat to medium-low. Simmer until the quinoa is tender and the liquid is absorbed, about 15 minutes. Keep warm.

3. Toss together the sweet potato, parsnips, carrots, oil, pepper, ¼ cup of the dill, and the remaining ½ teaspoon salt in a large bowl. Arrange the sweet potato mixture on a rimmed baking sheet coated with cooking spray. Bake at 400°F for 15 minutes. Stir in the apple wedges; bake for 20 minutes or until the vegetables are tender and lightly caramelized.

4. Place the quinoa mixture into each of 4 bowls; top evenly with the sweet potato mixture, sour cream, and remaining ¼ cup dill.

(serving size: 1 cup quinoa, 1 cup sweet potato mixture, 1 tablespoon dill, 1 tablespoon sour cream): CALORIES 533; FAT 14g (sat 2.6g, mono 6.9g, poly 3.6g); PROTEIN 15g; CARB 88g; FIBER 12g; SUGARS 17g (est. added sugars 0g); CHOL 5mg; IRON 5mg; SODIUM 678mg; CALCIUM 118mg

KALE, QUINOA, AND CHERRY SALAD

HANDS-ON: **10 MINUTES** TOTAL: **10 MINUTES** SERVES **6**

3 tablespoons extra-virgin olive oil

3 tablespoons cider vinegar

1 tablespoon honey

2 teaspoons Dijon mustard

¼ teaspoon freshly ground black pepper

¼ teaspoon kosher salt

1½ (6-ounce) packages baby kale

1½ (8.5-ounce) packages precooked quinoa and brown rice blend (such as Seeds of Change)

¾ cup fresh sweet cherries, pitted and halved

⅔ cup chopped fresh flat-leaf parsley

⅓ cup thinly sliced shallots

1 (15-ounce) can unsalted chickpeas, rinsed and drained

2 ounces goat cheese, crumbled (about ½ cup)

You can use leftover quinoa-rice blend to make fried rice or stir it into soups or stews.

Combine the first 6 ingredients in a medium bowl. Combine 1½ tablespoons of the oil mixture and the kale. Place the kale mixture on a platter. Stir the quinoa blend, cherries, parsley, shallots, and chickpeas into the remaining oil mixture. Top the kale mixture with the quinoa mixture and the cheese.

(serving size: about ⅔ cup kale mixture, ⅔ cup quinoa mixture, and about 1 tablespoon cheese): CALORIES 296; FAT 11.8g (sat 3.2g, mono 5.6g, poly 0.9g); PROTEIN 9g; CARB 40g; FIBER 5g; SUGARS 7g (est. added sugars 3g); CHOL 7mg; IRON 3mg; SODIUM 369mg; CALCIUM 135mg

SPINACH-QUINOA CAKES WITH BELL PEPPER RELISH

HANDS-ON: **50 MINUTES**   TOTAL: **1 HOUR, 10 MINUTES**   SERVES **4**

RELISH

- 2 red bell peppers, halved and seeded
- 2 tablespoons chopped fresh flat-leaf parsley
- 1 teaspoon balsamic vinegar
- ⅛ teaspoon kosher salt
- ⅛ teaspoon ground red pepper

CAKES

- 1½ teaspoons canola oil
- 1 cup chopped onion
- ¾ cup uncooked quinoa
- 1 tablespoon minced fresh garlic
- 1⅓ cups organic vegetable broth
- 2 cups spinach leaves, coarsely chopped
- 2 ounces goat cheese, crumbled (about ½ cup)
- ½ cup whole-wheat panko (Japanese breadcrumbs)
- ⅜ teaspoon kosher salt
- ½ teaspoon freshly ground black pepper
- 2 large eggs, lightly beaten
- Cooking spray

The quinoa mixture is very moist but will firm up beautifully in the oven. Press firmly when shaping the cakes, and be careful when transferring them to the hot baking sheet. Place them directly on the pan for crispier cakes, or use parchment paper for quicker cleanup.

1. Preheat the broiler to high.

2. Make the relish: Arrange the bell peppers, skin side up, on a foil-lined baking sheet. Broil 10 minutes or until charred. Remove the pan from the oven; wrap the peppers in foil. Let stand 10 minutes. Peel and finely chop. Combine the peppers, parsley, vinegar, ⅛ teaspoon salt, and ground red pepper.

3. Make the cakes: Heat a large saucepan over medium-high heat. Add the oil to the pan; swirl to coat. Add the onion; cook 4 minutes or just until tender, stirring frequently. Add the quinoa; cook 4 minutes or until toasted and lightly browned, stirring occasionally. Add the garlic; cook 30 seconds. Add the broth; bring to a boil. Cover and simmer 17 minutes or until the liquid is fully absorbed. Stir in the chopped spinach. Spread the hot quinoa mixture in a single layer on a baking sheet; cool 10 minutes.

4. Place a baking sheet in the oven. Reduce the oven temperature to 375°F.

5. Combine the quinoa mixture, cheese, panko, ⅜ teaspoon salt, black pepper, and eggs in a bowl, and toss well to combine. Let the mixture stand 5 minutes. Shape into 4 (4-inch) cakes.

6. Remove the preheated baking sheet from the oven; coat the pan with cooking spray. Place the cakes on the pan, and return to the oven. Bake at 375°F for 10 minutes on each side or until lightly browned and thoroughly heated. Top with the bell pepper relish.

(serving size: 1 quinoa cake and ¼ cup relish): **CALORIES** 299; **FAT** 9.9g (sat 3.3g, mono 3.2g, poly 2.2g); **PROTEIN** 14g; **CARB** 39g; **FIBER** 6g; **SUGARS** 7g (est. added sugars 0g); **CHOL** 100mg; **IRON** 4mg; **SODIUM** 543mg; **CALCIUM** 87mg

QUINOA-STUFFED HEIRLOOM TOMATOES WITH ROMESCO

HANDS-ON: **60 MINUTES** TOTAL: **1 HOUR, 30 MINUTES** SERVES **4**

ROMESCO

- 1 cup bottled roasted red bell peppers, rinsed and drained (about 5 ounces)
- ¼ cup unsalted dry-roasted almonds
- 1 tablespoon olive oil
- 1½ teaspoons red wine vinegar
- 1 teaspoon minced fresh garlic
- ⅛ teaspoon kosher salt
- ⅛ teaspoon ground red pepper
- ⅛ teaspoon freshly ground black pepper

FILLING

- 1 tablespoon olive oil
- ¼ cup thinly sliced onion
- 1 teaspoon minced fresh garlic
- 1 teaspoon minced peeled fresh ginger
- ¾ cup uncooked quinoa
- 1¾ cups organic vegetable broth
- ⅜ teaspoon kosher salt
- ¼ teaspoon freshly ground black pepper
- 3 tablespoons chopped fresh Italian parsley
- 2 tablespoons chopped fresh dill
- 1 (15-ounce) can unsalted chickpeas (garbanzo beans), rinsed, drained, and coarsely chopped
- 8 medium heirloom tomatoes

You can make the quick and easy pepper sauce ahead; refrigerate it in an airtight container for up to 4 days.

1. Make the romesco: Place the first 8 ingredients in a blender or food processor; process until smooth.

2. Make the filling: Heat a medium saucepan over medium-high heat. Add 1 tablespoon oil to the pan; swirl to coat. Add the onion; sauté 4 minutes or until the onion begins to brown. Add 1 teaspoon garlic and ginger; sauté 30 seconds, stirring constantly. Stir in the quinoa; cook 1 minute, stirring constantly. Add the broth, ⅜ teaspoon salt, and ¼ teaspoon black pepper; bring to a boil. Cover and simmer 20 minutes or until the quinoa is tender and the liquid is absorbed.

3. Combine the quinoa mixture, parsley, dill, and chickpeas in a bowl. Cut the tops off the tomatoes; set aside. Carefully scoop out the tomato pulp, leaving the shells intact; discard the pulp. Divide the quinoa mixture evenly among the tomato shells; replace the tomato tops. Spoon the romesco sauce on top of the stuffed tomatoes.

(serving size: 2 stuffed tomatoes and about ¼ cup sauce): CALORIES 387; **FAT** 15.4g (sat 1.7g, mono 8.7g, poly 3.8g); **PROTEIN** 14g; **CARB** 52g; **FIBER** 11g; **SUGARS** 10g (est. added sugars 0g); **CHOL** 0mg; **IRON** 3mg; **SODIUM** 614mg; **CALCIUM** 102mg

FARRO SALAD WITH ROASTED BEETS, WATERCRESS, AND POPPY SEED DRESSING

HANDS-ON: **15 MINUTES**   TOTAL: **1 HOUR, 45 MINUTES**   SERVES **4**

2 bunches small beets, trimmed

⅔ cup uncooked farro

3 cups water

¾ teaspoon kosher salt

3 cups trimmed watercress

½ cup thinly sliced red onion

2 ounces goat cheese, crumbled (about ½ cup)

2 tablespoons cider vinegar

2 tablespoons toasted walnut oil

2 tablespoons reduced-fat sour cream

1½ teaspoons poppy seeds

2 teaspoons honey

½ teaspoon freshly ground black pepper

2 garlic cloves, crushed

Farro is a wonderful base for this salad, but you can also substitute wheat berries or spelt. You'll need to cook them a little longer than the farro.

1. Preheat the oven to 375°F.

2. Wrap the beets in foil. Bake at 375°F for 1 hour and 30 mintues or until tender. Cool; peel and thinly slice.

3. While the beets roast, place the farro and 3 cups water in a medium saucepan; bring to a boil. Reduce the heat, and simmer 25 minutes or until the farro is tender. Drain and cool. Stir in ½ teaspoon of the salt.

4. Arrange 1½ cups of the watercress on a serving platter; top with half of the farro, ¼ cup of the onion, and half of the sliced beets. Repeat the layers with the remaining 1½ cups watercress, remaining farro, remaining ¼ cup onion, and remaining beets. Sprinkle the top with the cheese.

5. Combine the remaining ¼ teaspoon salt, vinegar, and remaining ingredients; stir well with a whisk. Place the salad on each of 4 plates. Drizzle the vinegar mixture over the salads.

(serving size: about 1¾ cups salad and about 3 tablespoons dressing): CALORIES 382; FAT 13.8g (sat 4.2g, mono 2.9g, poly 4.9g); PROTEIN 13g; CARB 53g; FIBER 12g; SUGARS 19g (est. added sugars 3g); CHOL 14mg; IRON 4mg; SODIUM 629mg; CALCIUM 153mg

Beets have a rich-hued flesh that's earthy yet sweet, dense yet tender. The beet greens, when fresh, are crisp-tender, bittersweet, and a little peppery, and they're also a great indicator of the root's freshness. If the greens are vibrant and healthy, you know the beet has been freshly picked. But it's best to cut the greens off after buying and refrigerate them separately since the greens pull moisture from the roots. The greens will also wilt within a few days, so use them quickly.

FARRO SALAD WITH CHERRY TOMATOES, ONIONS, AND ALMONDS

HANDS-ON: **10 MINUTES**   TOTAL: **38 MINUTES**   SERVES **4**

9 ounces uncooked pearled farro

1½ cups halved cucumber, sliced into half moons

1½ cups halved cherry tomatoes

½ cup vertically sliced red onion

½ cup chopped fresh flat-leaf parsley

¼ cup Multipurpose Vinaigrette

1 tablespoon mascarpone cheese

¼ cup lightly salted, smoked almonds, chopped

This whole-grain salad is ideal for summer when cucumbers and tomatoes are in season. Plus, you can make it ahead and serve it chilled or at room temperature.

1. Cook the farro according to the package directions, omitting the salt; drain in a colander. Rinse with cold water for 30 seconds; drain. Cool to room temperature.

2. Combine the cooked farro, cucumber, tomatoes, onion, and parsley in a large bowl.

3. Combine the vinaigrette and mascarpone in a bowl, stirring with a whisk. Pour over the farro mixture, tossing to combine. Top with the almonds.

(serving size: 1½ cups): **CALORIES** 375; **FAT** 16.7g (sat 3.3g, mono 7.7g, poly 1.8g); **PROTEIN** 12g; **CARB** 48g; **FIBER** 8g; **SUGARS** 3g (est. added sugars 0g); **CHOL** 9mg; **IRON** 3mg; **SODIUM** 217mg; **CALCIUM** 67mg

MULTIPURPOSE VINAIGRETTE

HANDS-ON: **10 MINUTES**   TOTAL: **10 MINUTES**   SERVES **8**

3 tablespoons red wine vinegar

2 tablespoons finely chopped shallots

2 teaspoons chopped thyme leaves

1½ teaspoons Dijon mustard

½ teaspoon light agave nectar

½ teaspoon freshly ground black pepper

¼ teaspoon kosher salt

2 garlic cloves, minced

¼ cup extra-virgin olive oil

Combine the first 8 ingredients in a small bowl, stirring with a whisk. Slowly drizzle the olive oil into the vinegar mixture, stirring constantly with a whisk.

(serving size: 1 tablespoon): **CALORIES** 69; **FAT** 6.7g (sat 0.9g, mono 4.9g, poly 0.7g); **PROTEIN** 0g; **CARB** 2g; **FIBER** 0g; **SUGARS** 1g (est. added sugars 0g); **CHOL** 0mg; **IRON** 0mg; **SODIUM** 144mg; **CALCIUM** 4mg

"FARROTTO" WITH BUTTERNUT, GRUYÈRE, AND HAZELNUTS

HANDS-ON: **50 MINUTES**   TOTAL: **1 HOUR, 20 MINUTES**   SERVES **4**

1 tablespoon olive oil

1½ cups thinly sliced leek (about 1 large)

1 cup uncooked farro

1 garlic clove, minced

½ cup white wine

4 cups water

4 cups (½-inch) cubed peeled butternut squash

1 tablespoon chopped fresh sage

¾ teaspoon kosher salt

½ teaspoon freshly ground black pepper

2 ounces vegetarian Gruyère cheese, grated (about ½ cup)

½ cup chopped hazelnuts, toasted

Cubes of butternut squash hold their shape and bite, and stand out wonderfully against the farro background in this dish. Grated Gruyère cheese and chopped hazelnuts add the perfect touch of fat and salt at the end.

1. Heat a Dutch oven over medium-high heat. Add the oil to the pan; swirl to coat. Add the leek; sauté 5 minutes or until tender, stirring frequently. Add the farro and garlic; cook for 1 minute, stirring constantly. Stir in the wine; cook 1 minute or until the wine evaporates.

2. Add 1 cup of the water to the pan; cook 8 minutes or until the liquid is nearly absorbed, stirring frequently. Add 2 more cups of the water, 1 cup at a time, stirring until each portion is absorbed before adding the next (about 30 minutes total). Stir in 1 cup of the water, squash, sage, salt, and pepper. Cover, reduce the heat, and simmer 30 minutes or until the squash is just tender, stirring occasionally. Stir in the cheese; sprinkle with the nuts. Serve immediately.

(serving size: about 1⅓ cups): CALORIES 468; **FAT** 18.5g (sat 3.8g, mono 10.5g, poly 1.9g); **PROTEIN** 15g; **CARB** 61g; **FIBER** 12g; **SUGARS** 5g (est. added sugars 0g); **CHOL** 16mg; **IRON** 4mg; **SODIUM** 420mg; **CALCIUM** 272mg

farro is an ancient wheat (also known as emmer) that has a tough outer husk; that exterior is what protects the grain's nutrients. It comes in a few varieties: pearled, semi-pearled, and whole. Pearled takes the least time to cook because it has no bran at all, meaning fewer nutrients. Semi-pearled has had some of the bran removed but retains some of the fiber, which allows for speedier cooking.Whole farro retains all the grain's nutrients, and takes the longest to cook. It also requires an overnight soak. Labels can sometimes be confusing, so when in doubt, follow the cooking directions on the package.

FARRO WITH SPICY TOMATO SAUCE

HANDS-ON: **40 MINUTES**   TOTAL: **40 MINUTES**   SERVES **4**

2 tablespoons olive oil

1 large yellow onion (about 14 ounces), chopped (about 2 cups)

6 garlic cloves, minced

1 small zucchini (about 7 ounces), chopped (about 1½ cups)

4 ounces chopped mushrooms (about 1½ cups)

2 tablespoons chopped fresh oregano

2 tablespoons tomato paste

4 cups chopped tomatoes (from 2 pounds tomatoes)

1 teaspoon kosher salt

½ teaspoon crushed red pepper or freshly ground black pepper

1½ teaspoons red wine vinegar

3 cups cooked farro

2 ounces fresh mozzarella cheese, diced (about ½ cup)

½ cup thinly sliced fresh basil

If you can, use fresh seasonal tomatoes to make this flavorful from-scratch sauce—it's worth it. We used pearled farro in this recipe because it's quick cooking, but you can certainly use whole-grain farro or wheat berries if you have the time.

1. Heat a large skillet over medium-high heat. Add the oil to the pan; swirl to coat. Add the onion and garlic; cook, stirring occasionally, 5 minutes or until lightly caramelized.

2. Add the zucchini and mushrooms; cook, stirring occasionally, until softened, about 4 minutes. Add the oregano and tomato paste; cook, stirring constantly, 1 minute. Add the tomatoes, salt, and red pepper. Bring to a boil; reduce the heat to medium-low, and simmer 12 minutes or until the tomatoes have started to break down and the mixture thickens slightly. Stir in the vinegar. Place the farro on each of 4 plates. Spoon the tomato sauce over the farro; top with the mozzarella and basil.

(serving size: ¾ cup farro, 1 cup tomato sauce, ½ ounce cheese, and 2 tablespoons basil): CALORIES 359; FAT 13.2g (sat 3.6g, mono 5g, poly 1g); PROTEIN 13g; CARB 61g; FIBER 11g; SUGARS 12g (est. added sugars 0g); CHOL 10mg; IRON 2mg; SODIUM 546mg; CALCIUM 79mg

VEGETARIAN MOUSSAKA

HANDS-ON: **25 MINUTES**   TOTAL: **1 HOUR, 19 MINUTES**   SERVES **4**

3 peeled eggplants, cut into ½-inch-thick slices (about 2½ pounds)

2 tablespoons extra-virgin olive oil

Cooking spray

2 cups chopped onion

4 garlic cloves, minced

½ cup uncooked bulgur

¼ teaspoon ground allspice

¼ teaspoon ground cinnamon

⅛ teaspoon ground cloves

2 cups organic vegetable broth

2 teaspoons chopped fresh oregano

1 (14.5-ounce) can no-salt-added diced tomatoes, undrained

1 tablespoon butter

2 tablespoons all-purpose flour

1 cup 1% low-fat milk

2 tablespoons finely grated vegetarian Parmesan cheese

¼ teaspoon salt

1 large egg, lightly beaten

In this meatless version of the classic Greek dish, bulgur wheat stands in for ground meat in a spiced-tomato filling surrounded by eggplant layers and topped with a béchamel sauce. The eggplant and bulgur pack this dish with fiber.

1. Preheat the broiler to high.

2. Brush the eggplant slices with 1 tablespoon of the oil. Place half of the eggplant on a foil-lined baking sheet coated with cooking spray; broil 5 inches from the heat for 5 minutes on each side or until browned. Repeat the procedure with the remaining eggplant. Set the eggplant aside.

3. Heat a large skillet over medium-high heat. Add the remaining 1 tablespoon oil to the pan; swirl to coat. Add the chopped onion to the pan; sauté 8 minutes. Add the garlic; sauté 1 minute. Add the bulgur; cook 3 minutes or until the bulgur is lightly toasted, stirring frequently. Add the ground allspice, cinnamon, and cloves; cook 1 minute, stirring constantly. Stir in the broth, oregano, and tomatoes. Bring to a boil; reduce the heat, and simmer 20 minutes or until thickened, stirring occasionally.

4. Melt the butter in a saucepan over medium heat. Add the flour; cook 1 minute, stirring constantly with a whisk until well blended. Gradually add the milk, stirring constantly with a whisk. Bring to a boil; reduce the heat to medium-low, and simmer 5 minutes or until thickened, stirring frequently. Stir in the cheese and salt. Remove from the heat, and cool slightly. Add the egg, stirring well with a whisk.

5. Preheat the oven to 350°F.

6. Arrange half of the eggplant in an 11 x 7–inch glass or ceramic baking dish coated with cooking spray. Spread the bulgur mixture evenly over the eggplant; arrange the remaining eggplant over the bulgur mixture. Top with the milk mixture. Bake at 350°F for 40 minutes, and remove from the oven. Increase the oven temperature to 475°F. Return the dish to the oven for 4 minutes or until the top is browned. Let stand for 10 minutes before serving.

CALORIES 343; **FAT** 13.1g (sat 4.1g, mono 6.4g, poly 1.3g); **PROTEIN** 12g; **CARB** 48g; **FIBER** 13g; **SUGARS** 15g (est. added sugars 0g); **CHOL** 57mg; **IRON** 2mg; **SODIUM** 541mg; **CALCIUM** 203mg

BULGUR-PEPPER PATTIES ♥

HANDS-ON: **10 MINUTES**   TOTAL: **40 MINUTES**   SERVES **6**

2¼ cups finely chopped peeled tomato

¾ cup uncooked fine bulgur

½ cup coarsely grated onion

¼ cup coarsely grated green bell pepper

1 teaspoon canned tomato puree

¾ cup shelled dry-roasted pistachios, finely ground

1 tablespoon finely chopped fresh flat-leaf parsley

2 teaspoons finely chopped fresh oregano

1 teaspoon ground Aleppo pepper

¾ teaspoon fine sea salt

Chopped fresh parsley (optional)

Lemon wedges (optional)

Be sure to use fine-ground bulgur in the patties for the best texture. Serve these with Aleppo-dusted yogurt and pita to round out this Mediterranean-inspired meal.

Combine the first 5 ingredients in a large bowl; let stand 15 minutes. Add the pistachios and the next 4 ingredients (through salt); mix well. Press the bulgur mixture into a (¼-cup) dry measuring cup; unmold onto a platter. Repeat with the remaining bulgur mixture to form 12 patties total. Chill for 15 minutes; shape each bulgur portion into a 2½-inch patty. Top with chopped parsley and serve with lemon wedges, if desired.

(serving size: 2 patties): **CALORIES** 167; **FAT** 7.5g (sat 0.8g, mono 3.6g, poly 2.2g); **PROTEIN** 6g; **CARB** 22g; **FIBER** 6g; **SUGARS** 4g (est. added sugars 0g); **CHOL** 0mg; **IRON** 1mg; **SODIUM** 296mg; **CALCIUM** 40mg

aleppo pepper is a red chile grown in Turkey and Syria near the northern Syrian city from which it gets its name, although it's also known as Halaby pepper. It's got a fruity, tart flavor that adds a gentle, smoldering heat to any dish it's added to. Try it in rice and pasta dishes, stews, and pizza. If you can't find Aleppo pepper, substitute ½ teaspoon paprika plus ½ teaspoon ground red pepper.

NORTH AFRICAN BULGUR PILAF V

HANDS-ON: **15 MINUTES**   TOTAL: **40 MINUTES**   SERVES **4**

1½ cups organic vegetable broth (such as Swanson)

1½ teaspoons ground cinnamon

1½ teaspoons ground cumin

1 teaspoon kosher salt

½ teaspoon cayenne pepper

1½ cups uncooked medium-grain bulgur

1 (15-ounce) can no-salt-added chickpeas, rinsed and drained

4 tablespoons olive oil

2 cups fresh cauliflower florets (about 8 ounces)

5 medium carrots, cut diagonally into ½-inch-thick slices (about 2 cups)

½ teaspoon freshly ground black pepper

Cooking spray

¼ cup chopped fresh flat-leaf parsley

¼ cup pomegranate arils

The chewy bulgur and roasted vegetables are bursting with bold, warm flavors in this filling dish. The parsley and pomegranate arils add a pop of color and freshness.

1. Preheat the oven to 450°F.

2. Bring the stock, ¾ teaspoon of the cinnamon. ¾ teaspoon of the cumin, ½ teaspoon of the salt, and ¼ teaspoon of the cayenne pepper to a boil in a medium saucepan over high heat. Stir in the bulgur. Cook 1 minute; cover, and remove from the heat. Let stand 15 minutes. Fluff with a fork. Stir in the chickpeas and 3 tablespoons of the oil.

3. Toss together the cauliflower, carrots, black pepper, and remaining 1 tablespoon oil, ¾ teaspoon each of the cinnamon and cumin, ½ teaspoon salt, and ¼ teaspoon cayenne in a large bowl. Arrange in a single layer on an aluminum foil-lined rimmed baking sheet coated with cooking spray. Bake at 450°F for 20 to 25 minutes or until caramelized, stirring halfway through. Place the bulgur mixture in each of 4 shallow bowls. Spoon the roasted vegetable mixture over the bulgur mixture. Top with the parsley and pomegranate arils.

(serving size: 1¼ cups bulgur mixture, ½ cup roasted vegetable mixture, 1 tablespoon parsley, and 1 tablespoon pomegranate arils): **CALORIES** 518; **FAT** 16.1g (sat 2.1g, mono 10g, poly 1.8g); **PROTEIN** 16g; **CARB** 82g; **FIBER** 15g; **SUGARS** 5g (est. added sugars 0g); **CHOL** 0mg; **IRON** 4mg; **SODIUM** 702mg; **CALCIUM** 134mg

MEDITERRANEAN BARLEY
WITH CHICKPEAS AND ARUGULA ⱱ

HANDS-ON: **11 MINUTES**   TOTAL: **31 MINUTES**   SERVES **4**

1 cup uncooked pearl barley

1 cup packed arugula leaves

1 cup finely chopped red bell pepper

3 tablespoons finely chopped sun-dried tomatoes, packed without oil

1 (15½-ounce) can no-salt-added chickpeas (garbanzo beans), rinsed and drained

2 tablespoons fresh lemon juice

2 tablespoons extra-virgin olive oil

1 teaspoon salt

½ teaspoon crushed red pepper

2 tablespoons chopped pistachios

This salad is delicious at room temperature and is a great make-ahead dish, as the flavor only gets better as the barley has time to absorb the dressing.

1. Cook the barley according to the package directions, omitting the salt. Combine the barley, arugula, bell pepper, tomatoes, and chickpeas in a large bowl.

2. Combine the lemon juice, oil, salt, and crushed red pepper, stirring with a whisk. Drizzle over the barley mixture, and toss. Sprinkle with the pistachios.

(serving size: 1¼ cups barley mixture and 1½ teaspoons pistachios): **CALORIES** 350; **FAT** 9.9g (sat 1.3g, mono 5.9g, poly 1.6g); **PROTEIN** 10g; **CARB** 57g; **FIBER** 12g; **SUGARS** 4g (est. added sugars 0g); **CHOL** 0mg; **IRON** 3mg; **SODIUM** 637mg; **CALCIUM** 72mg

barley comes in two forms: pearled and hulled. Pearled barley has been polished to remove the bran and possibly some of the endosperm layer of the grain. It's softer than the hulled form and cooks more quickly, but it's not a whole grain. Hulled barley has had the tough outermost hull removed, but is considered a whole grain because it still retains the nutrient-rich bran and endosperm. It's nuttier and chewier and takes longer to cook.

LENTIL-BARLEY BURGERS WITH FIERY FRUIT SALSA

HANDS-ON: **35 MINUTES** TOTAL: **2 HOURS** SERVES **4**

SALSA

¼ cup finely chopped
  pineapple

¼ cup finely chopped mango

¼ cup finely chopped
  tomatillo

¼ cup halved grape tomatoes

1 tablespoon fresh lime juice

1 serrano chile, minced

BURGERS

1½ cups water

½ cup dried lentils

Cooking spray

1 cup chopped onion

¼ cup grated carrot

2 teaspoons minced fresh
  garlic

2 tablespoons tomato paste

1½ teaspoons ground cumin

¾ teaspoon dried oregano

½ teaspoon chili powder

¾ teaspoon salt

¾ cup cooked pearl barley

½ cup panko (Japanese
  breadcrumbs)

¼ cup finely chopped fresh
  parsley

½ teaspoon coarsely ground
  black pepper

2 large egg whites

1 large egg

3 tablespoons canola oil

If you have leftover barley, this is a great opportunity to transform it into something new. Combined with lentils, veggies, and seasonings, it makes a hearty main-dish burger sans the bun. The fruit salsa adds bright flavors. Serve with lime wedges for added zest.

1. Make the salsa: Combine the first 6 ingredients in a bowl; cover and refrigerate.

2. Make the burgers: Combine 1½ cups water and the lentils in a saucepan; bring to a boil. Cover, reduce the heat, and simmer 25 minutes or until the lentils are tender. Drain. Place half of the lentils in a large bowl. Place the remaining lentils in a food processor; process until smooth. Add the processed lentils to the whole lentils in the bowl.

3. Heat a large nonstick skillet over medium-high heat. Coat the pan with cooking spray. Add the onion and carrot; sauté 6 minutes or until tender, stirring occasionally. Add the garlic; cook 1 minute, stirring constantly. Add the tomato paste, cumin, oregano, chili powder, and ¼ teaspoon of the salt; cook 1 minute, stirring constantly. Add the onion mixture to the lentils. Add the remaining ½ teaspoon salt, barley, and the next 5 ingredients (through egg); stir well. Cover and refrigerate 1 hour or until firm.

4. Divide the mixture into 8 portions, shaping each into a ½-inch-thick patty. Heat a large nonstick skillet over medium-high heat. Add 1½ tablespoons of the oil to the pan; swirl to coat. Add 4 patties; cook 3 minutes on each side or until browned. Repeat the procedure with the remaining 1½ tablespoons oil and 4 patties. Serve with the salsa.

(serving size: 2 patties and ¼ cup salsa): **CALORIES** 315; **FAT** 13g (sat 1.2g, mono 6.8g, poly 3.5g); **PROTEIN** 13g; **CARB** 40g; **FIBER** 10g; **SUGARS** 8g (est. added sugars 0g); **CHOL** 53mg; **IRON** 4mg; **SODIUM** 539mg; **CALCIUM** 60mg

CHEDDAR, BROCCOLI, AND BARLEY SWEET POTATOES

HANDS-ON: **12 MINUTES**   TOTAL: **1 HOUR, 22 MINUTES**   SERVES **6**

6 Perfect Roasted Sweet
  Potatoes
⅓ cup uncooked pearl barley
1½ tablespoons olive oil
1 tablespoon finely chopped
  fresh garlic
4½ cups coarsely chopped
  broccoli florets
  (about 1 large head)
¼ cup water
¼ teaspoon kosher salt
¼ teaspoon crushed red
  pepper
2 ounces cheddar cheese,
  shredded (about ½ cup)

Keep this simple recipe in your back pocket for nights you're looking for a hearty, nutritious dinner idea that has some kid-appeal.

1. Bake the potatoes according to the recipe instructions below.
2. Cook the barley according to the package directions, omitting the salt and fat.
3. Heat a large nonstick skillet over medium-high heat. Add the oil to the pan; swirl to coat. Add the garlic; cook 30 seconds, stirring constantly. Add the broccoli and ¼ cup water to the pan. Cover and cook 4 minutes or until crisp-tender. Stir in the cooked barley, salt, and pepper; uncover and cook 1 minute. Stir in the cheese. Top the potatoes with the barley-broccoli mixture.

(serving size: 1 potato and ½ cup topping): CALORIES 409; FAT 17.1g (sat 4g, mono 10.8g, poly 1.7g); PROTEIN 9g; CARB 58g; FIBER 10g; SUGARS 10g (est. added sugars 0g); CHOL 10mg; IRON 2mg; SODIUM 399mg; CALCIUM 168mg

PERFECT ROASTED SWEET POTATOES

HANDS-ON: **10 MINUTES**   TOTAL: **1 HOUR, 10 MINUTES**   SERVES **6**

6 (8-ounce) sweet potatoes
1½ teaspoons olive oil
⅜ teaspoon kosher salt
¼ teaspoon freshly ground
  black pepper

Preheat the oven to 400°F. Pierce the potatoes with a fork. Rub the potatoes with the olive oil; wrap each in foil. Place the potatoes on a jelly-roll pan; bake at 400°F for 1 hour or until tender. Partially split the potatoes in half lengthwise; fluff the flesh with a fork. Sprinkle evenly with the kosher salt and freshly ground black pepper.

(serving size: 1 potato): CALORIES 205; FAT 1.2g (sat 0.2g, mono 0g, poly 0g); PROTEIN 0g; CARB 0g; FIBER 0g; SUGARS 10g (est. added sugars 10g); CHOL 0mg; IRON 0mg; SODIUM 245mg; CALCIUM 0mg

BEER-BRUSHED TOFU SKEWERS WITH BARLEY

HANDS-ON: **45 MINUTES**   TOTAL: **45 MINUTES**   SERVES **4**

1 (12-ounce) bottle brown ale
¼ cup honey
½ teaspoon crushed red pepper
12 ounces water packed, extra-firm tofu, drained, cut into 1½-inch cubes, patted dry
Cooking spray
1 teaspoon freshly ground black pepper
¾ teaspoon kosher salt
1 zucchini (about 10 ounces), cut lengthwise into ½-inch-thick planks
1 pint cherry tomatoes, halved
3 cups loosely packed arugula (about 2½ ounces)
2 cups cooked barley
3 tablespoons extra-virgin olive oil
1 tablespoons sherry vinegar

Tofu get a grilled treatment in this recipe with a sweet brown beer glaze that's brushed on before and while it grills. The flavor and texture is a delicious contrast with the hearty, chewy, nutty barley.

1. Preheat the grill to high heat.

2. Bring the beer, honey, and red pepper to a boil in a 2-quart saucepan over medium-high heat, stirring occasionally. Cook, stirring occasionally, 20 to 25 minutes or until the mixture is reduced to ½ cup.

3. Thread the tofu onto 4 (6-inch) skewers. Coat the tofu with cooking spray. Sprinkle with ½ teaspoon of the black pepper and ¼ teaspoon of the salt. Brush the tofu and zucchini with the beer mixture. Arrange the tofu and zucchini in a single layer on a grill grate coated with cooking spray. Grill the tofu, brushing often with the beer mixture, 2 to 3 minutes per side or until grill marks appear. Cook the zucchini 3 to 4 minutes per side or until tender and grill marks appear. Remove from the grill; roughly chop the zucchini.

4. Toss together the zucchini, tomatoes, arugula, barley, oil, vinegar, and remaining ½ teaspoon each pepper and salt in a large bowl. Arrange the zucchini mixture on a platter. Top with the tofu skewers.

(serving size: 1⅓ cups barley mixture and 1 tofu skewer): CALORIES 382; FAT 16.7g (sat 2.2g, mono 11.5g, poly 2.4g); PROTEIN 12g; CARB 49g; FIBER 5g; SUGARS 22g (est. added sugars 17g); CHOL 0mg; IRON 3mg; SODIUM 384mg; CALCIUM 204mg

WHEAT BERRY, SPINACH, AND STRAWBERRY SALAD

HANDS-ON: **10 MINUTES**   TOTAL: **55 MINUTES**   SERVES **4**

2½ cups water

¾ cup uncooked hard winter wheat berries

3 tablespoons extra-virgin olive oil

1 tablespoon white wine vinegar

¾ teaspoon kosher salt

½ teaspoon freshly ground black pepper

1 tablespoon butter

⅓ cup sliced almonds

1½ ounces feta cheese, crumbled (about ⅓ cup)

1 tablespoon balsamic vinegar

6 cups fresh baby spinach

½ cup chopped fresh flat-leaf parsley

¼ cup chopped fresh basil

¼ cup halved strawberries

Because of their long cooking time, you may want to cook a big batch of wheat berries to have on hand for grain-based salads like this one, to stir into soups, as a base for stir-fries, or to mix into casseroles. They'll keep for about 5 days in the refrigerator and can be frozen for up to 2 months.

1. Bring 2½ cups water and the wheat berries to a boil in a saucepan over high heat. Reduce the heat, and simmer 45 minutes or until the wheat berries are tender but still chewy. Drain; rinse with cold water. Drain.

2. Combine the wheat berries, 1 tablespoon of the oil, white wine vinegar, ½ teaspoon of the salt, and ¼ teaspoon of the pepper in a large bowl; toss.

3. Melt the butter in a large skillet over medium-high heat. Add the almonds; cook 1 minute, stirring constantly. Remove the pan from the heat; stir in the wheat berry mixture and feta cheese. Combine the remaining 2 tablespoons oil, balsamic vinegar, remaining ¼ teaspoon salt, and remaining ¼ teaspoon pepper in a large bowl. Stir in the spinach, parsley, and basil. Place the spinach mixture on each of 4 plates; top with the wheat berry mixture and strawberries.

(serving size: about 2 cups spinach mixture, ⅓ cup wheat berry mixture, and 1 tablespoon strawberries): CALORIES 352; FAT 19.7g (sat 5.1g, mono 11.1g, poly 2.2g); PROTEIN 10g; CARB 37g; FIBER 8g; SUGARS 2g (est. added sugars 0g); CHOL 17mg; IRON 4mg; SODIUM 574mg; CALCIUM 134mg

wheat berries are whole-grain wheat kernels that have a sweet nutty flavor and an assertively chewy texture. They can be red or white, hard (higher protein) or soft (lower protein), and winter or spring, depending on when they are planted. Like other grains, the quicker-cooking pearled variety has had the outer bran removed, taking with it much of the fiber.

WHEAT BERRY SALAD WITH MELON AND FETA

HANDS-ON: **22 MINUTES**   TOTAL: **22 MINUTES**   SERVES **4**

- 3 tablespoons extra-virgin olive oil
- 2 tablespoons white wine vinegar
- ½ teaspoon kosher salt
- ½ teaspoon freshly ground black pepper
- ½ teaspoon tomato paste
- 1½ cups cooked wheat berries
- 1 cup sliced English cucumber
- 1 cup chopped watermelon
- 1 cup yellow grape tomatoes, halved
- 3 tablespoons chopped fresh mint
- 2 ounces feta cheese, crumbled (about ½ cup)
- 2 tablespoons unsalted sunflower seed kernels

This salad offers an intriguing mix of fresh, crunchy, and juicy fresh produce with chewy wheat berries and creamy cheese.

Combine the first 5 ingredients in a large bowl, stirring well with a whisk. Stir in the wheat berries; toss to coat. Stir in the cucumber, watermelon, tomatoes, and mint; toss to coat. Sprinkle with the cheese and sunflower seeds.

(serving size: about 1¼ cups): **CALORIES** 306; **FAT** 16.5g (sat 3.8g, mono 9.2g, poly 2.4g); **PROTEIN** 9g; **CARB** 31g; **FIBER** 5g; **SUGARS** 5g (est. added sugars 0g); **CHOL** 13mg; **IRON** 2mg; **SODIUM** 411mg; **CALCIUM** 103mg

english cucumber adds cool crispness to whatever dish it's added to, but a couple of its other particularly lovely characteristics are its thin skin and inconspicuous seeds. This low-maintenance vegetable requires no peeling or seeding.

WHEAT BERRY AND PORTOBELLO OVEN PILAF

HANDS-ON: **25 MINUTES**   TOTAL: **1 HOUR, 5 MINUTES**   SERVES **4**

2 tablespoons unsalted butter

3 portobello mushroom caps (about 6 ounces), gills removed, cut into 8 wedges

3 shallots (about 4 ounces), thinly sliced (about 1 cup)

1½ tablespoons chopped fresh thyme

¾ teaspoon freshly ground black pepper

½ teaspoon kosher salt

1 cup dry red wine

3 cups unsalted vegetable stock

1 cup uncooked wheat berries

1 tablespoon unsalted tomato paste

¾ cup toasted fresh breadcrumbs

2 tablespoons extra-virgin olive oil

2 tablespoons chopped fresh flat-leaf parsley

Wheat berries have a satisfying chew that pairs beautifully with the hearty, earthy mushrooms, which get deeply browned and buttery in the cast-iron skillet. The dish is finished with golden breadcrumbs and fresh parsley for a little crunch and color.

1. Preheat the oven to 400°F.

2. Melt the butter in a 10-inch cast-iron or other ovenproof skillet over medium-high heat. Add the portobellos; cook, stirring constantly, until lightly browned, about 4 minutes. Add the shallots, thyme, pepper, and salt; cook, stirring often, until the shallots are softened, about 3 minutes. Add the wine, and bring to a boil. Cook, stirring occasionally, 4 to 5 minutes or until reduced to ¼ cup. Stir in the stock, wheat berries, and tomato paste. Bring to a boil, stirring occasionally.

3. Transfer the pan to the oven, and bake at 400°F for 40 minutes or until the wheat berries are tender and the liquid is absorbed. Toss the breadcrumbs with the olive oil, and sprinkle over the portobello mixture. Top with the parsley.

(serving size: about 1¼ cups): CALORIES 525; FAT 16.3g (sat 5.1g, mono 6.5g, poly 1.1g); PROTEIN 16g; CARB 78g; FIBER 10g; SUGARS 7g (est. added sugars 0g); CHOL 15mg; IRON 3mg; SODIUM 645mg; CALCIUM 49mg

SHAVED APPLE AND FENNEL SALAD
WITH CRUNCHY SPELT ⓥ

HANDS-ON: **20 MINUTES**   TOTAL: **20 MINUTES**   SERVES **6**

3 tablespoons canola oil

2 tablespoons cider vinegar

1½ teaspoons sugar

1½ teaspoons whole-grain Dijon mustard

⅜ teaspoon kosher salt

¼ teaspoon freshly ground black pepper

1 fennel bulb, halved and cored

1 small green apple, quartered and cored

1 small red apple, quartered and cored

1 cup flat-leaf parsley leaves

1 cup Crunchy Fried Spelt

Simply put, apples and fennel are right together—the flavors are so complementary. Canola oil may seem like an odd choice, but it's a neutral oil that helps keep the flavors of this salad clean and straightforward; you can always use olive oil if you'd like the vinaigrette to assert itself a bit more. Garnish with fresh dill, if you'd like.

1. Combine the first 6 ingredients in a large bowl, stirring well with a whisk.

2. Cut the fennel and apples into ¹⁄₁₆-inch slices using a mandoline. Add the fennel, apples, parsley leaves, and Crunchy Fried Spelt to the vinaigrette; toss well to combine.

(serving size: about 1 cup): CALORIES 204; FAT 13.3g (sat 1g, mono 8g, poly 3.6g); PROTEIN 3g; CARB 21g; FIBER 4g; SUGARS 7g (est. added sugars 0g); CHOL 0mg; IRON 2mg; SODIUM 166mg; CALCIUM 43mg

CRUNCHY FRIED SPELT ⓥ

HANDS-ON: **30 MINUTES**   TOTAL: **2 HOURS, 30 MINUTES**   SERVES **18**

3 cups cooked spelt (about 1 cup uncooked grains)

6 cups canola oil or peanut oil

This technique (which works with any cooked grain) turns whole grains into nuggets of nutty flavor that are delicious anywhere you're craving a little crunch. And don't be concerned about frying—when the oil is heated to the right temperature, the food doesn't absorb much.

1. Line a jelly-roll pan with several layers of paper towels. Spread the spelt out into a thin layer on the paper towels. Let stand 1 to 2 hours to dry out the surface moisture, stirring the grains occasionally.

2. Heat the oil in a large Dutch oven over high heat until a thermometer submerged in the oil registers 375°F. (Do not use a smaller pot; the moisture in the grains will cause the oil to bubble up vigorously.) Add ½ cup spelt to the hot oil; cook 4 to 5 minutes or until the grains are browned and crisp. (Maintain oil temperature at 375°F, and fry in small batches.) Remove the fried spelt from the pan with a slotted spoon; drain on paper towels. Repeat with remaining spelt, ½ cup at a time.

(serving size: about 2 tablespoons): CALORIES 70; FAT 4.5g (sat 0.3g, mono 2.6g, poly 1.2g); PROTEIN 1g; CARB 7g; FIBER 1g; SUGARS 0g (est. added sugars 0g); CHOL 0mg; IRON 0mg; SODIUM 0mg; CALCIUM 0mg

BRUSSELS SPROUTS SALAD
WITH PICKLED RYE BERRIES ⓥ

HANDS-ON: **30 MINUTES**   TOTAL: **3 HOURS**   SERVES **8**

2 pounds whole Brussels
   sprouts
3 tablespoons toasted
   walnut oil
2 teaspoons cider vinegar
¾ teaspoon kosher salt
½ teaspoon freshly ground
   black pepper
½ cup slivered red onion
2 cups Pickled Rye Berries
½ cup dried cranberries
6 tablespoons chopped
   walnuts, toasted

*Soaking chewier whole grains (such as rye or wheat berries)
in a pickling brine gives them a tanginess that makes each bite
that much more enjoyable.*

1. Trim the bottoms off the sprouts; pull off the bigger leaves to
yield 8 cups. (Reserve the sprout "hearts" for another use.)
2. Combine the oil, vinegar, salt, and pepper in a large bowl. Add the
leaves and onion; toss gently to coat. Arrange the leaves on a platter;
sprinkle with the Pickled Rye Berries, cranberries, and toasted walnuts.

(serving size: about 1 cup): **CALORIES** 253; **FAT** 9.6g (sat 0.9g, mono 1.7g, poly 6g);
PROTEIN 8g; **CARB** 36g; **FIBER** 3g; **SUGARS** 9g (est. added sugars 2g); **CHOL** 0mg;
IRON 2mg; **SODIUM** 319mg; **CALCIUM** 47mg

PICKLED RYE BERRIES ⓥ

HANDS-ON: **10 MINUTES**   TOTAL: **2 HOURS, 30 MINUTES**   SERVES **8**

⅔ cup uncooked rye berries
3 cups cider vinegar
6 tablespoons sugar
2 teaspoons kosher salt
3 bay leaves
2 dried red chiles (optional)

*This recipe works best with "hard-shell" grains—those with
a chewy, closed texture (rye berries, wheat berries, spelt,
and kamut). Grains with a more "open" texture (such as farro
or barley) take on so much brine that they lose their own
nutty flavor.*

1. Cook the rye berries in a large pot of boiling water for 1 hour or until
chewy-tender. Drain and rinse with cold water; drain.
2. Combine the vinegar and remaining ingredients in the pan; bring
to a boil. Cook 3 minutes, stirring to dissolve the sugar. Add the
rye berries; simmer 2 minutes. Remove the pan from the heat; cool
to room temperature. Let stand at least 1 hour before serving. Store,
in the brine, in the refrigerator for up to 2 weeks (the flavor will
intensify the longer it stands).

(serving size: ¼ cup drained grains): **CALORIES** 121; **FAT** 0.7g (sat 0.1g, mono 0.1g, poly 0.3g);
PROTEIN 5g; **CARB** 23g; **FIBER** 0g; **SUGARS** 2g (est. added sugars 2g); **CHOL** 0mg;
IRON 1mg; **SODIUM** 124mg; **CALCIUM** 15mg

MILLET AND CORN PIE

HANDS-ON: **45 MINUTES** TOTAL: **2 HOURS, 45 MINUTES** SERVES **6**

2 tablespoons unsalted butter

2 cups fresh corn kernels (from 4 ears)

1 cup finely chopped onion (1 medium onion)

4 teaspoons chopped fresh thyme

4½ cups water

1 teaspoon kosher salt

1¼ cups uncooked millet, rinsed

4 ounces goat cheese, crumbled (about 1 cup)

Cooking spray

½ teaspoon freshly ground black pepper

This pie offers a refreshingly atypical grain-based meal option. Mild-flavored millet gets a boost from the sweet fresh corn and creamy goat cheese.

1. Cook the butter in a 3-quart saucepan over medium heat until bubbly, 1 to 2 minutes. Add corn, onion, and 1 tablespoon of the thyme; cook, stirring often, until softened but not yet beginning to brown, about 8 minutes. Add the water and salt; increase the heat to medium-high, and bring to a boil, stirring occasionally. Add the millet; cook, stirring often, 10 minutes. Reduce the heat to medium-low; simmer, stirring occasionally, until thickened but still slightly soupy, 8 to 10 minutes. Remove from the heat, and stir in the goat cheese.

2. Coat a 9½-inch deep-dish pie pan with cooking spray. Spoon the mixture into the pan, and smooth the top. Sprinkle with the pepper and the remaining 1 teaspoon thyme. Cover and chill until set, about 2 hours. Bring to room temperature before serving. Cut into wedges and serve.

(serving size: 1 wedge): **CALORIES** 293; **FAT** 10g (sat 5.6g, mono 2.3g, poly 1.3g); **PROTEIN** 10g; **CARB** 42g; **FIBER** 5g; **SUGARS** 3g (est. added sugars 0g); **CHOL** 19mg; **IRON** 2mg; **SODIUM** 418mg; **CALCIUM** 47mg

millet may be an ingredient in birdseed, but it's not just for the birds. This tiny, often overlooked grain has a mild, slightly sweet, slightly nutty flavor that gives it great versatility. (You can toast it in a skillet to bring out it's nuttiness.) It's small size means it cooks quickly, making it ideal for weeknight meals. Add it to salads, use it as a base for stir-fries, and serve it as a breakfast cereal.

RISOTTO PRIMAVERA

HANDS-ON: **40 MINUTES**   TOTAL: **40 MINUTES**   SERVES **4**

1 tablespoon olive oil

½ teaspoon salt

1 pint cherry tomatoes

3¼ cups water

2¼ cups organic vegetable broth (such as Swanson)

1½ cups chopped onion

1½ cups Arborio rice or other medium-grain rice

2 tablespoons white wine vinegar

½ cup frozen green peas

12 ounces asparagus, trimmed and cut into 1-inch pieces

2 ounces vegetarian Parmesan cheese (about ½ cup)

1 tablespoon fresh lemon juice

¼ teaspoon freshly ground black pepper

This risotto is studded with the color and vibrant flavor of fresh spring vegetables. It's not an expensive meal to prepare, but it's a wonderful option to serve to guests or for a special occasion.

1. Preheat the oven to 400°F. Line a jelly-roll pan with parchment paper.

2. Toss 1½ teaspoons of the olive oil, ⅛ teaspoon of the salt, and the tomatoes on the prepared pan. Bake at 400°F for 15 minutes or until the tomatoes burst.

3. Heat 3¼ cups water and the broth in a saucepan over medium heat (do not boil).

4. Heat a large Dutch oven over medium-high heat. Add the remaining 1½ teaspoons oil to the pan; swirl to coat. Add the onion to the pan; cook 5 minutes, stirring frequently. Add the rice; cook 1 minute. Stir in the vinegar; cook 30 seconds or until the liquid is absorbed, stirring constantly. Add the broth mixture, ½ cup at a time, stirring constantly until each portion is absorbed before adding the next (about 20 minutes total). Add the peas and asparagus to the pan with the last ½ cup of the broth mixture. Remove from the heat; grate 1 ounce cheese. Stir in the grated cheese, remaining ⅜ teaspoon salt, and juice. Spoon the risotto into each of 4 bowls; top evenly with the tomatoes. Shave the remaining cheese over each serving; sprinkle with the pepper.

CALORIES 430; FAT 8.2g (sat 2.6g, mono 3.6g, poly 0.7g); PROTEIN 16g; CARB 76g; FIBER 8g; SUGARS 8g (est. added sugars 0g); CHOL 13mg; IRON 3mg; SODIUM 734mg; CALCIUM 228mg

MAKING TRADITIONAL RISOTTO

1. Bring the cooking liquid to a simmer—when the liquid is in motion but almost no bubbles break the surface. Adding cold ingredients slows the release of starch.

2. Sautéing the grain infuses it with flavor and allows the risotto to simmer quickly once the liquid is added.

3. Stirring the rice constantly as you add the hot cooking liquid agitates the grain, causing it to release its starch, which creates the characteristic creaminess of this dish.

MUSHROOM AND ROASTED BUTTERNUT SQUASH RISOTTO

HANDS-ON: **25 MINUTES**   TOTAL: **50 MINUTES**   SERVES **4**

2 cups (¾-inch) cubed peeled butternut squash

3 tablespoons extra-virgin olive oil

Cooking spray

1 cup boiling water

½ ounce dried porcini mushrooms

2½ cups unsalted vegetable stock

1 (12-ounce) package sliced button mushrooms

½ cup chopped shallots

4 garlic cloves, minced

1 cup uncooked Arborio rice or other medium-grain rice

⅓ cup Madeira wine or dry sherry

1½ ounces vegetarian Parmesan cheese, grated (about 6 tablespoons)

½ teaspoon salt

⅛ teaspoon freshly ground black pepper

Roasting the squash deepens its flavor. Stir it in at the end so it retains it's shape in the risotto.

1. Preheat the oven to 450°F.

2. Combine the squash and 1 tablespoon of the oil in a bowl; toss to coat. Arrange the squash in a single layer on a baking sheet coated with cooking spray; bake at 450°F for 20 minutes or until lightly browned and tender, stirring after 10 minutes.

3. Combine 1 cup boiling water and the porcini mushrooms in a bowl; let stand 20 minutes. Strain through a cheesecloth-lined colander over a bowl. Reserve the liquid; chop the mushrooms.

4. Heat the stock in a saucepan over low heat (do not boil).

5. Heat a Dutch oven over medium-high heat. Add the remaining 2 tablespoons oil to the pan; swirl to pan. Add the button mushrooms; sauté 12 minutes or until the liquid evaporates and the mushrooms brown. Add the porcini mushrooms, shallots, and garlic; sauté 2 minutes. Add the rice; cook 30 seconds, stirring constantly. Add the reserved soaking liquid and wine; cook 3 minutes or until the liquid almost evaporates, stirring constantly.

6. Ladle in 1 cup of the stock; cook 2 minutes or until the liquid is nearly absorbed, stirring constantly. Continue adding the stock, ½ cup at a time, stirring constantly until each portion of the stock is absorbed before adding the next (about 26 minutes total). Stir in the reserved butternut squash, grated cheese, salt, and pepper.

(serving size: about 1½ cups): **CALORIES** 402; **FAT** 13.5g (sat 2.9g, mono 7.4g, poly 1.1g); **PROTEIN** 13g; **CARB** 58g; **FIBER** 5g; **SUGARS** 5g (est. added sugars 0g); **CHOL** 9mg; **IRON** 2mg; **SODIUM** 556mg; **CALCIUM** 184mg

ASPARAGUS AND LEMON
MICROWAVE RISOTTO

HANDS-ON: **15 MINUTES**   TOTAL: **32 MINUTES**   SERVES **4**

¾ cup chopped onion

2 tablespoons butter

1 tablespoon olive oil

2 garlic cloves, minced

1 cup uncooked Arborio rice or other medium-grain rice

3 cups unsalted vegetable stock

⅓ cup dry white wine

1 pound asparagus, trimmed and cut into ½-inch pieces

½ teaspoon grated lemon rind

1½ tablespoons fresh lemon juice

½ teaspoon salt

¼ teaspoon freshly ground black pepper

1½ ounces vegetarian Parmesan cheese, shaved (about 6 tablespoons)

Do not cover this risotto while microwaving, and be sure you're using at least a 2-quart bowl to allow plenty of room for the liquid to boil.

Combine the first 4 ingredients in a 2-quart microwave-safe glass bowl. Microwave at HIGH 3 minutes. Stir in the rice; microwave at HIGH 3 minutes. Stir in the stock and wine; microwave at HIGH 16 minutes, stirring for 30 seconds every 4 minutes. Add the asparagus; microwave at HIGH 2 minutes. Stir in the rind, juice, salt, pepper, and half of the cheese. Top with the remaining cheese.

(serving size: 1 cup): **CALORIES** 348; **FAT** 12.4g (sat 5.7g, mono 4.5g, poly 0.7g); **PROTEIN** 11g; **CARB** 48g; **FIBER** 4g; **SUGARS** 3g (est. added sugars 0g); **CHOL** 25mg; **IRON** 2mg; **SODIUM** 628mg; **CALCIUM** 161mg

GREEN CHILE-AND-TOMATILLO
MICROWAVE RISOTTO

HANDS-ON: **10 MINUTES**   TOTAL: **25 MINUTES**   SERVES **4**

½ cup diced yellow onion
(from 1 onion)

½ cup diced tomatillo
(from 3 small tomatillos)

½ cup diced poblano pepper
(from 1 medium pepper)

2 tablespoons olive oil

1 tablespoon minced fresh
garlic

¼ teaspoon crushed red
pepper

1 cup uncooked Arborio rice

2 tablespoons fresh lime juice

½ teaspoon kosher salt

½ teaspoon ground cumin

3 cups unsalted vegetable
stock

2 tablespoons ⅓-less-fat
cream cheese

2 ounces queso fresco,
crumbled (fresh Mexican
cheese; about ½ cup)

¼ cup firmly packed cilantro
leaves

Risottos often bring to mind long cook times and lots of stirring—not so with this version, which doesn't require any compromise in texture or flavor. If you like, you can use canned diced green chiles instead of the poblano pepper and tomatillos; the same tangy spiciness will come through.

Combine the onion, tomatillo, poblano, oil, garlic, and red pepper in a large microwave-safe bowl; cover with plastic wrap. Microwave at HIGH for 5 minutes or until the vegetables are tender. Stir in the rice, lime juice, salt, cumin, and 2¾ cups of the stock. Cover the bowl with plastic wrap; poke a hole in the plastic wrap to vent. Microwave at HIGH 15 to 16 minutes or until the liquid is absorbed and rice is tender. Add the cream cheese and remaining ¼ cup stock; stir until the cheese melts and the mixture is creamy. Top with the crumbled queso fresco and cilantro.

(serving size: 1 cup): CALORIES 329; FAT 11.7g (sat 3.5g, mono 6.1g, poly 1g); PROTEIN 11g; CARB 48g; FIBER 3g; SUGARS 2g (est. added sugars 0g); CHOL 15mg; IRON 1mg; SODIUM 487mg; CALCIUM 110mg

Tomatillos, despite their name, taste nothing like tomatoes. The tomatillo is used when it's still green. If it's turning yellow and the papery husk is browning, then the vegetable is past its prime. Tomatillos are frequently used in Mexican cuisine, where you'll often find they lend their very tart flavor to green sauces.

beans, eggs & soy

WHITE BEAN POT PIE
WITH WHOLE-WHEAT CRUST

HANDS-ON: **45 MINUTES**   TOTAL: **1 HOUR, 10 MINUTES**   SERVES **6**

6.5 ounces all-purpose flour
(about 1⅓ cups plus
2 tablespoons)

3 ounces white whole-wheat
flour (about ⅔ cup)

¼ teaspoon baking powder

1⅛ teaspoons salt

¼ cup vegetable shortening
(such as Earth Balance)

2 tablespoons cold unsalted
butter, cut into ½-inch
pieces

4 to 5 tablespoons ice-cold
water

1 teaspoon olive oil

1½ cups chopped carrots
(about 8 ounces)

1½ cups chopped turnips
(about 1 pound)

1 cup chopped fennel bulb
(about 1½ pounds)

1 cup sliced leeks (about
1 large)

1 tablespoon minced fresh
garlic

1 tablespoon finely chopped
fresh sage

2 teaspoons finely chopped
fresh rosemary

2 cups unsalted vegetable
stock

1 teaspoon freshly ground
black pepper

2 (15-ounce) cans unsalted
cannellini beans, rinsed
and drained

2 tablespoons fresh lemon
juice

Cooking spray

1 large egg white, lightly
beaten

This pot pie can also be made in a single-serving pie plate. You'll just need to cook it a bit longer. If you'd like, you can make the filling up to 3 days ahead and the crust up to 2 days ahead. For the crust, simply let it sit at room temperature for about 10 minutes before rolling. Instead of turnips, you can use rutabagas or potatoes.

1. Weigh or lightly spoon flours into dry measuring cups; level with a knife. Combine 1⅓ cups of the all-purpose flour, the whole-wheat flour, baking powder, and ½ teaspoon of the salt in a large bowl. Using your fingertips, gently incorporate the shortening and butter into the flour mixture until both are well distributed and small clumps begin to form. Stir 2 tablespoons of the ice-cold water into the flour mixture. Gently work in additional water, 1 teaspoon at a time, just until the dough begins to come together. Gently knead the dough 1 or 2 times to form a ball. Flatten the ball into a disk; wrap tightly in plastic wrap. Chill 20 minutes or up to 2 days.

2. Preheat the oven to 425°F.

3. Heat the oil in a Dutch oven over medium-high heat. Add the carrots, turnips, fennel, and leeks; cook until slightly softened, about 4 minutes. Cover, reduce the heat to medium, and cook, stirring occasionally, until crisp-tender, about 4 minutes. Uncover; add the garlic, sage, and rosemary, and cook, stirring often, until fragrant, about 1 minute. Sprinkle in the remaining 2 tablespoons flour, stirring constantly, and cook until incorporated, about 1 minute. Add the vegetable stock, pepper, and remaining ⅝ teaspoon salt, and bring to boil, stirring and scraping the bottom of the pan to loosen the browned bits. Stir in the beans and lemon juice. Reduce the heat to medium, and simmer until thickened, about 2 minutes, stirring often. Remove from the heat.

4. Coat 6 (10-ounce) ramekins with cooking spray. Roll out the dough on a lightly floured work surface to ⅛-inch thickness; cut the dough into 6 (4-inch) rounds. Spoon 1 cup filling into each ramekin, and top with a dough round, cutting small slits in the tops to vent. Brush the tops with the egg white. Place the ramekins on a rimmed baking sheet. Bake at 425°F for 20 to 25 minutes or until the crusts are light golden brown and the filling is bubbly.

(serving size: 1 pot pie): **CALORIES** 453; **FAT** 15.8g (sat 6g, mono 4.9g, poly 2.5g); **PROTEIN** 14g; **CARB** 63g; **FIBER** 11g; **SUGARS** 6g (est. added sugars 0g); **CHOL** 10mg; **IRON** 5mg; **SODIUM** 658mg; **CALCIUM** 119mg

BLACK BEAN CAKES
WITH GINGER-CILANTRO CREAM

HANDS-ON: **23 MINUTES**   TOTAL: **23 MINUTES**   SERVES **4**

2 tablespoons butter

½ cup finely chopped onion

1 tablespoon minced fresh garlic

¾ teaspoon ground cumin

¾ teaspoon kosher salt

½ teaspoon ground coriander

½ teaspoon crushed red pepper

½ teaspoon freshly ground black pepper

¼ cup panko (Japanese breadcrumbs)

1 tablespoon fresh lime juice

1 (14.5-ounce) can unsalted black beans, rinsed and drained

2 large eggs, lightly beaten

¼ cup reduced-fat sour cream

2 tablespoons finely chopped fresh cilantro

1 teaspoon grated peeled fresh ginger

Cilantro leaves (optional)

The black bean mixture is delicate, so be sure to turn the cakes gently so they don't fall apart. If they do, don't worry—you can press them back together. Serve with a simple salad of lettuce, sliced cucumbers and radishes, and carrot ribbons.

1. Heat a medium skillet over medium heat. Add 1 tablespoon of the butter; swirl until the butter melts. Add the onion and garlic; cook 4 minutes, stirring occasionally. Stir in the cumin, ½ teaspoon of the salt, coriander, red pepper, and ¼ teaspoon of the black pepper; cook 30 seconds, stirring. Remove from the heat. Stir in the panko and lime juice.

2. Place the beans in a bowl; coarsely mash with a fork. Stir in the eggs. Stir in the onion mixture. Divide the bean mixture into 4 portions, gently shaping each into a ½-inch-thick cake. Heat the pan over medium-high heat. Add the remaining 1 tablespoon butter to the pan; swirl until the butter melts. Add the cakes to the pan; cook 3 minutes on each side or until browned.

3. Combine the remaining ¼ teaspoon salt, the remaining ¼ teaspoon black pepper, sour cream, cilantro, and ginger. Serve with the cakes, and garnish with cilantro, if desired.

(serving size: 1 cake and about ¼ cup sauce): **CALORIES** 192; **FAT** 10.3g (sat 5.6g, mono 2.4g, poly 0.7g); **PROTEIN** 9g; **CARB** 16g; **FIBER** 4g; **SUGARS** 2g (est. added sugars 0g); **CHOL** 116mg; **IRON** 2mg; **SODIUM** 476mg; **CALCIUM** 86mg

GRILLED BEAN AND CHEESE–STUFFED POBLANOS

HANDS-ON: **15 MINUTES**   TOTAL: **27 MINUTES**   SERVES **4**

1 cup fresh or frozen corn kernels

⅔ cup chopped celery

½ teaspoon kosher salt

¼ teaspoon freshly ground black pepper

3.5 ounces cheddar cheese, shredded (about ¾ cup)

1 (15-ounce) can unsalted pinto beans, rinsed and drained

8 medium poblano peppers or Anaheim chiles (about 2 pounds)

1 tablespoon canola oil

4 lime wedges

The cheesy filling becomes extra gooey and melty as the peppers grill. Unlike with a lot of stuffed peppers, you don't need to roast these before stuffing. Poblanos are fairly mild, especially with the seeds removed. For even less heat, use Anaheim chiles.

1. Preheat the grill to high heat.

2. Combine the first 6 ingredients in a medium bowl. Remove the tops from the poblanos; reserve the tops. Scoop out the seeds; discard. Place about ½ cup bean mixture in each pepper. Replace the pepper tops; secure each with a 4-inch skewer. Brush the peppers evenly with the oil. Place the peppers on the grill rack; grill 12 minutes or until lightly charred, turning once after 6 minutes. Place the stuffed peppers on a platter; remove the skewers. Serve the stuffed peppers with the lime wedges.

(serving size: 2 stuffed peppers and 1 lime wedge): CALORIES 265; FAT 12.3g (sat 5.5g, mono 4.6g, poly 1.4g); PROTEIN 12g; CARB 29g; FIBER 6g; SUGARS 1g (est. added sugars 0g); CHOL 26mg; IRON 1mg; SODIUM 420mg; CALCIUM 218mg

poblanos are dark green, almost black, chile peppers. They're ideal for stuffing because they're rather large (4 to 5 inches long) with thick walls. Green Anaheim chiles, which get their name from the California city, have a milder flavor than poblanos and are a good substitute.

PEPPERED WHITE BEAN, KALE, AND EGG STACK

HANDS-ON: **30 MINUTES**   TOTAL: **30 MINUTES**   SERVES **4**

1 (14.5-ounce) can unsalted Great Northern beans, rinsed and drained

½ cup water

½ teaspoon grated lemon rind

⅜ teaspoon freshly ground black pepper

1 ounce vegetarian Parmesan cheese, grated (about ¼ cup)

2 teaspoons olive oil

5 cups chopped kale

½ teaspoon kosher salt

2 tablespoons white vinegar

4 large eggs

¼ cup chopped onion

2 teaspoons fresh lemon juice

1 teaspoon minced fresh cilantro

1 teaspoon minced fresh flat-leaf parsley

1 plum tomato, seeded and finely chopped

1 garlic clove, minced

This layered vegetarian dish boasts a nice array of textures and flavors. Great Northern beans are creamy and have a relatively neutral flavor, making them a wonderful base for this dish.

1. Combine the beans and ½ cup water in a saucepan; bring to a boil. Cook 4 minutes; remove from the heat. Stir in the rind, ⅛ teaspoon of the pepper, and cheese; coarsely mash.

2. Heat a Dutch oven over medium-high heat. Add 1 teaspoon of the oil to the pan; swirl to coat. Add the kale and ¼ teaspoon of the salt. Cook 3 minutes or until the kale wilts, stirring frequently. Remove the kale from the pan; keep warm.

3. Wipe the Dutch oven clean with a paper towel; return the pan to medium-high heat. Add water to the pan, filling two-thirds full; bring to a boil. Reduce the heat; simmer. Add the vinegar. Break each egg into a custard cup. Gently pour the eggs into the pan; cook 3 minutes or until the desired degree of doneness. Carefully remove the eggs using a slotted spoon; place on a paper towel–lined plate.

4. Combine the remaining 1 teaspoon oil, remaining ¼ teaspoon pepper, remaining ¼ teaspoon salt, onion, and remaining ingredients in a medium bowl. Place the bean mixture on each of 4 plates. Top with the kale, eggs, and tomato mixture.

(serving size: ⅓ cup bean mixture, ⅔ cup kale, 1 egg, and 3 tablespoons tomato mixture): CALORIES 264; FAT 10.5g (sat 3.2g, mono 4.1g, poly 1.6g); PROTEIN 16g; CARB 28g; FIBER 9g; SUGARS 2g (est. added sugars 0g); CHOL 192mg; IRON 4mg; SODIUM 493mg; CALCIUM 286mg

CHICKPEA-ROSEMARY CREPES
WITH PEPPER RELISH

HANDS-ON: **55 MINUTES**   TOTAL: **55 MINUTES**   SERVES **4**

CREPES

3.13 ounces chickpea (garbanzo bean) flour (about ¾ cup)

3 tablespoons all-purpose flour

2 teaspoons chopped fresh rosemary

1 teaspoon grated lemon rind

¼ teaspoon kosher salt

⅛ teaspoon baking soda

¾ cup water

2 tablespoons olive oil

2 large eggs, lightly beaten

FILLING

1 cup canned chickpeas (garbanzo beans), rinsed and drained

1 tablespoon 2% reduced-fat milk

2 teaspoons olive oil

2 teaspoons fresh lemon juice

¼ teaspoon freshly ground black pepper

Dash of salt

2 ounces goat cheese

½ garlic clove

RELISH

¼ cup diced yellow bell pepper

¼ cup diced red bell pepper

¼ cup diced orange bell pepper

2 tablespoons finely diced onion

1 teaspoon extra-virgin olive oil

½ teaspoon balsamic vinegar

¼ teaspoon kosher salt

¼ teaspoon freshly ground black pepper

Chickpea flour has more protein than wheat flour (a bonus for vegetarians) and gives these crepes a nutty flavor. Make the crepes in advance for speedier prep, and garnish with additional rosemary, if desired.

1. Make the crepes: Weigh or lightly spoon the chickpea flour into dry measuring cups; level with a knife. Combine the flours, rosemary, rind, ¼ teaspoon salt, and baking soda in a large bowl, stirring with a whisk. Add ¾ cup water, 2 tablespoons oil, and eggs; stir with a whisk. Let stand 30 minutes.

2. Make the filling: Place the chickpeas and next 7 ingredients (through garlic) in a food processor; process until smooth.

3. Make the relish: Place the yellow pepper and remaining ingredients in a medium bowl; toss gently to combine.

4. Heat an 8-inch crepe pan or nonstick skillet over medium-high heat. Pour about 2 tablespoons of the batter into the pan; quickly tilt the pan in all directions so the batter covers the pan with a thin film. Cook 30 seconds. Carefully lift the edge of the crepe with a spatula to test for doneness. Turn the crepe over when it can be shaken loose from the pan and the underside is lightly browned; cook 10 seconds. Place the crepe on a clean towel; keep warm. Repeat the procedure until all of the batter is used. Stack the crepes between single layers of paper towels to prevent sticking.

5. Spread 1 heaping tablespoon of the filling down the center of each crepe; roll up. Top with the relish.

(serving size: 3 crepes and 3 tablespoons relish): CALORIES 319; FAT 17.8g (sat 4.5g, mono 9.5g, poly 2.6g); PROTEIN 13g; CARB 26g; FIBER 3g; SUGARS 5g (est. added sugars 0g); CHOL 100mg; IRON 2mg; SODIUM 492mg; CALCIUM 71mg

chickpea flour, also known as garbanzo bean flour, is a gluten-free flour that gives baked goods a sweet, slightly bitter flavor. It can be used to thicken soups and sauces, too.

GREEK CUCUMBER AND
CHICKPEA BREAKFAST BOWL

HANDS-ON: **10 MINUTES**   TOTAL: **10 MINUTES**   SERVES **1**

1½ teaspoons extra-virgin
   olive oil

1½ teaspoons red wine vinegar

⅛ teaspoon freshly ground
   black pepper

Dash of kosher salt

½ cup unsalted canned
   chickpeas, rinsed and
   drained

2 tablespoons slivered
   roasted red bell peppers

2 pitted kalamata olives,
   chopped

½ cup thinly sliced cucumber

2 tablespoons crumbled feta
   cheese

2 teaspoons chopped fresh dill

Dill offers a fresh, herbaceous boost that livens up the canned chickpeas. This is a satisfying bowl of crunchy, creamy, chewy textures.

Combine the first 4 ingredients in a medium bowl, stirring with a fork or whisk. Add the chickpeas, bell peppers, and olives; toss to combine. Arrange the cucumber slices and chickpea mixture in a bowl; top with the cheese and dill.

CALORIES 255; FAT 11.6g (sat 3.1g, mono 5.6g, poly 0.8g); PROTEIN 9g; CARB 28g; FIBER 6g; SUGARS 3g (est. added sugars 0g); CHOL 13mg; IRON 2mg; SODIUM 467mg; CALCIUM 160mg

LENTIL AND MUSHROOM SHEPHERD'S PIE

HANDS-ON: **1 HOUR**   TOTAL: **1 HOUR, 30 MINUTES**   SERVES **6**

3 large garlic cloves

4 cups water

¾ cup uncooked brown lentils

3 thyme sprigs

1¼ teaspoons kosher salt

2 pounds Yukon Gold potatoes, cut into 1-inch pieces

½ cup reduced-fat sour cream

¼ cup 1% low-fat milk

1 teaspoon unsalted butter

½ teaspoon freshly ground black pepper

2 tablespoons olive oil

2 (8-ounce) package sliced cremini mushrooms

1 cup chopped yellow onions (about 6 ounces)

½ cup coarsely chopped carrots (about 2½ ounces)

¼ cup coarsely chopped celery (about 1½ ounces)

1 cup chopped cauliflower florets (about 4 ounces)

1 tablespoon lower-sodium soy sauce

2 tablespoons all-purpose flour

1½ cups unsalted vegetable stock

3 tablespoons chopped fresh flat-leaf parsley

Cooking spray

Pair this comforting dish with a green salad and toasted French bread for sopping up the sauce. You can make the mashed potatoes ahead and keep refrigerated, but let them warm up a bit at room temperature so that they're easily spreadable.

1. Smash 1 garlic clove, and place in a large saucepan with 4 cups water, lentils, and thyme sprigs over medium-high heat; bring to a boil. Reduce heat to medium-low; bring to a simmer. Cover and cook until lentils are tender but not mushy, 15 to 20 minutes. Drain lentils; discard thyme sprigs. Transfer lentils to a bowl; stir in ¼ teaspoon salt, and set aside.

2. Place the potatoes in a Dutch oven or large saucepan, and add enough cold water to cover by 1 inch. Bring the potatoes and water to a boil over high heat. Reduce the heat to medium; bring to a rapid simmer, and cook 15 to 20 minutes or until the potatoes are very tender. Drain and return the potatoes to the Dutch oven. Add the sour cream, milk, butter, ½ teaspoon of the salt, and ¼ teaspoon of the pepper; mash the potatoes until fully incorporated, and set aside.

3. Preheat the oven to 450°F.

4. Heat a large skillet over medium-high heat. Add the olive oil to the pan; swirl to coat. Add the mushrooms and cook, stirring often, until the mushrooms are deep golden brown and all the moisture is evaporated, 8 to 10 minutes. Chop the remaining 2 garlic cloves, and add to the pan with the onions, carrots, and celery. Cook, stirring often, until the vegetables are slightly softened and starting to brown, about 4 minutes. Add the cauliflower, soy sauce, and the remaining ½ teaspoon salt; stir to combine. Add the flour, and cook, stirring constantly, until the vegetables are fully coated, about 1 minute. Add the stock; stir to combine, and cook, stirring constantly, until the liquid thickens, about 2 minutes. Stir in the reserved lentils and 2 tablespoons of the parsley; remove from the heat.

5. Spoon the lentil mixture into a 3-quart baking dish coated with cooking spray. Spoon the mashed potatoes over the top, and gently spread almost to the edges of the dish. Lightly coat with cooking spray; sprinkle with the remaining ¼ teaspoon black pepper.

6. Bake at 450°F for 25 to 30 minutes or until the filling is bubbly and the potatoes are lightly browned. Sprinkle with the remaining 1 tablespoon parsley. Let stand 5 minutes before serving.

(serving size: about 1½ cups): **CALORIES** 323; **FAT** 8.4g (sat 2.8g, mono 3.6g, poly 0.7g); **PROTEIN** 13g; **CARB** 53g; **FIBER** 9g; **SUGARS** 8g (est. added sugars 0g); **CHOL** 13mg; **IRON** 3mg; **SODIUM** 572mg; **CALCIUM** 95mg

WHOLE ROASTED CARROTS WITH BLACK LENTILS AND GREEN HARISSA ▼

HANDS-ON: **20 MINUTES**   TOTAL: **50 MINUTES**   SERVES **6**

5 tablespoons olive oil

1½ cups chopped onion

1 tablespoon minced fresh garlic

3 cups unsalted vegetable stock

2 cups uncooked black lentils, rinsed

2 tablespoons plus 2 teaspoons Cajun seasoning

2 pounds large carrots

2 cups cilantro leaves

2 tablespoons rice wine vinegar

1 teaspoon salt

1 teaspoon sugar

1 teaspoon ground cumin

1 teaspoon ground coriander

1 teaspoon freshly ground black pepper

2 garlic cloves

2 jalapeño peppers, seeded

The homemade green harissa, a take on the classic Tunisian hot sauce, adds balancing tang.

1. Preheat the oven to 400°F.

2. Heat a medium saucepan over medium-high heat. Add 1 tablespoon of the olive oil to the pan; swirl to coat. Add ½ cup of the onion and the minced garlic; sauté 5 minutes or until golden. Add the stock, lentils, and 2 teaspoons of the Cajun seasoning; bring to a boil. Cover, reduce the heat, and simmer for 45 minutes or until the lentils are tender.

3. While the lentils simmer, combine the carrots, 2 tablespoons of the oil, and the remaining 2 tablespoons Cajun seasoning, tossing well to coat. Arrange the carrot mixture in a single layer on a baking sheet. Bake at 400°F for 30 minutes or until tender.

4. Place the remaining 1 cup onion, the remaining 2 tablespoons oil, cilantro, and the remaining ingredients in a blender; process until smooth.

5. Place the lentils on a serving dish; arrange the carrots on top. Serve with the harissa.

(serving size: about 5 ounces carrots, about 1 cup lentils, and about 3 tablespoons harissa): CALORIES 427; FAT 12.1g (sat 1.7g, mono 8.4g, poly 1.5g); PROTEIN 21g; CARB 64g; FIBER 14g; SUGARS 14g (est. added sugars 1g); CHOL 0mg; IRON 7mg; SODIUM 504mg; CALCIUM 72mg

Black lentils are small, quick to prepare, and stay firm after you cook them. You can use red lentils, which are also quick cooking, as a substitute.

RED LENTIL-RICE CAKES
WITH SIMPLE TOMATO SALSA

HANDS-ON: **42 MINUTES**   TOTAL: **1 HOUR, 10 MINUTES**   SERVES **6**

SALSA

3 cups chopped plum
   tomato (about 6 tomatoes)
¼ cup chopped fresh basil
1 tablespoon balsamic vinegar
2 teaspoons capers
¼ teaspoon salt

CAKES

5 cups water
1 cup dried small red lentils
½ cup uncooked basmati rice
2 tablespoons olive oil
½ cup finely chopped red
   bell pepper
½ cup finely chopped red
   onion
½ teaspoon fennel seeds,
   crushed
2 garlic cloves, minced
3 ounces part-skim
   mozzarella cheese,
   shredded (about ¾ cup)
¼ cup dry breadcrumbs
1 tablespoon chopped
   fresh basil
1 teaspoon salt
¼ teaspoon freshly ground
   black pepper
2 large egg whites, lightly
   beaten

Crisp on the outside and creamy on the inside, these salsa-topped, red lentil–rice cakes make a lovely entrée. They offer a great way to use leftover basmati rice; if you're starting with cooked rice, use about 1½ cups. Add mixed greens to the plate for even more color.

1. Make the salsa: Combine the first 5 ingredients; set aside at room temperature.

2. Make the cakes: Bring 4 cups of the water and the lentils to a boil in a medium saucepan. Reduce the heat, and simmer 20 minutes or until tender. Drain and rinse with cold water; drain. Place the lentils in a large bowl.

3. While the lentils simmer, combine the remaining 1 cup water and rice in a medium saucepan; bring to a boil. Cover, reduce the heat, and simmer 18 minutes or until the liquid is absorbed. Cool 10 minutes. Add the rice to the lentils.

4. While the rice simmers, heat a large nonstick skillet over medium-high heat. Add 1 teaspoon of the oil to the pan; swirl to coat. Add the bell pepper, onion, fennel seeds, and garlic to the pan; sauté 2 minutes or until tender. Cool 10 minutes. Add to the rice mixture. Add the mozzarella cheese and the remaining ingredients, stirring until well combined. Let stand for 10 minutes.

5. Wipe the pan clean with paper towels. Heat the pan over medium heat. Add 2 teaspoons of the oil to the pan; swirl to coat. Spoon half of the rice mixture by ⅓-cupfuls into the pan, spreading to form 6 (3-inch) circles; cook 5 minutes or until lightly browned. Carefully turn the cakes over; cook 5 minutes on the other side. Remove the cakes from the pan. Repeat the procedure with the remaining 1 tablespoon olive oil and the remaining rice mixture. Serve with the salsa.

(serving size: 2 cakes and ½ cup salsa): **CALORIES** 308; **FAT** 8.3g (sat 2.3g, mono 3.3g, poly 0.6g); **PROTEIN** 17g; **CARB** 44g; **FIBER** 7g; **SUGARS** 5g (est. added sugars 0g); **CHOL** 8mg; **IRON** 3mg; **SODIUM** 655mg; **CALCIUM** 138mg

MUJADARRA BAKE

HANDS-ON: **20 MINUTES**   TOTAL: **1 HOUR, 30 MINUTES**   SERVES **8**

2 tablespoons extra-virgin olive oil

2 cups thinly sliced red onion (about 6½ ounces)

1 cup finely chopped carrots (about 6 ounces)

½ cup finely chopped celery (about 2 ounces)

2 large garlic cloves, chopped

1 tablespoon ground cumin

1 teaspoon ground coriander

1 cup uncooked French green lentils

1 cup uncooked brown basmati rice

4 cups unsalted vegetable stock

1 teaspoon kosher salt

1 cup plain 2% reduced-fat Greek yogurt

2 ounces feta cheese, crumbled (about ½ cup)

1½ teaspoons grated lemon rind

1 cup loosely packed flat-leaf parsley leaves

1 cup coarsely chopped mint leaves

¼ cup chopped fresh chives

1 tablespoon fresh lemon juice

When preparing this one-pot meal, the cast-iron skillet will be very full and a bit tight, but the dish cooks well and easily.

1. Preheat the oven to 350°F.

2. Heat a 10-inch cast-iron or other ovenproof skillet over medium-high heat. Add 1 tablespoon of the oil to the pan; swirl to coat. Add the onions, carrots, celery, and garlic, and cook, stirring occasionally, until the onions soften, about 5 minutes. Add the cumin and coriander; cook, stirring constantly, until fragrant and toasted, about 1 minute. Add the lentils and brown rice; stir to combine. Add the stock and salt; bring to a boil.

3. Cover the pan, and transfer to the oven. Bake at 350°F for 50 minutes or until the rice, lentils, and vegetables are tender. Remove from the oven, and let stand, covered, 10 minutes.

4. Combine the yogurt, feta, and rind in a small bowl. Place the parsley, mint, chives, juice, and the remaining 1 tablespoon olive oil in a separate bowl, tossing to coat.

5. Spoon lentil mixture into each of 8 bowls; top with yogurt mixture and herb salad.

(serving size: about 1 cup lentils, 2 tablespoons yogurt, and ¼ cup herb salad):
CALORIES 265; FAT 7.6g (sat 2.3g, mono 3g, poly 0.5g); PROTEIN 12g; CARB 39g; FIBER 6g; SUGARS 5g (est. added sugars 0g); CHOL 10mg; IRON 3mg; SODIUM 501mg; CALCIUM 117mg

FRIED EGG AND AVOCADO TOASTS

HANDS-ON: **12 MINUTES**   TOTAL: **12 MINUTES**   SERVES **4**

1 teaspoon olive oil

4 large eggs

1 ripe peeled avocado, mashed

4 (1-ounce) slices hearty whole-grain bread, toasted

1 cup alfalfa sprouts

¼ teaspoon kosher salt

¼ teaspoon freshly ground black pepper

½ cup refrigerated fresh salsa

Sunny-side-up eggs, fresh sprouts, and salsa amp up avocado toast for a fast, no-fuss meal. It's a sure winner at breakfast, lunch, or dinner.

1. Heat a large nonstick skillet over medium heat. Add the oil to the pan; swirl to coat. Crack the eggs into the pan; cook 2 minutes. Cover and cook 2 minutes or until the desired degree of doneness.

2. Spread one-fourth of the mashed avocado evenly over each toast slice. Arrange ¼ cup sprouts over the mashed avocado on each toast slice. Top each toast slice with 1 fried egg. Sprinkle the eggs evenly with the salt and black pepper. Top each assembled avocado toast with 2 tablespoons fresh salsa.

(serving size: 1 toast): **CALORIES** 245; **FAT** 14.9g (sat 2.8g, mono 8g, poly 2.8g); **PROTEIN** 11g; **CARB** 19g; **FIBER** 7g; **SUGARS** 4g (est. added sugars 0g); **CHOL** 186mg; **IRON** 2mg; **SODIUM** 422mg; **CALCIUM** 57mg

VEGETARIAN BENEDICTS WITH THYME SABAYON

HANDS-ON: **55 MINUTES**   TOTAL: **55 MINUTES**   SERVES **4**

SAUCE
- 1 large egg
- 2 tablespoons 1% low-fat milk
- 1 tablespoon dry white wine
- 1 tablespoon fresh lemon juice
- 1 teaspoon chopped fresh thyme
- 2 teaspoons butter, chilled and cut into small pieces

BENEDICTS
- 2 (4-inch) portobello mushroom caps
- 1 teaspoon extra-virgin olive oil
- 4 small leaves Lacinato kale, trimmed and tough center ribs removed
- 2 multigrain English muffins, split
- 1 ounce aged Gouda cheese, shredded (about ¼ cup)
- 2 tablespoons white wine vinegar
- 4 large eggs
- ¼ teaspoon freshly ground black pepper

Fresh thyme is a welcome addition to this frothy, egg and wine–based sauce called sabayon. Substitute curly kale for Lacinato kale, if you like.

1. Make the sauce: Combine 1 egg and the next 4 ingredients (through thyme) in the top of a double boiler. Cook over simmering water until thick (about 9 minutes), stirring constantly with a whisk. Remove from the heat. Add the butter, 1 piece at a time, stirring with a whisk until thoroughly incorporated. Keep warm.

2. Make the Benedicts: Remove the brown gills from the undersides of the portobello mushrooms using a spoon; discard the gills. Remove and discard the stems. Cut the mushroom caps into ½-inch-thick slices.

3. Heat a large skillet over medium-high heat. Add the olive oil to the pan; swirl to coat. Add the mushrooms, and cook 3 minutes on each side or until browned. Keep warm.

4. Bring a large saucepan of water to a boil. Add the kale; cook 2 minutes or until just tender. Plunge the kale into ice water; drain well.

5. Preheat the broiler to high.

6. Place the muffin halves, cut sides up, on a baking sheet. Broil 1 minute or until browned. Top each muffin half with 1 tablespoon of the cheese. Broil 1 minute or until the cheese melts. Top the cheese with one kale leaf; broil 1 minute. Top the muffins evenly with the mushroom slices. Keep warm.

7. Add water to a large skillet, filling two-thirds full. Bring to a simmer. Add the vinegar. Break each egg into a custard cup, and pour gently into the pan. Cook 3 minutes or until the desired degree of doneness. Remove the eggs from the pan using a slotted spoon. Top each muffin half with 1 egg. Whisk the sauce over simmering water to reheat; spoon about 1½ tablespoons sauce evenly over each egg. Sprinkle with pepper. Serve immediately.

(serving size: 1 Benedict): **CALORIES** 242; **FAT** 12g (sat 4.7g, mono 4.6g, poly 1.3g); **PROTEIN** 14g; **CARB** 20g; **FIBER** 2g; **SUGARS** 2g (est. added sugars 0g); **CHOL** 278mg; **IRON** 3mg; **SODIUM** 307mg; **CALCIUM** 174mg

EGGS FLORENTINE OVER SEARED POLENTA

HANDS-ON: **25 MINUTES**   TOTAL: **25 MINUTES**   SERVES **4**

1 tablespoon olive oil

2 garlic cloves, sliced

5 ounces baby spinach leaves

4 (3 x 2-inch) slices refrigerated polenta

1 tablespoon white vinegar

5 large eggs

3 tablespoons canola mayonnaise (such as Hellmann's)

1 tablespoon fresh lemon juice

2 teaspoons water

2 teaspoons butter, melted

¼ teaspoon kosher salt

For an elegant weekend brunch, try this twist on classic Eggs Benedict. The seared polenta makes a hearty base in place of the traditional English muffin.

1. Heat a large skillet over medium-high heat. Add 1½ teaspoons of the olive oil to the pan; swirl to coat. Add the garlic; cook until golden; remove from the pan. Add the spinach, stirring until wilted; remove from the pan. Add the remaining 1½ teaspoons olive oil to the pan; swirl to coat. Add the polenta slices; cook 3 minutes on each side or until golden.

2. Add water to a large skillet, filling two-thirds full; bring to a boil. Reduce the heat; simmer. Add the vinegar. Break each egg into a custard cup, and pour each gently into the pan; cook 3 minutes or until the desired degree of doneness. Carefully remove the eggs from the pan using a slotted spoon.

3. Place 1 poached egg yolk, the mayonnaise, lemon juice, 2 teaspoons water, melted butter, and salt in a blender; process until blended. Place polenta slices on each of 4 plates. Top each polenta slice with the spinach, egg, sauce, and garlic.

(serving size: 1 polenta slice, ¼ cup spinach, 1 egg, 1½ tablespoons sauce, and one-fourth of the garlic): CALORIES 226; FAT 14g (sat 3.7g, mono 7g, poly 2.6g); PROTEIN 9g; CARB 13g; FIBER 2g; SUGARS 0g (est. added sugars 0g); CHOL 237mg; IRON 3mg; SODIUM 435mg; CALCIUM 71mg

POACHING EGGS

1. Fresh eggs are key to successful poached eggs. As eggs age, the whites become watery, so the fresher the egg, the more compactly it will poach. An older egg will leave you with little white whispies in the water.

2. A little bit of vinegar added to the water helps the whites set more quickly. Also, make sure the water is simmering, not boiling. Boiling water is too intense and will twist and toughen the egg.

3. If you don't have custard cups or ramekins, break each egg into a measuring cup. You can poach more than one egg at once—just be sure each egg has plenty of space around it for the water to circulate.

FLORENTINE FRITTATA
WITH BRUSCHETTA TOPPINGS

HANDS-ON: **15 MINUTES**   TOTAL: **35 MINUTES**   SERVES **6**

1½ cups coarsely chopped plum tomato

1 tablespoon chopped fresh basil

2 teaspoons balsamic vinegar

1 teaspoon olive oil

⅛ teaspoon crushed red pepper

1 garlic clove, minced

½ teaspoon salt

1½ cups (6 ounces) fat-free ricotta cheese

¼ teaspoon freshly ground black pepper

4 large eggs

4 large egg whites

Cooking spray

1 cup chopped red onion

1 (8-ounce) package presliced mushrooms

3 cups baby spinach leaves

Basil leaves (optional)

Frittatas offer a big wow factor without much effort. The dish goes from stovetop to oven, and emerges with a light, fluffy texture and beautiful browned edges.

1. Preheat the oven to 350°F.

2. Combine the first 6 ingredients and ¼ teaspoon of the salt in a small bowl.

3. Combine the fat-free ricotta, black pepper, remaining ¼ teaspoon salt, eggs, and egg whites in a medium bowl.

4. Heat an ovenproof skillet over medium-high heat. Coat the pan with cooking spray. Add the onion; sauté 2 minutes. Add the mushrooms; sauté 2 minutes. Add the spinach; sauté 1 minute. Stir in the egg mixture. Bake at 350°F for 20 minutes or until a wooden pick inserted in the center comes out clean. Top with the tomato mixture. Garnish with basil leaves, if desired.

(serving size: 1 frittata wedge and about ¼ cup tomato mixture): CALORIES 118; FAT 4.3g (sat 1.2g, mono 1.8g, poly 0.7g); PROTEIN 12g; CARB 8g; FIBER 2g; SUGARS 4g (est. added sugars 0g); CHOL 143mg; IRON 1mg; SODIUM 328mg; CALCIUM 131mg

HUEVOS RANCHEROS BURRITOS

HANDS-ON: **45 MINUTES**   TOTAL: **45 MINUTES**   SERVES **6**

½ cup chopped onion

3 large plum tomatoes, sliced

2 tablespoons plus 1 teaspoon olive oil

½ chipotle chile canned in adobo sauce, chopped

1 tablespoon adobo sauce

½ cup water

1 tablespoon fresh lime juice

¾ teaspoon chili powder

½ teaspoon kosher salt

½ teaspoon ground cumin

1 (14-ounce) can lower-sodium black beans, rinsed and drained

6 large eggs, lightly beaten

6 (8-inch) multigrain tortillas

6 (½-inch-thick) slices avocado

2 tablespoons chopped fresh cilantro

Roasting the vegetables gives our ranchero sauce intensely rich flavor in just 10 minutes. Be sure to use plum tomatoes, which are meaty and not overly juicy—this will ensure a thick sauce that won't make the burrito soggy.

1. Preheat the broiler to high.

2. Toss the onion and tomato with 1 tablespoon of the olive oil. Place on a baking sheet; broil 8 to 10 minutes or until the tomatoes are lightly charred around the edges, turning once. Transfer to a blender; add the chile and adobo sauce. Pulse until coarsely pureed.

3. While the tomato and onion roast, combine ½ cup water, lime juice, chili powder, salt, cumin, black beans, and 1 tablespoon of the olive oil in a medium saucepan over medium-high heat. Reduce the heat, and simmer about 10 minutes or until the beans are very tender. Partially mash the bean mixture; cool to room temperature.

4. Heat a large nonstick skillet over medium heat. Add the remaining 1 teaspoon olive oil to the pan; swirl to coat. Add the eggs; cook 3 to 4 minutes or until the eggs are soft and beginning to set, stirring frequently. Remove the pan from the heat.

5. Place the tortillas on a work surface. Spread the bottom third of each tortilla with 2½ tablespoons bean mixture. Divide the eggs evenly over the beans. Top the eggs with 2 tablespoons of the tomato sauce, 1 avocado slice, and 1 teaspoon cilantro. Roll up, jelly-roll style.

(serving size: 1 burrito): **CALORIES** 319; **FAT** 14.5g (sat 2.8g, mono 7.9g, poly 2g); **PROTEIN** 14g; **CARB** 35g; **FIBER** 8g; **SUGARS** 2g (est. added sugars 0g); **CHOL** 186mg; **IRON** 3mg; **SODIUM** 512mg; **CALCIUM** 117mg

freezing burritos will give you easy grab-and-go meals later on. To freeze the burritos, wrap each burrito in plastic wrap, and then place them in a large zip-top plastic freezer bag. Store them for up to 3 months. You can pull them out one at a time. Just unwrap them, and then rewrap them in a paper towel. Microwave at HIGH 3 to 4 minutes, turning once halfway through cooking.

CHIPOTLE CHILAQUILES

HANDS-ON: **28 MINUTES**   TOTAL: **33 MINUTES**   SERVES **4**

2 tablespoons canola oil

1½ cups chopped onion

2 cups chopped zucchini

5 garlic cloves, chopped

2 (14-ounce) cans unsalted diced tomatoes

3 tablespoons chopped fresh oregano

½ teaspoon kosher salt

2 ounces chopped chipotle chiles in adobo sauce

2 ounces baked tortilla chips

4 large eggs

2 tablespoons oregano leaves

¼ teaspoon freshly ground black pepper

1 avocado, peeled and diced

6 radishes, sliced

Chilaquiles is a traditional Mexican dish that's often served for breakfast or brunch. Traditionally, tortillas are fried and stirred into a homemade salsa. In this version, we opt for tortilla chips to save time. Serve this immediately because the tortilla chips— since they're not fried—will quickly become soggy.

1. Preheat the broiler to high.

2. Heat a large cast-iron or other ovenproof skillet over medium heat. Add the canola oil to the pan; swirl to coat. Add the onion; cook 4 minutes. Add the zucchini and chopped garlic; cook 4 minutes. Add the tomatoes, 3 tablespoons chopped fresh oregano, salt, and chiles. Cook 4 minutes; remove from the heat. Stir in the tortilla chips. Level the surface. Make 4 indentations in the surface; crack 1 egg into each. Broil 5 minutes or until the whites are set. Remove from the oven. Sprinkle the 2 tablespoons fresh oregano leaves and pepper over the eggs. Serve immediately with the diced avocado and radishes.

(serving size: 1½ cups chilaquiles mixture, 1 egg, ¼ avocado, and ¼ cup radishes): CALORIES 384; FAT 23.1g (sat 3.5g, mono 13.7g, poly 4.2g); PROTEIN 12g; CARB 36g; FIBER 9g; SUGARS 11g (est. added sugars 1g); CHOL 186mg; IRON 3mg; SODIUM 552mg; CALCIUM 150mg

canned chipotles in adobo sauce are jalapeños that have been smoked, dried, and then rehydrated. Canned in a pureed mix of tomato, vinegar, garlic, and other spices, they bring smoky depth and a bit of heat wherever they go. Stir them into mayo or sour cream to drizzle over tacos, or add them to braises or stews for smokiness.

BROCCOLINI, RED PEPPER, AND ROASTED GARLIC FRITTATA

HANDS-ON: **35 MINUTES** TOTAL: **45 MINUTES** SERVES **4**

2 tablespoons canola oil

11 to 12 garlic cloves (from 1 large bulb)

6 large eggs, lightly beaten

½ cup low-fat cottage cheese

1 (8-ounce) bunch Broccolini

1 medium-sized red bell pepper, sliced into thin strips

½ cup vertically sliced sweet onion

2 tablespoons chopped fresh flat-leaf parsley

1 tablespoon chopped fresh oregano

½ teaspoon kosher salt

¼ teaspoon freshly ground black pepper

Salsa (optional)

Combining the eggs, cottage cheese, and roasted garlic in a food processor helps distribute the roasted garlic throughout the mixture for maximum flavor. You can substitute broccoli rabe or broccoli florets in place of the Broccolini, if you like. Serve this colorful frittata with a simple salad or oven-roasted potatoes.

1. Heat a small saucepan over medium-low heat; add the oil and garlic, and cook, stirring occasionally and adjusting the heat as needed to keep the garlic from browning too quickly, 25 to 30 minutes or until the garlic is very soft. Drain the oil into a small bowl, and reserve. Place the garlic cloves, eggs, and cottage cheese in a food processor; process until smooth. Transfer the mixture to a medium bowl.

2. Preheat the broiler with the oven rack 6 inches from the heat. Trim the Broccolini stems; cut the tops into bite-sized pieces. Heat a 10-inch nonstick ovenproof skillet over medium-high heat. Add 1½ teaspoons of the reserved garlic oil to the pan; swirl to coat. Add the Broccolini stems, pepper, and onion, and cook, stirring often, 5 minutes or until the vegetables are slightly tender. Add the Broccolini tops, and cook 5 to 6 minutes or until the Broccolini is bright green and the pepper and onion are tender. Fold the vegetable mixture, parsley, oregano, salt, and black pepper into the egg mixture.

3. Heat the skillet over medium-high heat. Add 1½ teaspoons of the reserved garlic oil to the pan; swirl to coat. Pour the egg-and-vegetable mixture into the pan, and cook 30 seconds. Reduce the heat to medium-low, and cook, without stirring, until the eggs are partially cooked, about 4 minutes.

4. Transfer the pan to the oven, and broil until the eggs are thoroughly cooked and the top of the frittata is slightly browned, about 5 minutes. Remove from the oven, and run a spatula around the edges of the frittata to loosen. Cut the frittata into 8 wedges. Serve immediately, with salsa, if desired.

(serving size: 2 wedges): **CALORIES** 222; **FAT** 15.1g (sat 3.2g, mono 7.3g, poly 3.5g); **PROTEIN** 15g; **CARB** 12g; **FIBER** 2g; **SUGARS** 5g (est. added sugars 0g); **CHOL** 282mg; **IRON** 2mg; **SODIUM** 457mg; **CALCIUM** 128mg

SUPER CRUNCHY TOFU TACOS

HANDS-ON: **16 MINUTES**   TOTAL: **46 MINUTES**   SERVES **4**

1 (14-ounce) package water-packed extra-firm tofu, drained

½ teaspoon salt

¼ teaspoon freshly ground black pepper

2 tablespoons canola oil

2 tablespoons unsalted cashews

¼ cup rice wine vinegar

3 tablespoons water

1½ tablespoons sugar

1½ cups (2-inch) julienne-cut carrots

1½ cups (2-inch) julienne-cut peeled daikon radish

2 tablespoons canola mayonnaise

1½ teaspoons Sriracha (hot chile sauce, such as Huy Fong)

1 teaspoon rice wine vinegar

8 (6-inch) corn tortillas

¼ cup diagonally sliced green onions

1. Cut the tofu lengthwise into 2 (1-inch-thick) slices. Cut each slice lengthwise into 4 (1-inch-thick) strips. Place the tofu on several layers of paper towels. Cover the tofu with additional paper towels; top with a cast-iron skillet or other heavy pan. Let stand 15 minutes, pressing down occasionally. Remove the paper towels.

2. Heat a large skillet over medium-high heat. Sprinkle the tofu with the salt and pepper. Add the canola oil to the pan; swirl to coat. Add the tofu to the pan; cook 10 minutes or until browned, turning to brown all sides. Remove the tofu from the pan, and drain on paper towels. Add the cashews to the pan; cook 30 seconds or until the nuts are just beginning to brown. Remove the nuts with a slotted spoon, and coarsely chop. Cut the tofu strips crosswise into 1-inch cubes. Combine ¼ cup vinegar, 3 tablespoons water, and sugar in a small saucepan; bring to a boil. Remove from the heat; add the carrots and radish. Let stand 15 minutes; drain. Combine the mayonnaise, Sriracha, and 1 teaspoon vinegar in a small bowl, stirring with a whisk.

3. Working with 1 tortilla at a time, heat the tortillas over medium-high heat directly on the eye of a burner for about 15 seconds on each side or until lightly charred. Arrange about ¼ cup carrot mixture in the center of each tortilla; top with 4 tofu pieces, about ½ teaspoon cashews, about 1 teaspoon mayonnaise mixture, and 1½ teaspoons green onions.

(serving size: 2 tacos): CALORIES 375; **FAT** 17.7g (sat 1.6g, mono 10.9g, poly 3.2g); **PROTEIN** 13g; **CARB** 43g; **FIBER** 7g; **SUGARS** 11g (est. added sugars 5g); **CHOL** 0mg; **IRON** 3mg; **SODIUM** 460mg; **CALCIUM** 256mg

PRESSING TOFU

1. Don't skip pressing tofu. In order to get a crisp, browned exterior, the excess water needs to be removed.

2. If you skip pressing it, you'll end up with a softer texture and minimal browning, as seen here. You can skip pressing it if you plan to blend it.

3. When you do press tofu, this crisp, browned crust is the result. It's worth the time investment.

SESAME BARLEY WITH GREENS AND TERIYAKI TOFU ▽

HANDS-ON: **30 MINUTES**   TOTAL: **2 HOURS**   SERVES **4**

3 cups water
½ cup uncooked pearl barley
¼ cup rice wine vinegar
3 tablespoons brown sugar
3 tablespoons lower-sodium soy sauce
4 teaspoons dark sesame oil
2 teaspoons finely grated peeled fresh ginger
2 garlic cloves, minced
6 cups thinly sliced Swiss chard (about 1 bunch)
1 (14-ounce) package water-packed extra-firm tofu, drained
¼ teaspoon crushed red pepper
Cooking spray
4 teaspoons toasted sesame seeds
2 green onions, thinly sliced

1. Bring 3 cups water to a boil in a medium, heavy saucepan. Add the barley; reduce the heat, and simmer 30 minutes or until the barley is tender. Drain and cool slightly.

2. Combine the vinegar, 1 tablespoon of the brown sugar, 1 tablespoon of the soy sauce, 1 tablespoon of the oil, 1 teaspoon of the ginger, and 1 garlic clove in a large bowl, stirring well with a whisk. Add the chard and barley; toss well to coat. Cover and chill 1 hour.

3. While the barley mixture chills, cut the tofu crosswise into 5 (1-inch-thick) slices. Place the tofu on several layers of paper towels. Cover with additional paper towels; top with a cast-iron skillet or other heavy pan. Let stand 20 minutes, pressing down occasionally.

4. Preheat the oven to 375°F.

5. Cut each tofu slice into ½-inch cubes. Combine the remaining 1 teaspoon sesame oil, remaining 2 tablespoons brown sugar, remaining 2 tablespoons soy sauce, remaining 1 teaspoon ginger, remaining garlic clove, and pepper in a medium bowl, stirring well with a whisk. Add the tofu; toss to combine. Let stand 10 minutes.

6. Arrange the tofu in a single layer on a foil-lined baking sheet coated with cooking spray. Bake at 375°F for 30 minutes or until the tofu is browned on all sides, stirring three times.

7. Place the barley mixture on each of 4 plates, and top with the tofu. Sprinkle evenly with the sesame seeds and onions.

(serving size: 1 cup barley mixture and ½ cup tofu): CALORIES 299; FAT 12.5g (sat 1.5g, mono 6.7g, poly 3.3g); PROTEIN 15g; CARB 37g; FIBER 6g; SUGARS 12g (est. added sugars 10g); CHOL 0mg; IRON 4mg; SODIUM 530mg; CALCIUM 257mg

baking tofu in the oven is an easy, hands-off way to prepare it. It crisps up nicely while still maintaining its creamy interior. Once it's cooled, the texture becomes firm and chewy. If you're serving the tofu immediately, toss it with cornstarch, which draws out more moisture and makes it crispier. But, if you're planning on cooling it to use in other dishes, skip the cornstarch, as the exterior won't stay crispy once it's chilled.

GRILLED EGGPLANT AND TOFU STEAKS
WITH STICKY HOISIN GLAZE ⩔

HANDS-ON: **45 MINUTES**   TOTAL: **45 MINUTES**   SERVES **4**

1 (14-ounce) package
  extra-firm tofu, drained

⅓ cup ketchup

3 tablespoons hoisin sauce

1½ tablespoons lower-sodium
  soy sauce

1½ tablespoons rice vinegar

1½ tablespoons minced fresh
  garlic

1 tablespoon minced peeled
  fresh ginger

1 serrano chile, finely
  chopped

2 tablespoons peanut oil

2 (1-pound) eggplants, cut
  lengthwise into ½-inch-thick
  slices

⅛ teaspoon kosher salt

Cooking spray

¼ cup diagonally sliced green
  onions

2 teaspoons sesame seeds,
  toasted

*We turned up the flavor with this Chinese-style barbecue dish.
It captures the essence of great barbecue without relying on meat.*

1. Place the tofu on several layers of paper towels. Cover the tofu with additional paper towels; top with a cast-iron skillet or other heavy pan. Let stand 20 minutes, pressing down occasionally. Cut the tofu crosswise into 8 (½-inch-thick) slices.

2. While tofu stands, combine the ketchup and next 6 ingredients (through chile) in a saucepan; bring to a boil. Reduce the heat to medium-low; cook until reduced to 1 cup (12 minutes), stirring occasionally. Set aside ½ cup.

3. Preheat the grill to medium-high heat.

4. Brush the oil over the tofu and eggplant; sprinkle with the salt. Place the eggplant on a grill rack coated with cooking spray, and grill 2 minutes. Turn the eggplant over, and brush with 2 tablespoons of the same sauce; grill 2 minutes. Turn the eggplant over; brush with 2 tablespoons of the sauce. Cook 2 minutes on each side.

5. Add the tofu to the grill; grill 3 minutes. Turn the tofu over, and brush with 2 tablespoons of the sauce; grill 3 minutes. Turn the tofu over and brush with 2 tablespoons of the sauce; grill for 1 minute on each side. Sprinkle with the onions and sesame seeds. Serve with the eggplant and ½ cup reserved sauce.

(serving size: about 3 eggplant slices, 2 tofu slices, and 2 tablespoons sauce): **CALORIES** 286; **FAT** 14.3g (sat 2.6g, mono 4.7g, poly 6.4g); **PROTEIN** 13g; **CARB** 29g; **FIBER** 9g; **SUGARS** 16g (est. added sugars 2g); **CHOL** 0mg; **IRON** 3mg; **SODIUM** 630mg; **CALCIUM** 124mg

SWEET AND SOUR TOFU-VEGETABLE STIR-FRY ⱽ

HANDS-ON: **25 MINUTES**   TOTAL: **40 MINUTES**   SERVES **4**

1 (14-ounce) package water-packed extra-firm tofu, drained

¾ cup water

⅓ cup rice vinegar

2 tablespoons sugar

4 garlic cloves, minced

2 tablespoons dry sherry

2 tablespoons ketchup

2 tablespoons finely chopped hot red chile (with seeds), such as red jalapeño or Thai chile

1 tablespoon cornstarch

1½ tablespoons lower-sodium soy sauce

2 tablespoons canola oil

½ teaspoon salt

1 red bell pepper, seeded and cut into ¼-inch-thick slices

2 carrots, diagonally cut into ⅛-inch-thick slices

1 (8-ounce) bunch Broccolini, cut into florets and stems cut into ½-inch pieces

2 cups cooked brown rice

This dish is mildly spicy; to make it extra kid-friendly, omit the chiles from the sweet and sour sauce.

1. Place the tofu in a shallow dish. Place the paper towels on top, and weight with a cast-iron skillet or other heavy pan. Let stand 20 minutes, pressing down occasionally. Discard the liquid, and cut the tofu into 2 x ¼-inch pieces.

2. While the tofu stands, combine ½ cup of the water, vinegar, and sugar in a small saucepan, stirring to dissolve sugar. Stir half of the garlic into the sugar mixture. Stir in the sherry, ketchup, and chile. Cook the mixture over medium heat until boiling. Remove from the heat; stir in the cornstarch, stirring with a whisk until smooth. Stir in the soy sauce.

3. Heat a large cast-iron skillet or wok over high heat. Add 1 tablespoon of the oil; swirl to coat. Add the tofu in an even layer; cook, without stirring, 2 minutes. Turn the tofu; cook 2 minutes. Place on a plate; sprinkle with the salt.

4. Add 1 teaspoon of the oil to the pan; swirl to coat. Add the bell pepper; stir-fry 2 minutes. Add the remaining garlic; stir-fry 10 to 20 seconds. Remove to the plate with the tofu. Add the remaining 2 teaspoons oil to the pan; swirl to coat. Add the carrots; stir-fry 1 minute. Add the Broccolini; stir-fry 3 minutes. Add the remaining ¼ cup water; cook 3 minutes or until the water evaporates. Return the tofu mixture to the pan. Add the sauce mixture; stir to coat. Place the rice on each of 4 plates. Place the tofu mixture over the rice.

(serving size: ½ cup rice and about 1½ cups tofu mixture): **CALORIES** 382; **FAT** 14g (sat 1.9g, mono 5.9g, poly 5.9g); **PROTEIN** 15g; **CARB** 47g; **FIBER** 4g; **SUGARS** 13g (est. added sugars 6g); **CHOL** 4mg; **IRON** 3mg; **SODIUM** 569mg; **CALCIUM** 141mg

WASABI PEA TOFU
WITH RED CABBAGE AND LEEKS

HANDS-ON: **35 MINUTES**   TOTAL: **35 MINUTES**   SERVES **4**

2 (14-ounce) packages water-packed extra-firm tofu, drained

¼ cup canola oil

12 ounces thinly sliced red cabbage

4 leeks, white and light green parts thinly sliced

1 teaspoon kosher salt

¾ teaspoon freshly ground black pepper

1 cup wasabi peas

1 large egg, lightly beaten

This dish is spectacular, as wasabi peas make a delicious breading for tofu. Surprisingly, they lose their bite when cooked but provide intriguing flavor and crunch in the slightly sweet, salty crust. Look for cans of the peas in the Asian food section of your supermarket or in the bulk bin of some large grocery stores. A few crushed peas get sprinkled on top of the finished dish for added crunch and a pop of pungency.

1. Cut each tofu block crosswise into 4 slices. Place the tofu on several layers of paper towels. Cover the tofu with additional paper towels; top with a cast-iron skillet or other heavy pan. Let stand 15 minutes, pressing down occasionally.

2. While the tofu stands, heat a large skillet over medium heat. Add 1 tablespoon of the oil to the pan; swirl to coat. Add the cabbage and leeks to the pan; cook 8 minutes or until crisp-tender, stirring occasionally. Stir in ½ teaspoon of the salt and ¼ teaspoon of the pepper. Keep warm.

3. Place ¾ cup of the peas in the bowl of a food processor; process until very finely ground and powdery. Place the ground peas in a shallow dish. Place the egg in another shallow dish. Sprinkle the tofu with the remaining ½ teaspoon salt and remaining ½ teaspoon pepper, pressing gently to adhere.

4. Heat a large skillet over medium-high heat. Add 2 tablespoons of the oil to pan; swirl to coat. Dredge 1 side of each tofu slice in the ground peas; dip in the egg. Dredge the same side of the tofu a second time in the ground peas. Arrange the tofu slices, dredged side down, in the pan; cook 5 minutes or until browned. Add the remaining 1 tablespoon oil to the pan; turn the tofu slices over, and cook 2 minutes.

5. Place the remaining ¼ cup peas in a zip-top plastic bag; lightly crush with a rolling pin or a small heavy pan. Place the cabbage mixture on each of 4 plates. Top with the tofu and sprinkle with the crushed peas.

(serving size: about 1¼ cups cabbage mixture, 2 tofu slices, and about 1 tablespoon crushed peas): **CALORIES** 450; **FAT** 26.9g (sat 4.7g, mono 12.7g, poly 8.9g); **PROTEIN** 24g; **CARB** 29g; **FIBER** 4g; **SUGARS** 8g (est. added sugars 0g); **CHOL** 47mg; **IRON** 6mg; **SODIUM** 607mg; **CALCIUM** 244mg

BBQ TEMPEH KEBABS ▼

HANDS-ON: **7 MINUTES**   TOTAL: **36 MINUTES**   SERVES **4**

1 tablespoon olive oil

1 tablespoon lower-sodium soy sauce

8 ounces tempeh (cut into 16 pieces)

¼ cup barbecue sauce

1 large zucchini, cut into 1-inch pieces

16 grape tomatoes

16 (1-inch) squares yellow bell pepper

Cooking spray

1 tablespoon sliced green onions

Barbecue sauce (optional)

Skewered food is always a favorite—the entrée and side are all together on one skewer, no utensils or washing up required. Turn the skewers occasionally as they grill so they'll char evenly.

1. Preheat the grill to medium-high heat.

2. Combine the olive oil, soy sauce, and tempeh. Let stand 20 minutes. Add ¼ cup barbecue sauce; toss.

3. Thread the tempeh, zucchini, grape tomatoes, and bell pepper alternately onto 8 (8-inch) skewers. Place the skewers on a grill rack coated with cooking spray. Grill 9 minutes or until browned, turning the skewers occasionally for an even char. Sprinkle with the chopped green onions. Serve with additional barbecue sauce, if desired.

Note: If using wooden skewers, soak them in water for 20 minutes before grilling.

(serving size: 2 skewers): **CALORIES** 220; **FAT** 10g (sat 1.8g, mono 4.2g, poly 2.6g); **PROTEIN** 14g; **CARB** 23g; **FIBER** 2g; **SUGARS** 10g (est. added sugars 3g); **CHOL** 0mg; **IRON** 2mg; **SODIUM** 333mg; **CALCIUM** 101mg

Tempeh is fermented soybeans packed into cakes. The process of fermentation breaks down the soybeans' natural sugars to form lactic acid, which not only imparts a very sour, pungent flavor, it also inhibits bad bacteria. Tempeh also contains probiotics, which are live good-for-your-gut bacteria that improve digestion and enhance immune health.

TEMPEH AND BROCCOLINI STIR-FRY

HANDS-ON: **30 MINUTES**   TOTAL: **30 MINUTES**   SERVES **4**

½ pound Broccolini

6 tablespoons chopped green onions

4½ tablespoons rice vinegar

3 tablespoons lower-sodium soy sauce

2 tablespoons hoisin sauce

2 teaspoons honey

¼ teaspoon crushed red pepper

5 teaspoons canola oil

1 (8-ounce) package tempeh, cut into ½-inch cubes

1 cup diagonally cut snow peas

2⅔ cups hot cooked long-grain white rice

3 tablespoons chopped unsalted, dry-roasted peanuts

It's best to prep all your ingredients before you start cooking. Stir-frying is a very quick cooking method that leaves little downtime. For a whole-grain base, use brown rice.

1. Cook the Broccolini in boiling water for 2 minutes or until crisp-tender. Drain and plunge the Broccolini into ice water; drain. Squeeze dry. Cut into 1-inch pieces.

2. Combine 3 tablespoons of the green onions and the next 5 ingredients (through red pepper) in a bowl.

3. Heat a large, heavy skillet or wok over medium-high heat. Add 1 tablespoon of the oil to the pan; swirl to coat. Add the tempeh; stir-fry for 5 minutes or until golden brown on all sides. Remove the tempeh from the pan; keep warm. Add the remaining 2 teaspoons oil to the pan; swirl to coat. Add the Broccolini and snow peas; stir-fry 2 minutes, stirring occasionally. Add the tempeh and vinegar mixture to the pan; bring to a boil. Spoon the rice into each of 4 bowls; top with the tempeh mixture. Sprinkle with the remaining 3 tablespoons green onions and peanuts.

(serving size: ⅔ cup rice, 1¼ cups tempeh mixture, and about 2 teaspoons peanuts): **CALORIES** 411; **FAT** 16g (sat 2.3g, mono 7.3g, poly 5.1g); **PROTEIN** 19g; **CARB** 51g; **FIBER** 8g; **SUGARS** 8g (est. added sugars 4g); **CHOL** 0mg; **IRON** 4mg; **SODIUM** 558mg; **CALCIUM** 140mg

TEMPEH WITH CHARRED PEPPERS AND KALE ▽

HANDS-ON: **22 MINUTES**   TOTAL: **22 MINUTES**   SERVES **4**

¼ cup canola oil

1 (14-ounce) package tempeh, cut into (⅓-inch-thick) slices

2 tablespoons lower-sodium soy sauce

1 cup vertically sliced onion

1 red bell pepper, thinly sliced

4 cups thinly sliced Lacinato kale (about 1 bunch)

½ teaspoon kosher salt

¼ teaspoon freshly ground black pepper

1 tablespoon cider vinegar

Tempeh, a soybean-based veggie protein, is a great option for sandwiches and wraps because of its firm texture and incredible flavor adaptability. We love it here with a quick soy sauce hit, layered over earthy kale.

1. Heat a large cast-iron skillet over medium-high heat. Add 2 tablespoons of the oil to the pan. Add the tempeh; cook 4 minutes, turning to brown evenly. Drizzle the soy sauce into the pan. Immediately remove the tempeh from the pan; keep warm.

2. Increase the heat to high. Add the remaining 2 tablespoons oil to the pan; swirl to coat. Add the onion and bell pepper. Cook 3 minutes, stirring occasionally. Add the kale, salt, and pepper to the pan; cook 1 minute, tossing to combine. Add the vinegar to the kale mixture; toss to coat. Place the kale mixture on each of 4 plates; top with the tempeh.

(serving size: about ½ cup kale mixture and one-fourth of tempeh): CALORIES 384; FAT 25.4g (sat 3.3g, mono 11.9g, poly 8g); PROTEIN 22g; CARB 23g; FIBER 3g; SUGARS 3g (est. added sugars 0g); CHOL 0mg; IRON 4mg; SODIUM 569mg; CALCIUM 214mg

pizza & tarts

ROASTED ASPARAGUS, MUSHROOM, AND ONION PIZZAS

HANDS-ON: **51 MINUTES**   TOTAL: **1 HOUR, 31 MINUTES**   SERVES **8**

24 ounces refrigerated fresh pizza dough

2 pounds cremini mushrooms, quartered

2 small red onions, each cut into 12 wedges

Cooking spray

1 pound asparagus spears, trimmed and cut into thirds

2 tablespoons cornmeal

⅔ cup lower-sodium marinara sauce (such as Dell'Amore)

5 ounces fresh mozzarella cheese, torn into small pieces (about 1¼ cups)

3 ounces fontina cheese, shredded (about ¾ cup)

1½ tablespoons extra-virgin olive oil

1½ tablespoons balsamic vinegar

¾ teaspoon crushed red pepper

¼ cup basil leaves

¼ teaspoon kosher salt

If you'd like to freeze this pizza, you'll want to partially bake it before freezing, as it helps draw moisture out of the vegetables and set the crust so it stays nice and crisp. Follow the directions through Step 4, and then bake it for 5 minutes. Cool the partially baked pizza completely, and then wrap it tightly in heavy-duty foil. Freeze it for up to 2 months. You can use any hearty vegetables you like, but skip more delicate items like fresh tomatoes, as they won't hold up as well in the freezer. To reheat it, unwrap the pizza; bake directly on the oven rack at 450°F for 20 minutes or until the crust is browned and crisp. Top with the oil mixture, basil, and salt.

1. Divide the dough in half. Let stand at room temperature, covered, for 30 minutes.

2. While the dough stands, place 2 heavy baking sheets in the oven. Preheat the oven to 500°F (keep the pans in the oven as it preheats).

3. Combine the mushrooms and onions on a jelly-roll pan; coat with cooking spray. Bake at 500°F for 15 minutes. Add the asparagus to the pan; bake at 500°F for 15 minutes. Remove from the oven; cool.

4. Roll each piece of dough into a 15 x 9–inch rectangle on a lightly floured work surface. Carefully remove the baking sheets from the oven; sprinkle with the cornmeal. Arrange the dough on the baking sheets; coat with cooking spray. Bake at 500°F for 8 minutes. Spread ⅓ cup sauce over each crust, leaving a ½-inch border. Top evenly with the vegetable mixture and cheeses.

5. Bake at 500°F for 10 to 11 minutes or until the crust is lightly browned.

6. Combine the oil, vinegar, and pepper in a small bowl; drizzle over the pizzas. Sprinkle with the basil and salt. Cut each pizza into 8 pieces.

(serving size: 2 pieces): **CALORIES** 397; **FAT** 12.6g (sat 5g, mono 5.2g, poly 1.2g); **PROTEIN** 18g; **CARB** 53g; **FIBER** 9g; **SUGARS** 5g (est. added sugars 0g); **CHOL** 27mg; **IRON** 3mg; **SODIUM** 571mg; **CALCIUM** 100mg

SPRING VEGETABLE PIZZA WITH GREMOLATA

HANDS-ON: **20 MINUTES**   TOTAL: **30 MINUTES**   SERVES **4**

12 ounces refrigerated fresh pizza dough

Cooking spray

1 large fennel bulb with stalks

1 tablespoon olive oil

½ cup frozen green peas

1½ cups (3-inch) pieces asparagus, cut in half lengthwise

5 garlic cloves, thinly sliced

⅔ cup part-skim ricotta cheese

3½ tablespoons 2% reduced-fat milk

½ teaspoon freshly ground black pepper

1½ ounces vegetarian Parmesan cheese, grated (about 6 tablespoons)

¼ teaspoon kosher salt

2 tablespoons chopped fresh flat-leaf parsley

1 tablespoon grated lemon rind

1 large garlic clove, minced

Serve this pizza loaded with fennel, green peas, asparagus, and more on a weeknight for a flavorful family-favorite meal. Reheated leftover wedges are an easy at-work lunch or a tasty snack for kids the next day.

1. Place a pizza stone or heavy baking sheet in the oven. Preheat the oven to 500°F (keep the pizza stone or baking sheet in the oven as it preheats).

2. Place the dough in a microwave-safe bowl coated with cooking spray. Cover and microwave at MEDIUM (50% power) for 45 seconds. Let stand 5 minutes.

3. Remove the stalks from the fennel bulb; reserve 1 tablespoon of the fronds. Cut the bulb into thin slices. Heat a large skillet over medium-high heat. Add the oil to the pan; swirl to coat. Rinse the peas in cold water to thaw; drain. Add the peas, fennel bulb, asparagus, and sliced garlic to the pan; sauté 2 minutes.

4. Roll the dough into a 14-inch circle on a lightly floured surface; pierce the entire surface liberally with a fork. Carefully remove the pizza stone from the oven. Arrange the dough on the pizza stone. Combine the ricotta, milk, pepper, and Parmesan cheese; spread evenly over the pizza, leaving a ½-inch border. Bake at 500°F for 5 minutes. Carefully remove the pizza stone from the oven. Top the pizza with the pea mixture. Bake at 500°F for 5 minutes or until the crust is browned and crisp. Remove from the oven; sprinkle evenly with the salt. Combine the reserved fennel fronds, parsley, rind, and minced garlic; sprinkle over the pizza. Cut into 8 wedges.

(serving size: 2 wedges): **CALORIES** 399; **FAT** 11.5g (sat 4.3g, mono 4.4g, poly 1g); **PROTEIN** 20g; **CARB** 53g; **FIBER** 10g; **SUGARS** 5g (est. added sugars 0g); **CHOL** 23mg; **IRON** 3mg; **SODIUM** 682mg; **CALCIUM** 320mg

gremolata traditionally is a combination of garlic, lemon rind, and parsley. It has a fresh flavor that brightens any dish. You can pair it with simple roasted vegetables, creamy beans, meats, poultry, seafood, or pizzas, as we've done in this recipe.

BROCCOLI SKILLET PIZZA

HANDS-ON: **20 MINUTES**   TOTAL: **35 MINUTES**   SERVES **4**

10 ounces refrigerated fresh whole-grain pizza dough

1 (12-ounce) package microwave-in-bag fresh broccoli florets

2 tablespoons canola oil

3 cups part-skim ricotta cheese

3 ounces vegetarian Parmesan cheese, grated (about ¾ cup)

1 garlic clove, grated

Crushed red pepper

Microwave-in-bag fresh vegetables help this meal come together quickly. A hot cast-iron skillet crisps the bottom of the crust while the surface gets golden brown under the broiler—no baking required.

1. Let the dough stand at room temperature, covered, for 15 minutes.

2. Preheat the broiler to high.

3. Microwave the broccoli according to the package directions. Carefully open the bag; cool slightly. Halve or quarter the larger florets. Combine the broccoli and 1 tablespoon of the oil in a bowl; toss well to coat.

4. Place the cheeses and garlic in a bowl; stir to combine (mixture will be thick).

5. Heat a 12-inch cast-iron or other ovenproof skillet over medium-high heat. Roll the dough into a 10½-inch circle. Add the remaining 1 tablespoon oil to the pan; swirl to coat. Remove the pan from the heat. Fit the dough into the pan, pressing slightly up the sides of the pan. Spread the cheese mixture evenly over the dough. Return the pan to medium-high heat; cook 2 minutes or until browned on the bottom. Place the pan in the oven; broil 2 minutes or until the cheese is lightly browned. Top the pizza with the broccoli mixture; broil 1 minute. Remove the pan from the oven. Sprinkle with the red pepper. Cut into 8 wedges.

(serving size: 2 wedges): **CALORIES** 377; **FAT** 18.4g (sat 5.6g, mono 5.4g, poly 2.2g); **PROTEIN** 20g; **CARB** 37g; **FIBER** 5g; **SUGARS** 1g (est. added sugars 0g); **CHOL** 32mg; **IRON** 1mg; **SODIUM** 572mg; **CALC** 420mg

refrigerated fresh pizza dough
is a fast way to get pizzeria-quality pizza at home. It's available in the bakery section of most supermarkets. It's always a good idea to let the dough rest at room temperature for 15 to 30 minutes before working with it, but if it starts to retract as you're trying to shape it, cover it and let it rest for an additional 5 to 10 minutes. The gluten should relax more, allowing you to stretch it.

CAPRESE PIZZA

HANDS-ON: **20 MINUTES**   TOTAL: **45 MINUTES**   SERVES **4**

12 **ounces refrigerated fresh pizza dough**

1½ **cups grape tomatoes, halved**

2 **tablespoons olive oil**

3 **tablespoons balsamic vinegar**

1 **tablespoon cornmeal**

3 **garlic cloves, minced**

3.25 **ounces fresh mozzarella cheese, thinly sliced**

Cooking spray

½ **teaspoon kosher salt**

¼ **teaspoon freshly ground black pepper**

¼ **cup basil leaves**

1. Let the dough stand at room temperature, covered, for 30 minutes.

2. Preheat the broiler to high. Line a baking sheet with parchment paper.

3. Combine the tomatoes and 1 tablespoon of the oil on the prepared baking sheet; toss to coat the tomatoes. Broil 10 minutes or until the tomatoes begin to brown.

4. Bring the vinegar to a simmer in a small saucepan over medium heat; simmer 10 minutes or until reduced by half.

5. Place a pizza stone or heavy baking sheet in the oven. Preheat the oven to 500°F (keep the pizza stone or baking sheet in the oven as it preheats).

6. Roll the dough into a 14-inch circle on a lightly floured surface; pierce the dough liberally with a fork. Remove the pizza stone from oven. Sprinkle the cornmeal over the pizza stone. Place the dough on the pizza stone; bake at 500°F for 5 minutes.

7. Remove the stone from oven. Combine the remaining oil and garlic; brush evenly over the crust, leaving a 1-inch border. Top with the tomatoes and cheese. Spray the border of the crust with cooking spray. Bake at 500°F for 12 minutes or until the cheese melts and the crust browns. Sprinkle with the salt and pepper. Drizzle with the vinegar; sprinkle with the basil. Cut into 8 wedges.

(serving size: 2 wedges): **CALORIES** 385; **FAT** 15.2g (sat 5.1g, mono 7.3g, poly 1.5g); **PROTEIN** 12g; **CARB** 47g; **FIBER** 7g; **SUGARS** 3g (est. added sugars 0g); **CHOL** 17mg; **IRON** 1mg; **SODIUM** 676mg; **CALCIUM** 22mg

USING A PIZZA STONE

1. A pizza stone is one way to create a crispy thin-crust pizza. Sprinkling the stone with cornmeal makes the dough easier to remove.

2. Prick the dough with a fork to prevent the dough from bubbling up as it prebakes.

3. Prebake the dough for 5 minutes before adding the toppings—or go longer if you like a really crisp crust. This helps seal the crust, protecting it from becoming soggy.

VEGGIE PIZZAS WITH CAULIFLOWER CRUST

HANDS-ON: **25 MINUTES**   TOTAL: **1 HOUR**   SERVES **2**

1 cauliflower head, roughly chopped (about 3 pounds)

Cooking spray

2 teaspoons olive oil

½ cup presliced cremini mushrooms

½ cup sliced red bell pepper

½ cup thinly sliced fresh basil

¼ teaspoon freshly ground black pepper

⅛ teaspoon kosher salt

3 garlic cloves, minced

2½ ounces part-skim mozzarella cheese, shredded (about ⅔ cup)

2 large egg whites

½ ounce vegetarian Parmesan cheese, grated (about 2 tablespoons)

½ cup thinly sliced seeded tomatoes

⅔ cup baby spinach

1. Preheat the oven to 375°F. Line a baking sheet with parchment paper.

2. Place half of the cauliflower in a food processor; pulse 10 to 15 times or until finely chopped (like rice). Transfer the cauliflower to the prepared baking sheet. Repeat the procedure with the remaining cauliflower. Coat the cauliflower with cooking spray. Bake at 375°F for 25 minutes, stirring once. Cool.

3. Increase the oven temperature to 450°F.

4. Heat a large skillet over medium-high heat. Add 1 teaspoon oil; swirl to coat. Add the mushrooms and bell pepper; sauté 5 minutes or until tender.

5. Place the cauliflower in a clean kitchen towel. Squeeze until very dry. Combine the cauliflower, the remaining 1 teaspoon oil, ¼ cup of the basil, ⅛ teaspoon of the black pepper, salt, garlic, 2 ounces of the mozzarella cheese, egg whites, and Parmesan cheese in a bowl. Press the cauliflower mixture into 2 (8-inch) circles on a baking sheet lined with parchment paper. Coat the crusts with cooking spray.

6. Bake the crusts at 450°F for 22 minutes or until browned. Remove the pan from the oven; top the crusts evenly with the mushroom mixture, tomatoes, spinach, remaining ¼ cup basil, remaining ⅛ teaspoon black pepper, and remaining mozzarella cheese. Bake an additional 7 minutes or until the cheese melts.

(serving size: 1 pizza): **CALORIES** 346; **FAT** 15.4g (sat 6.3g, mono 5.3g, poly 1.1g); **PROTEIN** 26g; **CARB** 33g; **FIBER** 11g; **SUGARS** 14g (est. added sugars 0g); **CHOL** 29mg; **IRON** 3mg; **SODIUM** 626mg; **CALCIUM** 493mg

MAKING A CAULIFLOWER CRUST

1. Process the raw cauliflower until it's a rice-like consistency.

2. When you think you can't squeeze anymore water out of the cooked cauliflower, keep squeezing. If it's not very dry, the crust will be mushy.

3. Since a cauliflower crust is more delicate than traditional dough, lining the baking sheet with parchment paper prevents it from sticking.

CRUNCHY WHOLE-WHEAT VEGGIE PIZZAS

HANDS-ON: **22 MINUTES**   TOTAL: **25 MINUTES**   SERVES **4**

1 tablespoon olive oil

8 ounces sliced mushrooms

3 garlic cloves, minced

1 medium zucchini, thinly sliced

4 (8-inch) whole-wheat flour tortillas (such as Mission)

Cooking spray

½ cup unsalted tomato sauce

½ teaspoon dried oregano

Dash of salt

6 ounces part-skim mozzarella cheese, shredded (about 1½ cups)

This recipe is a real kid-pleaser. The whole-wheat tortillas serve as quick pizza crusts. Broil them in batches so the tops of each pizza get melty and browned. Sprinkle with fresh oregano leaves, if you'd like.

1. Preheat the broiler to high.

2. Heat a large skillet over medium-high heat. Add the oil to the pan; swirl to coat. Add the mushrooms, garlic, and zucchini; sauté 6 minutes or until tender and the mushroom liquid evaporates.

3. Arrange 2 of the tortillas on a baking sheet; coat the tortillas with cooking spray. Broil 2 minutes or until browned. Place, browned sides down, on a work surface. Repeat with the remaining 2 tortillas.

4. Combine the tomato sauce, oregano, and salt in a microwave-safe bowl; microwave at HIGH 30 seconds. Spoon 2 tablespoons of the sauce on the unbrowned side of each tortilla.

5. Divide the vegetables evenly over the tortillas; sprinkle each with about ⅓ cup cheese. Place 2 pizzas on a baking sheet. Broil 2 minutes or until the cheese melts. Repeat with the remaining pizzas.

(serving size: 1 pizza): **CALORIES** 320; **FAT** 16g (sat 6.4g, mono 6.3g, poly 1.5g); **PROTEIN** 17g; **CARB** 30g; **FIBER** 4g; **SUGARS** 4g (est. added sugars 0g); **CHOL** 28mg; **IRON** 1mg; **SODIUM** 656mg; **CALCIUM** 321mg

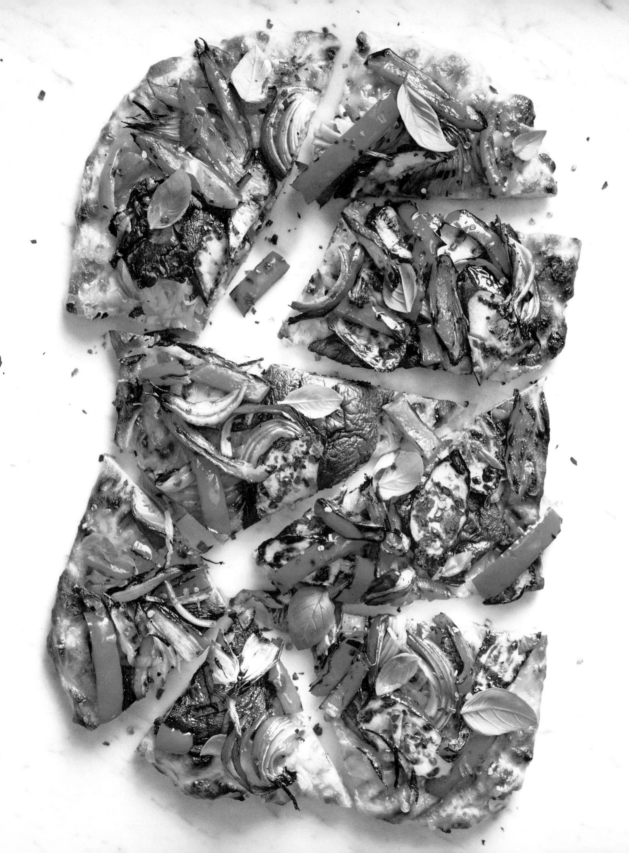

GRILLED VEGETABLE AND FONTINA PIZZA

HANDS-ON: **28 MINUTES**   TOTAL: **35 MINUTES**   SERVES **4**

2 portobello mushroom caps

1 tablespoon chopped fresh garlic

1 large red bell pepper, cut into ½-inch strips

1 medium zucchini, cut diagonally into ½-inch-thick slices

1 red onion, cut into ½-inch wedges (root end intact)

5 teaspoons extra-virgin olive oil

¼ teaspoon kosher salt

¼ teaspoon black pepper

Cooking spray

8 ounces refrigerated fresh pizza dough

4 ounces fontina cheese, shredded (about 1 cup)

¼ cup basil leaves

½ teaspoon crushed red pepper

When done right, grilling pizza yields crisp, well-charred pies that have a wonderfully smoky flavor—one of the major perks of grilling. This pizza is ideal as a simple main dish, but it also makes for a lovely summery party appetizer.

1. Preheat the grill to high heat.

2. Remove the brown gills from the undersides of the mushrooms with a spoon; discard. Combine the mushrooms, garlic, bell pepper, zucchini, onion, and oil in a bowl; toss to coat. Sprinkle with the salt and pepper. Arrange the vegetables on a grill rack coated with cooking spray; grill 8 minutes or just until tender. Slice the mushrooms.

3. Roll the dough into a 12-inch oval on a lightly floured surface. Place the dough on the grill rack; grill 2 minutes on each side or until lightly browned.

4. Sprinkle the cheese over the crust, leaving a ½-inch border around the edges. Arrange the vegetable mixture over the cheese. Grill the pizza for 3 minutes or until the cheese melts. Sprinkle the pizza with the basil leaves and red pepper. Cut into 8 pieces.

(serving size: 2 pieces): CALORIES 344; FAT 16.1g (sat 6g, mono 6.5g, poly 2.2g); PROTEIN 14g; CARB 38g; FIBER 3g; SUGARS 5g (est. added sugars 0g); CHOL 31mg; IRON 3mg; SODIUM 693mg; CALCIUM 173mg

GRILLING PIZZAS

1. Since the dough spends so little time on the grill, you'll want to have all your ingredients ready to go before you start. Place the dough directly on the grill grates. It should start to bubble up within 15 seconds.

2. You can shift and rotate it so it cooks evenly, but this whole process should take only a couple minutes per side.

3. Add the toppings and cheese and place it back on the grill until the cheese is melted. Add any fresh herbs once the pie is off the grill to prevent wilting.

SUMMER VEGGIE PIZZA

HANDS-ON: **33 MINUTES**   TOTAL: **45 MINUTES**   SERVES **4**

8 ounces refrigerated fresh
    pizza dough

2 tablespoons olive oil

2 garlic cloves, crushed

1 cup sliced onion

1 red bell pepper, cut into
    thin strips

8 ounces asparagus, trimmed
    and cut into 1-inch pieces

2 ears shucked corn

1 tablespoon cornmeal

3 ounces part-skim
    mozzarella cheese,
    shredded (about ¾ cup)

½ teaspoon kosher salt

½ teaspoon crushed red
    pepper

⅓ cup small thyme leaves

Most refrigerated fresh pizza dough comes in 1-pound balls, so use half to make this thin-crust pizza and freeze the other half to use later. Just thaw it overnight in the refrigerator before use.

1. Preheat the oven to 500°F.

2. Let the dough stand at room temperature, covered, for 30 minutes.

3. Heat a small skillet over medium heat. Add 4 teaspoons of the olive oil and garlic to the pan; cook 2 minutes or until fragrant (do not brown). Remove the garlic from the oil, and discard the garlic. Remove the garlic oil from the pan. Increase the heat to medium-high. Add the remaining 2 teaspoons oil to the pan; swirl to coat. Add the onion and bell pepper; sauté 5 minutes. Place the onion mixture in a bowl, and add the asparagus. Cut the corn from the cob; add the corn to the vegetable mixture.

4. Scatter the cornmeal over a lightly floured surface; roll the dough into a 13-inch circle on the prepared surface. Transfer the dough to a baking sheet; brush with the garlic oil. Top with the vegetable mixture, leaving a ½-inch border; sprinkle the cheese, salt, and pepper over the top. Bake at 500°F for 15 minutes or until golden. Sprinkle with the thyme. Cut into 8 wedges.

(serving size: 2 wedges): CALORIES 362; **FAT** 13.5g (sat 3.6g, mono 6.2g, poly 2.2g); **PROTEIN** 14g; **CARB** 50g; **FIBER** 4g; **SUGARS** 7g (est. added sugars 0g); **CHOL** 11mg; **IRON** 4mg; **SODIUM** 728mg; **CALCIUM** 185mg

SUNNY-SIDE-UP PIZZA

HANDS-ON: **30 MINUTES**   TOTAL: **30 MINUTES**   SERVES **6**

1 pound refrigerated fresh pizza dough

Cooking spray

2 tablespoons olive oil

2 garlic cloves, minced

6 large eggs

⅛ teaspoon kosher salt

4 cups mâche or baby spinach

¼ cup thinly sliced red onion

3 tablespoons balsamic vinaigrette

2 ounces vegetarian Parmesan cheese, shaved (about ½ cup)

⅜ teaspoon freshly ground black pepper

This pizza is a delicious take on breakfast for dinner. Chilled dough needs to rest 15 to 30 minutes at room temperature to allow the gluten to relax and allow you to stretch and shape it without it retracting. You can save time by using the microwave instructions in this recipe.

1. Preheat the oven to 450°F.

2. Place the dough in a microwave-safe bowl coated with cooking spray. Cover and microwave at MEDIUM (50% power) for 45 seconds. Let stand 5 minutes. Roll the dough into a 14-inch circle. Place on a pizza pan; pierce with a fork. Combine 1½ tablespoons of the oil and the garlic; brush over the dough. Bake at 450°F for 14 minutes.

3. Heat a large nonstick skillet over medium heat. Add the remaining 1½ teaspoons oil; swirl to coat. Crack the eggs into the pan, and cook 4 minutes or until the whites are set. Sprinkle with the salt.

4. Combine the mâche, onion, and vinaigrette. Arrange on the crust; top with the eggs, cheese, and pepper. Cut into 6 wedges.

(serving size: 1 wedge): **CALORIES** 372; **FAT** 15.2g (sat 3.8g, mono 5.9g, poly 2.6g); **PROTEIN** 17g; **CARB** 39g; **FIBER** 6g; **SUGARS** 1g (est. added sugars 0g); **CHOL** 194mg; **IRON** 3mg; **SODIUM** 611mg; **CALCIUM** 192mg

COOKING EGGS SUNNY SIDE UP

1. A sunny side up egg is a fried egg that hasn't been flipped over. The yolk is still runny, shiny, and yellow, and the whites are fully cooked but just barely. Using a nonstick pan prevents sticking; then add a thin layer of oil—you don't need much.

2. Using medium heat is ideal. You want the eggs to cook slowly to prevent the whites from becoming tough. Crack the eggs into the pan.

3. If you want your whites a little firmer, tilt the pan slightly and spoon the oil over the whites. Keep doing this until the whites are as done as you'd like.

APPLE, GOAT CHEESE, AND PECAN PIZZA

HANDS-ON: **20 MINUTES**   TOTAL: **20 MINUTES**   SERVES **6**

Cooking spray
- 1 (1-pound) six-grain pizza crust (such as Rustic Crust Tuscan Six Grain)
- 3 cups thinly sliced Fuji apple (about 8 ounces)
- 4 ounces goat cheese, crumbled (about 1 cup)
- 2 teaspoons chopped fresh thyme
- 1 tablespoon extra-virgin olive oil
- 2 teaspoons Dijon mustard
- 1 teaspoon fresh lemon juice
- 1½ teaspoons honey
- 2 cups baby arugula
- 3 tablespoons chopped pecans, toasted

This pizza blends a variety of flavors and textures for a delicious outside-the-box option. Crumbled feta is a savory substitute for the goat cheese in this recipe. Use a premade six-grain crust or any premade thin crust you like.

1. Preheat the oven to 450°F. Coat a baking sheet with cooking spray.

2. Place the pizza crust on the prepared baking sheet. Arrange the apple slices evenly over the crust; top with the cheese. Sprinkle the thyme evenly over the cheese. Bake at 450°F for 8 minutes or until the cheese melts and begins to brown.

3. Combine the oil and next 3 ingredients (through honey) in a medium bowl, stirring with a whisk. Add the arugula; toss gently to coat. Sprinkle the pecans evenly over the pizza; top with the arugula mixture. Cut the pizza into 6 pieces.

(serving size: 1 piece): **CALORIES** 305; **FAT** 9.6g (sat 3.3g, mono 4.1g, poly 1.1g); **PROTEIN** 11g; **CARB** 45g; **FIBER** 3g; **SUGARS** 7g (est. added sugars 1g); **CHOL** 9mg; **IRON** 1mg; **SODIUM** 408mg; **CALCIUM** 44mg

DEEP-DISH MUSHROOM AND ONION PIZZA

HANDS-ON: **35 MINUTES**   TOTAL: **2 HOURS, 30 MINUTES**   SERVES **6**

1¼ teaspoons dry yeast

½ teaspoon sugar

¾ cup warm water

5 tablespoons olive oil

9 ounces all-purpose flour
(about 2 cups)

¼ cup semolina flour

⅝ teaspoon salt

Cooking spray

1½ cups thinly vertically sliced
onion

1 tablespoon minced fresh
garlic

½ teaspoon dried oregano

¼ teaspoon freshly ground
black pepper

1 (8-ounce) package
presliced mushrooms

¾ cup lower-sodium marinara
sauce

1 bay leaf

1 ounce vegetarian Parmesan
cheese, grated (about
¼ cup)

5 ounces part-skim
mozzarella cheese,
shredded (about 1¼ cups)

Basil leaves (optional)

This pizza delivers the deep-dish texture and doughiness that makes this style of pie so crave worthy. The order of ingredients—adding the marinara onto the filling—helps the crust from becoming wet and soggy as it bakes.

1. Dissolve the yeast and sugar in ¾ cup warm water in the bowl of a stand mixer; let stand 5 minutes. Add 3 tablespoons of the oil. Weigh or lightly spoon 7.9 ounces (about 1¾ cups) of the all-purpose flour into dry measuring cups; level with a knife. Add 7.9 ounces of the all-purpose flour, semolina, and ⅜ teaspoon of the salt to the yeast mixture; mix at medium-low speed with a dough hook until smooth (about 4 minutes). Turn the dough out onto a lightly floured surface. Knead until smooth and elastic (about 5 minutes), gradually adding the remaining ¼ cup all-purpose flour. Place the dough in a large bowl coated with cooking spray, turning to coat the top. Cover and let rise in a warm place (85°F), free from drafts, 1½ hours or until doubled in size.

2. Heat a large skillet over medium-high heat. Add 1 tablespoon of the oil; swirl to coat. Add the onion; cook 3 minutes or just until tender. Stir in the garlic; cook 30 seconds, stirring constantly. Add the oregano, ⅛ teaspoon of the salt, pepper, and mushrooms. Cook 6 minutes or until the mushrooms release their moisture.

3. Combine the remaining ⅛ teaspoon salt, marinara, and bay leaf in a saucepan. Bring to a boil; reduce heat, and simmer 5 minutes. Discard the bay leaf.

4. Preheat the oven to 425°F. Place the oven rack in the bottom third of the oven.

5. Coat the bottom and sides of a 10-inch springform pan with the remaining 1 tablespoon oil. Punch the dough down; turn the dough out onto a lightly floured surface. Gently press the dough into a 13-inch circle. Carefully lift the dough and place in the prepared pan. Press the dough into the bottom and halfway up the sides of the pan. Sprinkle the Parmesan evenly over the dough. Top with the mushroom mixture. Spread the marinara mixture over the mushroom mixture. Sprinkle with the mozzarella. Bake at 425°F for 28 minutes or until the crust and cheese are browned. Let stand 5 minutes. Garnish with fresh basil leaves, if desired. Cut into 6 wedges.

(serving size: 1 wedge): **CALORIES** 409; **FAT** 17.9g (sat 4.7g, mono 9.4g, poly 1.5g); **PROTEIN** 15g; **CARB** 47g; **FIBER** 3g; **SUGARS** 4g (est. added sugars 0g); **CHOL** 19mg; **IRON** 3mg; **SODIUM** 627mg; **CALCIUM** 271mg

SPINACH AND FETA QUICHE
WITH QUINOA CRUST

HANDS-ON: **15 MINUTES**   TOTAL: **1 HOUR, 10 MINUTES**   SERVES **4**

CRUST

- 2 cups cooked quinoa, chilled
- ⅛ teaspoon freshly ground black pepper
- 1 large egg, beaten
- Cooking spray

FILLING

- 1 teaspoon canola oil
- ½ onion, thinly sliced
- 1 (5-ounce) package baby spinach
- ½ cup 1% low-fat milk
- ½ teaspoon kosher salt
- ¼ teaspoon freshly ground black pepper
- ¼ teaspoon crushed red pepper
- 4 large eggs
- 2 large egg whites
- 1½ ounces feta cheese, crumbled (about ⅓ cup)

The cooked quinoa creates a deliciously crisp crust on this cheesy quiche that's also gluten free and packed with protein and fiber.

1. Preheat the oven to 375°F.

2. Make the crust: Combine the quinoa, pepper, and egg in a bowl, stirring well. Press the mixture into the bottom and up the sides of a 9-inch pie plate coated with cooking spray. Bake at 375°F for 20 minutes; cool.

3. Make the filling: Heat a nonstick skillet over medium heat. Add the oil; swirl to coat. Add the onion; sauté 3 minutes. Add the spinach; sauté 3 minutes. Remove from the heat; cool.

4. Combine the milk and the next 5 ingredients (through egg whites) in a bowl; stir with a whisk. Arrange the spinach mixture in the crust; pour the egg mixture over the spinach. Sprinkle with the feta. Bake at 375°F for 35 minutes. Let stand 5 minutes. Cut into 4 wedges.

(serving size: 1 wedge): CALORIES 276; FAT 11.6g (sat 4.1g, mono 4.1g, poly 2.6g); PROTEIN 17g; CARB 25g; FIBER 4g; SUGARS 4g (est. added sugars 0g); CHOL 243mg; IRON 4mg; SODIUM 501mg; CALCIUM 180mg

TOMATO-LEEK PIE WITH QUINOA CRUST

HANDS-ON: **35 MINUTES** TOTAL: **1 HOUR** SERVES **4**

1 cup uncooked quinoa
½ cup almond meal
1 tablespoon cornstarch
¾ teaspoon kosher salt
2 tablespoons olive oil
1 large egg, lightly beaten
Cooking spray
2 cups thinly sliced leeks
2 garlic cloves, minced
1 pound heirloom tomatoes, seeded and sliced
1 teaspoon chopped fresh thyme
2 large egg whites, lightly beaten
1 ounce vegetarian Parmesan cheese, grated (about ¼ cup)

The two-slice portion of this summer pie is nice and hearty: For a lighter lunch or brunch for eight people, serve one slice with a simple spinach salad. Toss 2 teaspoons chopped fresh thyme into the crust for extra flavor.

1. Preheat the oven to 350°F.

2. Place the quinoa on a jelly-roll pan. Bake at 350°F for 10 minutes or until golden brown; cool. Place half of the quinoa in a food processor; pulse 30 seconds. Transfer to a large bowl. Add the remaining toasted quinoa, almond meal, cornstarch, and ¼ teaspoon of the salt; stir to combine. Add 1 tablespoon of the oil and egg; stir until the mixture is crumbly but holds together when pressed. Press into the bottom and up the sides of a 9-inch pie plate coated with cooking spray. Bake at 350°F for 5 minutes.

3. Heat a medium skillet over medium-high heat. Add the remaining 1 tablespoon oil to the pan; swirl to coat. Add the leeks; sauté 3 minutes. Add the garlic; sauté 1 minute. Combine the leek mixture, tomatoes, thyme, and remaining ½ teaspoon salt in a medium bowl; let stand 5 minutes. Add the egg whites, stirring to combine.

4. Arrange the tomato mixture in the crust; sprinkle with the cheese. Bake at 350°F for 15 minutes or until the filling is set. Let stand 10 minutes. Cut into 8 wedges.

(serving size: 2 wedges): **CALORIES** 408; **FAT** 19.7g (sat 3.3g, mono 11.1g, poly 4.4g); **PROTEIN** 17g; **CARB** 43g; **FIBER** 7g; **SUGARS** 7g (est. added sugars 0g); **CHOL** 53mg; **IRON** 4mg; **SODIUM** 493mg; **CALCIUM** 158mg

leeks are the mildest relative of the onion family and have a clean, slightly sweet and grassy flavor. They're available year-round, but they're at their peak in the spring and fall. Wash them thoroughly before using since dirt is easily trapped in their many layers.

MUSHROOM, BUTTERNUT, AND PISTACHIO TART ♥

HANDS-ON: **35 MINUTES** TOTAL: **1 HOUR, 15 MINUTES** SERVES **6**

5 tablespoons unsalted shelled pistachios

6 ounces all-purpose flour (about 1⅓ cups)

1¼ teapoons kosher salt

6 tablespoons all-natural vegan buttery spread (such as Earth Balance), frozen

2 tablespoons ice water

Cooking spray

1 cup rinsed and drained unsalted cannellini beans

2 tablespoons chopped fresh thyme

2 tablespoons chopped fresh sage

2 tablespoons extra-virgin olive oil

¾ teaspoon freshly ground black pepper

16 ounces cremini mushrooms, quartered

1 cup thinly sliced red onion

2 garlic cloves, sliced

2 cups (½-inch) cubed butternut squash (about 10½ ounces)

¾ cup unsalted vegetable stock

1 tablespoon red wine vinegar

¼ cup loosely packed flat-leaf parsley leaves

This hearty, earthy, fall-inspired tart is best served immediately, but you can prepare the crust in advance. Leave the crust unbaked, wrap it well in plastic wrap, and freeze it for up to a week. You can substitute any other white beans in place of the cannellini, if you like.

1. Preheat the oven to 400°F.

2. Place the pistachios in a food processor; process until finely ground. Weigh or lightly spoon the flour into dry measuring cups; level with a knife. Add the flour and ¼ teaspoon of the salt to the food processor; pulse to combine. Cut the buttery spread into ½-inch cubes; add to the processor, and pulse until the mixture resembles coarse meal, about 6 times. Add the ice water, 1 tablespoon at a time, and pulse until the dough just starts to come together but is still crumbly. Lightly coat a 9-inch square or round tart pan with a removable bottom with cooking spray. Press the dough firmly onto the bottom and up the sides of the prepared pan. Freeze 10 minutes. Bake in 400°F until golden brown, about 30 minutes. Cool completely on a wire rack, about 30 minutes.

3. While the crust cools, wipe the food processor clean with a paper towel. Add the beans, 1 tablespoon of the thyme, 1 tablespoon of the sage, 1 tablespoon of the olive oil, and ¼ teaspoon each of the salt and pepper to the food processor. Process until smooth. Spread the bean mixture evenly in the bottom of the cooled tart shell.

4. Heat a large nonstick skillet over medium-high. Add the remaining 1 tablespoon oil to the pan; swirl to coat. Add the mushrooms and onion; cook, stirring often, until the onion is tender, about 7 minutes. Add the garlic; cook, stirring often, until the mushrooms are browned, about 3 minutes. Add the squash, stock, and remaining 1 tablespoon each of thyme and sage to the pan. Bring to a boil; cover and reduce the heat to medium. Cook until the squash is almost tender, about 8 minutes. Uncover and cook, stirring occasionally, until the liquid is nearly evaporated, about 7 minutes. Stir in the vinegar and the remaining ¾ teaspoon salt and ½ teaspoon pepper. Spoon the squash mixture evenly over the bean mixture in the tart shell. Sprinkle with the parsley. Cut into 6 slices.

(serving size: 1 slice): **CALORIES** 365; **FAT** 19.7g (sat 3.3g, mono 11.1g, poly 4.4g); **PROTEIN** 9g; **CARB** 41g; **FIBER** 5g; **SUGARS** 4g (est. added sugars 0g); **CHOL** 0mg; **IRON** 3mg; **SODIUM** 575mg; **CALCIUM** 80mg

FRESH TOMATO TART WITH WHIPPED RICOTTA

HANDS-ON: **25 MINUTES**   TOTAL: **1 HOUR, 5 MINUTES**   SERVES **6**

CRUST
1 cup uncooked quinoa
½ cup almond meal
1 tablespoon cornstarch
¼ teaspoon kosher salt
3 tablespoons olive oil
1 large egg
Cooking spray

FILLING
3 medium heirloom tomatoes (1¼ pounds), cut into ¼-inch-thick slices
1 pint heirloom grape tomatoes, halved lengthwise
1 tablespoon olive oil
⅔ cup sliced shallots (from 2 medium)
3 garlic cloves, sliced
1 cup part-skim ricotta cheese
1 tablespoon chopped fresh thyme
¾ teaspoon kosher salt
½ teaspoon freshly ground black pepper
¼ cup fresh basil

The sweetness and bright acidity of in-season tomatoes shine in this tart. You can make the crust a day in advance, but you should put the tart together just before you plan to serve it. The crust will begin to soften from the ricotta and the juices from the tomatoes if the tart isn't served within a couple of hours.

1. Make the crust: Preheat the oven to 350°F. Spread the quinoa evenly on a rimmed baking sheet. Bake at 350°F until golden brown, about 10 minutes. Cool completely, about 10 minutes.

2. Place half of the quinoa in a food processor; process until partially ground, about 30 seconds. Transfer to a medium bowl. Add the almond meal, cornstarch, salt, and remaining quinoa; stir to combine. Add the oil and egg; stir until the mixture is crumbly but holds together when pressed. Lightly coat a 9-inch round tart pan with a removable bottom with cooking spray. Press the mixture on the bottom and up the sides of the prepared pan. Bake at 350°F until golden and crisp, 15 to 20 minutes. Cool completely on a wire rack, about 30 minutes.

3. While the crust cools, make the filling: Arrange the tomatoes on a baking sheet lined with several layers of paper towels; let stand 30 minutes.

4. Heat a small nonstick skillet over medium heat. Add 1 teaspoon of the oil to the pan; swirl to coat. Add the shallots and garlic; cook, stirring often, until softened and beginning to brown, about 5 minutes. Remove from the heat; cool 5 minutes.

5. Combine the ricotta, thyme, and ¼ teaspoon of the salt in a medium bowl. Beat with an electric mixer at medium speed until slightly fluffy, about 1 minute. Spread ½ cup of the ricotta mixture in the bottom of the tart shell. Layer half of the tomatoes on top of the ricotta; drizzle with 1 teaspoon of the olive oil, and sprinkle with ¼ teaspoon each of the salt and pepper. Top evenly with the shallot mixture and remaining tomatoes, oil, salt, and pepper. Sprinkle with the basil. Cut the tart into 6 wedges; top each with about 2 tablespoons of the remaining ricotta mixture.

(serving size: 1 wedge): **CALORIES** 271; **FAT** 20.1g (sat 4.1g, mono 8.3g, poly 2.3g); **PROTEIN** 14g; **CARB** 33g; **FIBER** 6g; **SUGARS** 7g (est. added sugars 0g); **CHOL** 44mg; **IRON** 3mg; **SODIUM** 399mg; **CALCIUM** 180mg

GRITS AND GREENS TART

HANDS-ON: **30 MINUTES**   TOTAL: **1 HOUR, 10 MINUTES**   SERVES **6**

4.5 ounces all-purpose flour
(about 1 cup)

¼ cup fine yellow cornmeal

¾ teaspoon kosher salt

3 tablespoons unsalted
butter, melted

1 tablespoon ice water

1 large egg white

Cooking spray

1 (1-pound) bunch collard
greens (7 cups chopped)

1 tablespoon olive oil

1 cup sliced yellow onion

2 tablespoons apple cider
vinegar

2 ounces part-skim
mozzarella cheese,
shredded (about ½ cup)

½ cup 1% low-fat milk

3 large eggs

¾ cup diced tomato (from
1 medium tomato)

Hot sauce (optional)

This Southern-inspired tart isn't particularly eggy—the custard really just helps bind the collard green filling. The greens still have a nice bite to them, and the cornmeal in the crust lends additional crunch. It's best not to buy prechopped collard greens for this recipe. Those packages contain pieces of tough stem that won't become tender with the short cooking time in this recipe. You can use turnip greens, kale, or another hearty green in place of the collards.

1. Preheat the oven to 375°F.

2. Weigh or lightly spoon the flour into a dry measuring cup; level with a knife. Place the flour, cornmeal, and ¼ teaspoon of the salt in a food processor; pulse until combined. Whisk the butter, water, and egg white in a small bowl; drizzle over the mixture in the food processor, and pulse until the mixture begins to stick together. (Do not allow it to form a ball.) Lightly coat a 9-inch pie plate with cooking spray. Press the mixture onto the bottom and up the sides of the prepared pan. Bake at 375°F until lightly browned, about 20 minutes. Cool on a wire rack 15 minutes.

3. Remove the stems from the collard greens; discard the stems. Coarsely chop the leaves. Heat a large skillet over medium-high heat. Add the oil to the pan; swirl to coat. Add the onion; cook, stirring often, until the onion is softened and beginning to brown, about 5 minutes. Add the greens; cook, stirring constantly, until wilted, about 4 minutes. Remove from the heat, and stir in the vinegar.

4. Whisk together the cheese, milk, eggs, and the remaining ½ teaspoon salt in a medium bowl. Spoon the greens mixture into the prepared piecrust. Pour the cheese mixture evenly over the greens mixture. Bake at 375°F until lightly browned and set, about 20 minutes. Top with the diced tomatoes. Cut into 6 slices. Serve with hot sauce, if desired.

(serving size: 1 slice): CALORIES 274; **FAT** 13g (sat 5.9g, mono 4.6g, poly 1.2g); **PROTEIN** 11g; **CARB** 28g; **FIBER** 3g; **SUGARS** 3g (est. added sugars 0g); **CHOL** 115mg; **IRON** 2mg; **SODIUM** 364mg; **CALCIUM** 227mg

sides

SAUTÉED SUGAR SNAP PEAS
WITH LEMON AND MINT ▽

HANDS-ON: **12 MINUTES**   TOTAL: **12 MINUTES**   SERVES **4**

4 teaspoons olive oil

¾ pound sugar snap peas, trimmed

¼ teaspoon kosher salt

¼ teaspoon crushed red pepper

2 green onions (green and light green parts only), thinly sliced

½ teaspoon grated lemon rind

2 teaspoons chopped fresh mint

Mint adds a fresh finish to this side dish, but fresh chopped thyme or oregano leaves will also pair well with the snap peas. The onions and rind are added at the end so they won't burn.

1. Heat a large skillet over medium-high heat. Add 2 teaspoons of the oil to the pan; swirl to coat.

2. Add half of the snap peas, ⅛ teaspoon of the salt, and ⅛ teaspoon of the pepper to the pan; sauté 1½ minutes, stirring and tossing constantly.

3. Add half of the onions to the pan; sauté 1 more minute or until the peas are crisp-tender. Toss in ¼ teaspoon of the rind, and remove from the pan. Repeat the procedure with the remaining oil, peas, salt, pepper, onions, and rind. Garnish with the mint.

(serving size: ¾ cup): **CALORIES** 44; **FAT** 2.3g (sat 0.3g, mono 1.6g, poly 0.2g); **PROTEIN** 1g; **CARB** 4g; **FIBER** 1g; **SUGARS** 6g (est. added sugars 0g); **CHOL** 0mg; **IRON** 1mg; **SODIUM** 80mg; **CALC** 30mg

when sautéing vegetables, small, thin vegetables work best. If you have large or thick vegetables, cut them into smaller pieces so they can cook quickly and thoroughly. And be sure you don't overcrowd the pan. As soon as the vegetables hit the pan surface, the temperature will fall; if there are too many vegetables, the temperature will drop too much and moisture will be trapped, causing the vegetables to steam rather than sauté. Stirring and tossing keeps the food moving and helps maintain even, high heat. The motion also allows the juices to quickly evaporate so the food cooks in dry heat.

GRILLED EGGPLANT
WITH MOROCCAN SPICES

HANDS-ON: **35 MINUTES**   TOTAL: **1 HOUR, 45 MINUTES**   SERVES **6**

1 teaspoon coriander seeds

1 teaspoon cumin seeds

½ teaspoon freshly ground black pepper

Dash of ground red pepper

Dash of ground cinnamon

¾ cup plain low-fat yogurt

2 tablespoons extra-virgin olive oil

1 tablespoon chopped fresh mint

1 tablespoon chopped fresh flat-leaf parsley

2 (1-pound) eggplants

Cooking spray

⅜ teaspoon kosher salt

Mint leaves

You can paint slices of eggplant with olive oil and grill them over coals for this French–Moroccan dish. The only trick is to cook the eggplant over a gentle fire, so the texture is soft and creamy. Alternatively, you may cook it on a stovetop grill, baked, or pan-fried. Be sure to let the eggplant marinate in the sauce for at least an hour.

1. Preheat the grill to medium heat.

2. Combine the coriander and cumin seeds in a small skillet over medium heat; cook 1½ minutes or until toasted. Combine the coriander mixture, black pepper, red pepper, and cinnamon in a small bowl. Place the spice mixture in a spice grinder; process until finely ground (you can also crush with a mortar and pestle). Combine ½ teaspoon spice mixture, yogurt, 1 tablespoon of the oil, mint, and parsley in a small bowl, stirring with a whisk.

3. Partially peel the eggplant lengthwise with a vegetable peeler, leaving long stripes. Cut the eggplants crosswise into ½-inch-thick slices; lightly coat with cooking spray. Sprinkle evenly with the remaining spice mixture, pressing to adhere. Arrange the eggplant on a grill rack coated with cooking spray; grill 5 minutes on each side or until just tender. Place the eggplant on a platter; cool to room temperature. Spread the yogurt mixture evenly over the eggplant. Cover with foil, and let stand at room temperature at least 1 hour. Drizzle with the remaining 1 tablespoon oil. Sprinkle with the salt and mint.

(serving size: about 3 eggplant slices): **CALORIES** 100; **FAT** 5.5g (sat 1g, mono 3.5g, poly 0.6g); **PROTEIN** 3g; **CARB** 11g; **FIBER** 5g; **SUGARS** 6g (est. added sugars 0g); **CHOL** 2mg; **IRON** 1mg; **SODIUM** 146mg; **CALCIUM** 78mg

SWEET AND SOUR ROASTED NAPA CABBAGE WEDGES ⓥ

HANDS-ON: **6 MINUTES**   TOTAL: **21 MINUTES**   SERVES **4**

2 tablespoons olive oil

2 tablespoons cider vinegar

1 tablespoon brown sugar

1 teaspoon whole-grain Dijon mustard

1 teaspoon grated garlic

¼ teaspoon salt

½ teaspoon freshly ground black pepper

1 head napa (Chinese) cabbage, cut lengthwise into quarters

Cooking spray

Caramelizing cabbage under the broiler draws out its natural sugars and deepens the flavor of the glaze. Preheat the roasting pan to jump-start the browning process.

1. Place a large roasting pan in the oven. Preheat the oven and pan to 450°F.

2. Combine the first 7 ingredients in a small bowl.

3. Coat the cut sides of the cabbage with cooking spray. Place the cabbage, cut sides down, on the preheated pan; bake at 450°F for 6 minutes. Turn the cabbage onto the other cut side; bake an additional 6 minutes. Remove the pan from the oven. Heat the broiler to high. Brush the cabbage evenly with the oil mixture; broil 3 minutes or until browned and caramelized.

(serving size: 1 wedge): **CALORIES** 95; **FAT** 6.8g (sat 0.9g, mono 4.9g, poly 0.7g); **PROTEIN** 2g; **CARB** 6g; **FIBER** 2g; **SUGARS** 4g (est. added sugars 2g); **CHOL** 0mg; **IRON** 0mg; **SODIUM** 194mg; **CALC** 64mg

cabbage adds color, crunch, and pungent flavor to dishes when raw, but softens, mellows, and sweetens when cooked. It's in season in late spring through the summer. Look for a firm head that seems heavy for its size and doesn't appear dry or cracked. Store it whole in a produce bag in the coldest part of your refrigerator; it'll keep for up to 2 weeks. Once cut though, it remains usable for only a few days.

TEQUILA SLAW
WITH LIME AND CILANTRO

HANDS-ON: **5 MINUTES**   TOTAL: **5 MINUTES**   SERVES **6**

¼ cup canola mayonnaise
(such as Hellmann's)

3 tablespoons fresh lime juice

1 tablespoon silver tequila

2 teaspoons sugar

¼ teaspoon kosher salt

⅓ cup thinly sliced green
onions

¼ cup chopped fresh cilantro

1 (14-ounce) package
coleslaw

Grab a bag of packaged coleslaw mix, and you've saved yourself the time of slicing cabbage and shredding carrots. A splash of tequila adds spirit and complexity (we urge you not to leave it out), while lime juice's zing perks up earthy cabbage.

Whisk together the first 5 ingredients in a large bowl. Add the remaining ingredients; toss.

(serving size: about ⅔ cup): **CALORIES** 59; **FAT** 2.5g (sat 0g, mono 1.6g, poly 0.9g); **PROTEIN** 1g; **CARB** 6g; **FIBER** 2g; **SUGARS** 4g (est. added sugars 1g); **CHOL** 0mg; **IRON** 0mg; **SODIUM** 173mg; **CALCIUM** 37mg

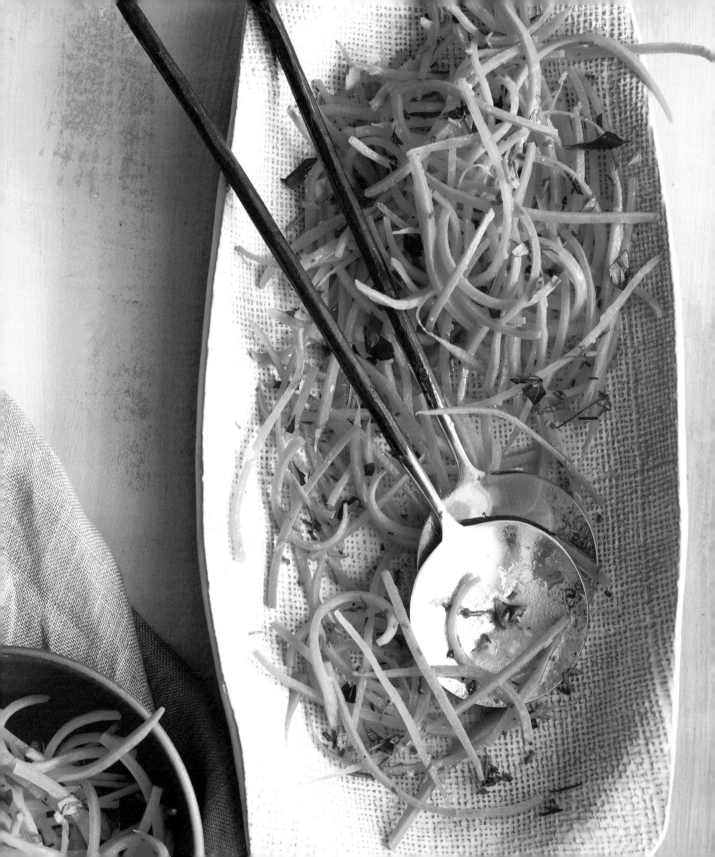

GRATED CARROT SALAD ▽

HANDS-ON: **20 MINUTES**   TOTAL: **1 HOUR, 20 MINUTES**   SERVES **6**

2 pounds medium-sized carrots, peeled

⅜ teaspoon kosher salt

1½ teaspoons grated lemon rind

2 tablespoons fresh lemon juice

1 teaspoon Dijon mustard

Dash of ground red pepper

2 garlic cloves, grated

¼ cup extra-virgin olive oil

¼ teaspoon freshly ground black pepper

2 tablespoons thinly sliced fresh chives

Chopped fresh parsley (optional)

Other possible herbs to sprinkle are dill, tarragon, and chervil. To make the salad more of a meal, garnish with thin slices of dry-cured ham or prosciutto, some watercress, and a hard-cooked egg. For the best texture, cut the carrots by hand with a mandoline, or with the julienne disk of a food processor.

1. Cut the carrots into a fine julienne with the julienne blade of a mandoline or a sharp knife. Place the carrots in a bowl; refrigerate until ready to use.

2. One hour before serving, sprinkle the carrots with ¼ teaspoon salt. Combine the rind, juice, Dijon mustard, red pepper, and garlic in a small bowl, stirring with a whisk. Gradually add the oil, stirring constantly with a whisk. Stir in the remaining ⅛ teaspoon salt and black pepper. Add half of the vinaigrette to the carrot mixture; toss to coat. Let stand 1 hour. Add the remaining vinaigrette to the carrot mixture; toss to coat. Sprinkle with the chives and, if desired, parsley.

(serving size: about 1⅓ cups): **CALORIES** 146; **FAT** 9.4g (sat 1.3g, mono 6.6g, poly 1.1g); **PROTEIN** 2g; **CARB** 16g; **FIBER** 4g; **SUGARS** 7g (est. added sugars 0g); **CHOL** 0mg; **IRON** 1mg; **SODIUM** 245mg; **CALCIUM** 54mg

RIPE SUMMER TOMATO GRATIN WITH BASIL

HANDS-ON: **12 MINUTES**   TOTAL: **50 MINUTES**   SERVES **8**

2 (1-ounce) slices whole-grain bread

6 tablespoons extra-virgin olive oil

2 tablespoons finely chopped fresh flat-leaf parsley

1 teaspoon finely chopped fresh thyme

⅜ teaspoon kosher salt

⅜ teaspoon freshly ground black pepper

1 ounce vegetarian Parmesan cheese, grated (about ¼ cup)

4 pounds sweet ripe tomatoes, mixed colors if possible

¼ cup torn basil leaves

1 tablespoon red wine vinegar

3 garlic cloves, minced

1 large shallot, finely diced

2 tablespoons small basil leaves (optional)

Ripe tomatoes and basil are baked together and topped with garlicky breadcrumbs for a savory take on a fruit crumble. Take care not to cook the tomatoes too long: This dish tastes best if they are still a bit firm. Garnish, if you can, with basil leaves of different shapes and colors, both green and purple.

1. Preheat the oven to 400°F.

2. Tear the bread with your hands to form coarse crumbs; spread in an even layer on a baking sheet. Bake at 400°F for 3 minutes or until lightly toasted. Combine the breadcrumbs, 2 tablespoons of the oil, parsley, thyme, ⅛ teaspoon of the salt, ⅛ teaspoon of the pepper, and the Parmesan cheese in a bowl.

3. Cut the tomatoes into ½-inch-thick slices. Place the tomatoes in a shallow dish; sprinkle with the remaining ¼ teaspoon salt and the remaining ¼ teaspoon pepper. Add the remaining ¼ cup oil, torn basil, vinegar, garlic, and shallots; toss gently to coat.

4. Arrange the tomato slices in a shallow 3- to 4-quart glass or ceramic baking dish. Pour any of the remaining liquid from the bowl over the tomatoes. Bake at 400°F for 15 minutes (tomatoes should still be firm). Sprinkle the breadcrumb mixture evenly over the tomatoes. Bake at 400°F for 10 minutes or until the breadcrumbs are golden. Remove the dish from the oven; let stand 10 minutes before serving. Garnish with small basil leaves, if desired.

(serving size: about ¾ cup): **CALORIES** 169; **FAT** 11.8g (sat 2g, mono 7.5g, poly 1.4g); **PROTEIN** 4g; **CARB** 13g; **FIBER** 3g; **SUGARS** 7g (est. added sugars 0g); **CHOL** 3mg; **IRON** 1mg; **SODIUM** 165mg; **CALCIUM** 81mg

fresh tomatoes are one of summer's most perfect offerings. Be sure to seek out local tomatoes, as their flavor truly is unrivaled by anything found in the supermarket. When buying, look for tomatoes with bright, shiny skin and firm flesh that yields slightly when you gently press with your finger. Never store tomatoes in the refrigerator. The cold temperature destroys the flavor and makes the texture mealy. They're best stored at room temperature out of direct sunlight.

PESTO POTATO SALAD

HANDS-ON: **20 MINUTES**   TOTAL: **32 MINUTES**   SERVES **6**

1½ pounds fingerling potatoes, cut into ¾-inch slices

2 tablespoons white wine vinegar

1 cup basil leaves

½ cup chopped fresh parsley

1½ ounces vegetarian Parmesan cheese, shaved (about 6 tablespoons)

2 tablespoons plain 2% reduced-fat Greek yogurt

1½ tablespoons olive oil mayonnaise (such as Hellmann's)

1 tablespoon roasted, salted sunflower seed kernels

1 tablespoon water

2½ teaspoons fresh lemon juice

⅜ teaspoon kosher salt

1 garlic clove, crushed

1 tablespoon olive oil

2 cups baby arugula

1 cup cherry tomatoes, halved

2 tablespoons chopped fresh dill

We start with a pot of cold water, and then add a tablespoon of vinegar to help the potatoes hold their shape. To make this ahead, complete steps 1 and 2, and refrigerate. Toss together the arugula mixture just before serving.

1. Place the potatoes in a saucepan; cover with cold water to 2 inches above the potatoes. Add 1 tablespoon vinegar. Bring to a boil; reduce the heat, and simmer 10 minutes or until tender. Drain; let stand 10 minutes.

2. Place the basil, parsley, 1 ounce of the cheese, yogurt, mayonnaise, sunflower seeds, remaining 1 tablespoon vinegar, 1 tablespoon water, 1½ teaspoons of the juice, salt, and garlic in a food processor; pulse 8 to 10 times or until smooth. Place the potatoes in a medium bowl. Add the pesto; toss to coat.

3. Combine the remaining 1 teaspoon lemon juice and oil in a medium bowl, stirring with a whisk. Add the arugula, tomatoes, and remaining 0.5 ounce cheese; toss to coat. Place the salad on each of 6 plates. Top each salad with the potato mixture. Sprinkle evenly with the dill.

(serving size: about ½ cup salad and ½ cup potato mixture): CALORIES 174; FAT 7.9g (sat 1.9g, mono 2.7g, poly 2.3g); PROTEIN 6g; CARB 21g; FIBER 3g; SUGARS 3g (est. added sugars 0g); CHOL 8mg; IRON 2mg; SODIUM 238mg; CALCIUM 138mg

ROASTED POTATO SALAD
WITH CREAMY DIJON VINAIGRETTE ⱱ

HANDS-ON: **10 MINUTES**   TOTAL: **40 MINUTES**   SERVES **8**

2 pounds Yukon gold potatoes, cut into wedges

3 tablespoons extra-virgin olive oil

2 tablespoons sliced garlic

1 teaspoon minced fresh thyme

¾ teaspoon kosher salt

¾ teaspoon freshly ground black pepper

1½ tablespoons white wine vinegar

2 tablespoons minced shallots

2 teaspoons Dijon mustard

1½ teaspoons chopped fresh tarragon

Here's a new twist on potato salad—a warm dish of golden-brown potato wedges with a creamy-tangy dressing drizzled on top. You can also serve it at room temperature.

1. Place a large heavy baking sheet in the oven. Preheat the oven to 400°F. (Do not remove the pan while the oven preheats.)

2. Combine the potatoes, 1½ tablespoons of the oil, garlic, and thyme in a medium bowl; toss to coat. Arrange the potato mixture on the preheated baking sheet, and sprinkle with ½ teaspoon each of the salt and black pepper. Bake at 400°F for 30 minutes or until browned and tender, turning after 20 minutes.

3. Combine the remaining 1½ tablespoons oil, remaining ¼ teaspoon salt, remaining ¼ teaspoon pepper, vinegar, shallots, Dijon mustard, and tarragon in a small bowl, stirring well with a whisk. Drizzle the dressing over the potatoes.

(serving size: about ¾ cup potatoes and about 2 teaspoons dressing): **CALORIES** 145; **FAT** 5.1g (sat 0.7g, mono 3.7g, poly 0.5g); **PROTEIN** 3g; **CARB** 22g; **FIBER** 2g; **SUGARS** 0g (est. added sugars 0g); **CHOL** 0mg; **IRON** 1mg; **SODIUM** 218mg; **CALCIUM** 7mg

ROASTING VEGETABLES

1. Few techniques do as much as roasting to build big intense flavors with so little effort. This simple cooking method causes the water in the vegetables to evaporate, concentrating the natural sugars and creating a beautiful browned crust. Cut the vegetables in uniform, bite-sized pieces so they'll cook evenly.

2. Toss the vegetables in a little oil or butter along with your seasonings. They should be evenly coated but not dripping in oil. This imparts rich flavor but also helps the vegetables crisp up.

3. Be sure to spread the vegetables in a single layer in the pan. Vegetables need air circulation to draw out as much moisture as possible. If the pan is too crowded, moisture can get trapped, making the vegetables soggy. Preheating the pan in the oven gives the vegetables a jump start on cooking.

THREE-BEAN SALAD ▼

HANDS-ON: **40 MINUTES**   TOTAL: **1 HOUR**   SERVES **6**

1 medium-sized red bell pepper

¾ cup frozen shelled edamame (green soybeans), thawed

8 ounces haricots verts, trimmed

1½ cups cooked, shelled fresh chickpeas (garbanzo beans)

½ teaspoon kosher salt

½ teaspoon freshly ground black pepper

¼ cup minced shallots

3 tablespoons flat-leaf parsley leaves

1½ tablespoons oregano leaves

2 tablespoons fresh lemon juice

1 tablespoon Dijon mustard

1 tablespoon extra-virgin olive oil

Canned beans may be a busy cook's best friend, and dried beans a healthy staple, but for a short seasonal window, fresh shelling beans, like the chickpeas called for in this recipe, offer a glorious middle ground. They cook much quicker than dried, and their flavor and texture are superior to canned. Try fresh chickpeas in this vibrant salad, where they combine with edamame (conveniently bought shelled and frozen) and slender haricots verts for a lovely summer side.

1. Preheat the broiler to high.

2. Cut the bell pepper in half lengthwise; discard the seeds and membranes. Place the pepper halves, skin sides up, on a foil-lined baking sheet; flatten with your hand. Broil for 10 minutes or until blackened. Place in a paper bag; fold to close tightly. Let stand 10 minutes. Peel and chop.

3. Cook the edamame and haricots verts in boiling water for 4 minutes; rinse with cold water, and drain.

4. Combine the bell pepper, edamame mixture, chickpeas, salt, and pepper in a medium bowl. Combine the shallots and remaining ingredients, stirring well with a whisk. Drizzle the dressing over the bean mixture; toss.

(serving size: about ⅔ cup): **CALORIES** 255; **FAT** 6.3g (sat 0.7g, mono 2.5g, poly 1.6g); **PROTEIN** 13g; **CARB** 38g; **FIBER** 11g; **SUGARS** 8g (est. added sugars 0g); **CHOL** 0mg; **IRON** 4mg; **SODIUM** 244mg; **CALCIUM** 89mg

TAHIREE VEGETABLE AND RICE CASSEROLE ⛉

HANDS-ON: **15 MINUTES**   TOTAL: **55 MINUTES**   SERVES **16**

¼ cup canola oil

2 teaspoons cumin seeds

½ teaspoon whole peppercorns

½ teaspoon cracked peppercorns

½ teaspoon coriander seeds

9 cardamom pods

6 whole cloves

3 bay leaves

3 dried red chiles de arbol

1 large onion, halved and thinly sliced

2 teaspoons kosher salt

1¼ pounds cauliflower florets (about ½ large head)

2 large red potatoes, cut into 1-inch cubes

1 (12-ounce) sweet potato, cut into ½-inch cubes

1 teaspoon ground turmeric

2 cups basmati rice

1 cup frozen petite green peas

4 cups water

1 teaspoon roasted ground cumin

½ teaspoon garam masala

This ancient dish traces its roots to India's Kayastha community, who developed it as a unique variation of biryani. In tahiree, rice and other elements cook together, while biryani rice is cooked separately, and then layered with meat and vegetables. Toasting the rice draws out its fragrance and adds nuttiness. Garam masala goes in at the end so it doesn't get bitter.

Combine the first 9 ingredients in a large Dutch oven over medium-high heat; cook, stirring frequently, about 2½ minutes or until the cumin seeds brown. Add the onion and 1 teaspoon of the salt; sauté 2 minutes. Stir in the cauliflower, potatoes, and turmeric; reduce the heat to medium, and cook 1 minute. Add the rice; cook 1 minute, stirring occasionally. Stir in the peas and 4 cups water. Bring to a boil; reduce the heat to low. Stir in the ground cumin, garam masala, and remaining 1 teaspoon salt; cover and cook 20 minutes. Turn off the heat; let stand 5 minutes. Fluff and serve immediately.

(serving size: 1 cup): CALORIES 172; FAT 3.8g (sat 0.3g, mono 2.2g, poly 1g); PROTEIN 4g; CARB 31g; FIBER 3g; SUGARS 3g (est. added sugars 0g); CHOL 0mg; IRON 1mg; SODIUM 279mg; CALCIUM 32mg

SUPER SAVORY WILD RICE PILAF

HANDS-ON: **30 MINUTES**   TOTAL: **1 HOUR, 40 MINUTES**   SERVES **10**

3 tablespoons butter

3 cups finely chopped onion

6 garlic cloves, minced

1½ cups uncooked wild rice

1 cup uncooked long-grain brown rice

1½ tablespoons chopped fresh thyme

4 cups unsalted vegetable stock

1 teaspoon kosher salt

1 teaspoon freshly ground black pepper

2 bay leaves

½ cup chopped fresh flat-leaf parsley

This twist on a traditional rice pilaf uses a mix of wild rice and long-grain brown rice. Be sure to use long-grain rice, as the firm grains stay distinct and separate after cooking, which makes them ideal for pilafs.

Melt the butter in a large Dutch oven over medium-low heat. Add the onion; cook 8 minutes. Add the garlic; cook 4 minutes, stirring occasionally. Increase the heat to medium-high. Add the rices and thyme; cook 1 minute, stirring frequently. Stir in the stock, salt, pepper, and bay leaves; bring to a boil. Reduce the heat to low, cover, and simmer 1 hour or until the rice is tender (do not stir). Remove the pan from the heat; let stand 10 minutes. Remove the bay leaves; discard. Fluff the rice mixture with a fork. Sprinkle with the parsley.

(serving size: about ⅔ cup): **CALORIES** 217; **FAT** 4.4g (sat 2.4g, mono 1.2g, poly 0.5g); **PROTEIN** 7g; **CARB** 39g; **FIBER** 3g; **SUGARS** 3g (est. added sugars 0g); **CHOL** 9mg; **IRON** 1mg; **SODIUM** 325mg; **CALCIUM** 31mg

seasonal produce guide

When you use fresh fruits, vegetables, and herbs, you don't have to do much to make them taste great. Although many fruits, vegetables, and herbs are available year-round, you'll get better flavor and prices when you buy what's in season. This guide helps you choose the best produce so you can create tasty meals all year long.

SPRING

FRUITS
Bananas
Blood oranges
Coconuts
Grapefruit
Kiwifruit
Lemons
Limes
Mangoes
Navel oranges
Papayas
Passion fruit
Pineapples
Strawberries
Tangerines
Valencia oranges

VEGETABLES
Artichokes
Arugula
Asparagus
Avocados
Baby leeks
Beets
Belgian endive
Broccoli
Cauliflower
Dandelion greens
Fava beans
Green onions
Green peas
Kale
Lettuce
Mushrooms
Radishes
Red potatoes
Rhubarb
Snap beans
Snow peas
Spinach
Sugar snap peas
Sweet onions
Swiss chard

HERBS
Chives
Dill
Garlic chives
Lemongrass
Mint
Parsley
Thyme

SUMMER

FRUITS
Apricots
Blackberries
Blueberries
Boysenberries
Cantaloupes
Casaba melons
Cherries
Crenshaw melons
Figs
Grapes
Guava
Honeydew melons
Mangoes
Nectarines
Papayas
Peaches
Plums
Raspberries
Strawberries
Watermelons

VEGETABLES
Avocados
Beans: snap, pole,
   and shell
Beets
Bell peppers
Cabbage
Carrots
Celery
Chile peppers
Collards
Corn
Cucumbers
Eggplant
Green beans
Jicama
Lima beans
Okra
Pattypan squash
Peas
Radicchio
Radishes
Summer squash
Tomatoes

HERBS
Basil
Bay leaves
Borage
Chives
Cilantro
Dill
Lavender
Lemon balm
Marjoram
Mint
Oregano
Rosemary
Sage
Summer savory
Tarragon
Thyme

FALL

FRUITS
Apples
Cranberries
Figs
Grapes
Pears
Persimmons
Pomegranates
Quinces

VEGETABLES
Belgian endive
Bell peppers
Broccoli
Brussels sprouts
Cabbage
Cauliflower
Eggplant
Escarole
Fennel
Frisée
Leeks
Mushrooms
Parsnips
Pumpkins
Red potatoes
Rutabagas
Shallots
Sweet potatoes
Winter squash
Yukon gold potatoes

HERBS
Basil
Bay leaves
Parsley
Rosemary
Sage
Tarragon
Thyme

WINTER

FRUITS
Apples
Blood oranges
Cranberries
Grapefruit
Kiwifruit
Kumquats
Lemons
Limes
Mandarin oranges
Navel oranges
Pears
Persimmons
Pomegranates
Pomelos
Tangelos
Tangerines
Quinces

VEGETABLES
Baby turnips
Beets
Belgian endive
Brussels sprouts
Celery root
Escarole
Fennel
Frisée
Jerusalem
   artichokes
Kale
Leeks
Mushrooms
Parsnips
Potatoes
Rutabagas
Sweet potatoes
Turnips
Watercress
Winter squash

nutritional information

HOW TO USE IT AND WHY

At *Cooking Light,* our team of food editors, experienced cooks, and registered dietitians builds recipes with wwhole foods and whole grains, and bigger portions of plants and seafood than meat. We emphasize oil-based fats more than saturated, and we promote a balanced diet low in processed foods and added sugars (those added during processing or preparation).

Not only do we focus on quality ingredients, but we also adhere to a rigorous set of nutrition guidelines that govern calories, saturated fat, sodium, and sugar based on various recipe categories. The numbers in each category are derived from the most recent set of USDA Dietary Guidelines for Americans, as shown in the following chart. As you look through our numbers, remember that the nutrition stats included with each recipe are for a single serving.

When we build recipes, we look at each dish in context of the role it plays in an average day: A one-dish meal that fills a plate with protein, starch, and vegetables will weigh more heavily in calories, saturated fat, and sodium than a recipe for roasted chicken thighs. Similarly, a bowl of ice cream may contain more than half of your daily added sugar recommendation, but balances out when the numbers are folded into a day's worth of healthy food prepared at home.

When reading the chart, remember that recommendations vary by gender and age; other factors, including lifestyle, weight, and your own health—for example, if you're pregnant or breast-feeding or if you have genetic factors such as risk for hypertension—all need consideration. Go to choosemyplate.gov for your own individualized plan.

IN OUR NUTRITIONAL ANALYSIS, WE USE THESE ABBREVIATIONS

sat	saturated fat	**carb**	carbohydrates	**mg**	milligram
mono	monounsaturated fat	**chol**	cholesterol	**est.**	estimated (added sugars)
poly	polyunsaturated fat	**g**	gram		

DAILY NUTRITION GUIDE

	Women ages 25 to 50	Women over 50	Men ages 25 to 50	Men over 50
Calories	2,000	2,000*	2,700	2,500
Protein	50 g	50 g	63 g	60 g
Fat	65 g*	65 g*	88 g*	83 g*
Saturated Fat	20 g*	20 g*	27 g*	25 g*
Carbohydrates	304 g	304 g	410 g	375 g
Fiber	25g to 35 g	25 g to 35 g	25 g to 35 g	25 g to 35 g
Added Sugars	38g	38g	38g	38g
Cholesterol	300 mg*	300 mg*	300 mg*	300 mg*
Iron	18 mg	8 mg	8 mg	8 mg
Sodium	2,300 mg*	1,500 mg*	2,300 mg*	1,500 mg*
Calcium	1,000 mg	1,200 mg	1,000 mg	1,000 mg

*Or less, for optimum health

Nutritional values used in our calculations either come from The Food Processor, Version 10.4 (ESHA Research), or are provided by food manufacturers.

metric equivalents

COOKING/OVEN TEMPERATURES

	Fahrenheit	Celsius	Gas Mark
Freeze Water	32° F	0° C	
Room Temp.	68° F	20° C	
Boil Water	212° F	100° C	
Bake	325° F	160° C	3
	350° F	180° C	4
	375° F	190° C	5
	400° F	200° C	6
	425° F	220° C	7
	450° F	230° C	8
Broil			Grill

LIQUID INGREDIENTS BY VOLUME

¼ tsp	=					1 ml	
½ tsp	=					2 ml	
1 tsp	=					5 ml	
3 tsp	=	1 Tbsp	=	½ fl oz	=	15 ml	
2 Tbsp	=	⅛ cup	=	1 fl oz	=	30 ml	
4 Tbsp	=	¼ cup	=	2 fl oz	=	60 ml	
5⅓ Tbsp	=	⅓ cup	=	3 fl oz	=	80 ml	
8 Tbsp	=	½ cup	=	4 fl oz	=	120 ml	
10⅔ Tbsp	=	⅔ cup	=	5 fl oz	=	160 ml	
12 Tbsp	=	¾ cup	=	6 fl oz	=	180 ml	
16 Tbsp	=	1 cup	=	8 fl oz	=	240 ml	
1 pt	=	2 cups	=	16 fl oz	=	480 ml	
1 qt	=	4 cups	=	32 fl oz	=	960 ml	
				33 fl oz	=	1000 ml	= 1 l

DRY INGREDIENTS BY WEIGHT

(To convert ounces to grams, multiply the number of ounces by 30.)

1 oz	=	¹⁄₁₆ lb	=	30 g
4 oz	=	¼ lb	=	120 g
8 oz	=	½ lb	=	240 g
12 oz	=	¾ lb	=	360 g
16 oz	=	1 lb	=	480 g

LENGTH

(To convert inches to centimeters, multiply inches by 2.5.)

1 in	=				2.5 cm	
12 in	=	1 ft		=	30 cm	
36 in	=	3 ft	= 1 yd	=	90 cm	
40 in	=				100 cm	= 1 m

EQUIVALENTS FOR DIFFERENT TYPES OF INGREDIENTS

Standard Cup	Fine Powder (ex. flour)	Grain (ex. rice)	Granular (ex. sugar)	Liquid Solids (ex. butter)	Liquid (ex. milk)
1	140 g	150 g	190 g	200 g	240 ml
¾	105 g	113 g	143 g	150 g	180 ml
⅔	93 g	100 g	125 g	133 g	160 ml
½	70 g	75 g	95 g	100 g	120 ml
⅓	47 g	50 g	63 g	67 g	80 ml
¼	35 g	38 g	48 g	50 g	60 ml
⅛	18 g	19 g	24 g	25 g	30 ml

index